NORTHERN
'Q'

NORTHERN
'Q'

THE HISTORY OF
ROYAL AIR FORCE LEUCHARS

IAN SMITH WATSON

FONTHILL

Fonthill Media Language Policy

Fonthill Media publishes in the international English language market. One language edition
is published worldwide. As there are minor differences in spelling and presentation, especially
with regard to American English and British English, a policy is necessary to define which form
of English to use. The Fonthill Policy is to use the form of English native to the author. Ian Smith
Watson was born and educated in England and now lives in Hertfordshire; therefore British
English has been adopted in this publication.

Fonthill Media Limited
Fonthill Media LLC
www.fonthillmedia.com
office@fonthillmedia.com

First published in the United Kingdom
and the United States of America 2015

British Library Cataloguing in Publication Data:
A catalogue record for this book is available from the British Library

Copyright © Ian Smith Watson 2015

ISBN 978-1-78155-192-9

Typeset in 10.5pt on 13pt Sabon Lt Std
Printed and bound by CPI Group (UK) Ltd, Croydon, CR0 4YY

CONTENTS

Acknowledgements

During the writing of Northern 'Q', I was aware that at some stage, given the subject matter, assistance from those who could provide first-hand testimony of RAF life while stationed at Leuchars would be vital. I was therefore relieved and grateful that the following people readily stepped up to the plate to provide their personal recollections and photographs. With my utmost appreciation, I give special thanks to Ed Durham, ex-222, 74 and 23 Squadrons, who got the ball rolling by passing my plea for information to all across the retired fighter pilot world, and for providing some rare shots from his time at Leuchars; to John Walmsley, for providing both photos and a first-hand account of intercept duties; to Jerry Parr, Gareth Jones, Steve Pickering and Keith Arkwright, for their insight and interesting memories of their time serving in north-east Fife; and to Paul Warren, for providing a very extensive detail of operational flying from Leuchars in the F-4 Phantom, and an abundance of photos not only from air intercepts but also of Soviet sea traffic and squadron badges.

I am particularly indebted to Barry Mayner. John Walmsley brought Barry to my attention and opened up a vein of detail going back to the Javelin era, together with a treasure chest of rare pictures. Steve Gyles provided accounts of his operational tours at Leuchars, flying both the Lightning and Phantom, and of his appreciation of the efficacy of that great life-saving invention of Martin-Baker, the ejector seat. Hugh Alexander at the National Archives Image Library was uber-efficient as usual in sorting out my myriad request for photos. Bob Offord supplied photos of 23 Squadron during the early Lightning era. Eric Lothian provided one of the more humorous memories from outside the station and touching upon the all-important golfing community. Neil Glen, who served on 74 Squadron and lived in St Andrews at the time, brought to my attention an unintended event connecting the base with the local golfing

Live QRA scramble during the 1988 airshow, QRA launches became a regular feature of the Leuchars airshow in the 1970s and 1980s. (*Fergel Goodman*)

community. Andy Renwick gave valuable assistance with photographs from the Department of Research and Information Service at the RAF Museum at Hendon. Likewise, Lee Barton took the time to meet a rather vague request for photos from Leuchars, but sorted a quite comprehensive list from the Air Historical Branch—which was much appreciated. Ian McBride (74 and 43 Squadrons, former CO of the latter) assisted with the Tiger Meet information, and Roger Colebrook (43 Squadron) also provided assistance and a rare shot or two. My thanks also go to Harry Drew, for his recollection of the early days of 11 Squadron.

Finally, I would like to record my gratitude to all the photographers: Michael Clarke, Richard Frial, Fergal Goodman, Jeremy Hughes, Colin Lourie, Andy McEwen, Charles E. MacKay, Peter R. March, Peter Nicholson, Trevor Thornton, Richard Vandervord and John Wharam.

Introduction

While driving along the M5 through the Mendips on the afternoon of Monday 18 July 2011, rather than listen to a CD as normal, I had tuned into the radio as I was eagerly awaiting the advertised address to Parliament by Dr Liam Fox, the Defence Secretary. Dr Fox was to reveal the conclusions of the second planning round to the SDSR (Strategic Defence and Security Review), perhaps more easily recognisable as the Defence Basing Review. There had been a good deal of speculation since the end of 2010, as the government had determined that the RAF would require no more than three main operating bases for its post-SDSR fighter/ attack force. This placed four such bases in the frame, one of which would end up without a chair once the music stopped.

I was already resigned to hearing that of the four RAF bases in question—Marham, Coningsby, Lossiemouth and Leuchars—the last named was to transfer to the Army. In its centenary year as a home for military aviation, Leuchars was now caught in the maelstrom of political expediency, misplaced priority, hidden agenda and the perennial rounds of defence cuts. Even before announcing the RAF withdrawal, Dr Fox, his voice charged with a note of satisfaction on a job well done, listed a number of Army units to move in.

The focus on preserving a single air base in Scotland had shifted from Leuchars to the far more remote base at Lossiemouth quite suddenly, following local protests, despite the proposal to move the Army onto the vacated sites. It is not often that the closure of a military establishment causes much of a response or the flaring of opinions, but recently UK military bases in Scotland have been placed in the centre of wider political arguments, especially in view of their impact on local economic circumstances, and have prompted further discord, were it possible, between the Scottish Nationalists and the UK Government in Westminster.

Arguably, Leuchars has the longest surviving pedigree in the history of British aviation if the arrival of a balloon unit of the Royal Engineers at Tentsmuir Forest is taken as the starting point. However, the acquisition of additional land slightly further south marked the true beginning of the air base, initially in the hands of the Royal Naval Air Service (RNAS) and later transferred to the RAF for the purpose of training Fleet aircrew. During the Second World War, Leuchars was transferred to the newly formed Coastal Command to become a maritime/anti-submarine warfare base. After the war, with the Cold War shift in defence strategy, the base served for more than six decades as an air defence fighter station and the sole home to the UK's northern air defence Quick Reaction Alert (Interceptor) Force—the Northern QRA.

So the story begins when manned flight was but six years old and still very much a mystery, and suitable plots of land were being purchased around much of the developed world in order to establish bases from which to launch and recover the new heavier-than-air flying machines. Few of those pioneer aerodromes survive to this day, many having gone on to lead new lives as industrial and housing estates, whilst others have been returned to rolling fields and wooded copses. Many of today's airfields sprung up in later years, their location being governed by other criteria. Leuchars is one airfield that has always found itself ideally suited to one military aviation function or another, from the first day of its establishment through to its most recent role as one of the RAF's dwindling frontline operational bases and home to its latest high-performance combat type, the Eurofighter Typhoon.

Powered flight arrived on Britain's shores in 1909, and it was two years later when the Royal Engineers began operating hot air balloons from Tentsmuir Forest on the edge of the present-day airfield. The RNAS, the first to establish Leuchars as an aerodrome, arrived in 1916, prior to which fields belonging to Reres Farm stood on this location. The farm itself survived a while longer, but eventual expansion saw it abandoned, and the station was just about ready for full operational use by 1918. At the end of the First World War, the RAF was established as the world's first independent military air arm.

Regarded as a rather odd and newfangled outfit, basing its rank system on a mix of those from the Army (enlisted ranks) and the Navy (commissioned ranks), the RAF had to battle against the prejudices of the two senior arms in order to secure its continued existence. Success in advancing the arguments in its favour required convincing all of the need to establish airfields—sizeable chunks of land with accompanying infrastructure—with a view towards long-term policy for establishing the service and its assets. With this taking shape, and with the move to subsume the air elements of the other services into the new independent air arm, the RAF moved into Leuchars in 1920, with the responsibility to continue the work of the Fleet at Leuchars by training aircrew essentially to serve its air requirements.

This was the original intention behind selecting Leuchars as a base to support maritime operations for the RNAS. However, with the independent air force established under peacetime conditions, the other two services' involvement with air power was now overseen by the junior service. Therefore the Fleet Air Arm (FAA) was, until shortly before the outbreak of the Second World War, an arm of the RAF not the Royal Navy, and training crews for service on the Navy's carriers became the station's stock-in-trade throughout the 1920s and '30s.

In 1938, Leuchars was handed to the recently formed Coastal Command, and anti-submarine and other air maritime operations were the station's lot throughout the war, but despite valuable operations against German shipping being flown by aircraft from Leuchars, the station and its units did not attract too much media attention. The immediate post-war years brought an inevitable reassessment of the country's defence arrangements, but the maritime role remained at Leuchars for the immediate future.

By the end of the 1940s, Western defence analysis caught up with the growing threat from the East, driven by the fear of Soviet hegemony and, to be fair to the Kremlin, their concerns about the likelihood of a resurgent German military threat rather than that from the USA, the UK or anywhere else.

For the next fifty years or so, Leuchars-based fighters stood guard over the most vulnerable section of UK airspace, the Atlantic north-eastern approaches. During this uncertain period of stand-off between NATO and the Warsaw Pact, the demands placed on NATO's Northern QRA role were met jointly as part of a triangle made up of the Royal Norwegian Air Force, the USAF 57th Fighter Interceptor Squadron, based at Keflavik in Iceland, and, of course, the Leuchars squadrons, to ensure the guard was never lowered. The Norwegians naturally are the first NATO partner to greet Soviet westbound sorties, and the Americans to provide an extension of coverage in light of the possibility of such long-range aircraft from the USSR having a free run across the Atlantic to the edge of US airspace. On occasion, this has taken place through some rather tense times when the Domesday clock has been moved an extra minute or two towards the midnight hour.

Since 1991, the Cold War stand-off has receded but not ended, although the early post-Cold War years brought about a sharp remission in the demand on the squadrons standing Northern 'Q'. The first decade following the collapse of the USSR did not quite bring the age of prosperity and peaceful accord that we were all expecting, and the second decade brought new threats to the fore, from Al-Qaeda to growing difficulties with a number of countries outside the Western democracies taking a path towards religious hegemony and seeking to pursue expansion through the waging of war by means of international terrorism and insurgence in vulnerable nations. A return to greater military reliance is once again a growing and unwelcome cause for concern in the western hemisphere, where dependence on global economic co-operation is more heavily relied on as the means by which to exert political pressure. Meanwhile, recent events have seen RAF interceptors responding to a noticeable rise in the number of Russian long-range reconnaissance bomber patrols and the possible threat of hijacked airliners.

Whatever the future holds, Britain's defence posture is being shaped not by what it needs but by what it can afford, given its increasing population and addiction to state services and intervention. This is not to suggest that Russian intentions towards the West are necessarily belligerent once more, but as this Introduction is written, the RAF Fighter Wing is in the process of departing Leuchars and heading further north to Lossiemouth—a move determined by political expedience rather than strategic planning. Moreover, as this book goes to press, the outcome of the Scottish independence referendum continues to have repercussions. The result, to maintain the union, is not a happy one for many, and the possibility of rolling back more than 300 years of British history continues to cast a shadow over the long-term future of British defence arrangements.

But whatever may come, the history of RAF Leuchars remains unique—having stood sentinel at the approaches to the West's northern gateway through the uncertain years of the Cold War—a task of renewed relevance today, now transferred to Lossiemouth in Moray.

1

Ploughshares to Propellers

The hitherto accepted means of going aloft for any reason at all, the hot air balloon, remained the method of choice from the military point of view in 1911, with the arrival of the balloon unit at Tentsmuir Forest on the Fife coast, just a mile or so north of the Eden Estuary which separated the Old Course at St Andrews from Reres Farm. The concept of aeroplanes as tools of war was still far removed from what concentrated the minds and drove the demands of both the War Office and the Admiralty. They may or may not have known it, but they were only three years away from the first of two global conflicts unparalleled in history. Nothing that the British Army or the Royal Navy had experienced in the past could have allowed them to predict or prepare for what was around the corner.

Other than this, there was as yet nothing to mark the presence of aviation in military terms, although airfields were beginning to become established. The Army took a significant step forward in this regard when, in November 1911, the Committee on Imperial Defence formally considered how best to address the question of conducting air operations, whether with balloons or aeroplanes, on a more established footing in the future. It did not take long to conclude that what was needed was the establishment of a new corps—the Royal Flying Corps (RFC)—which would incorporate the RE balloon unit, a part of which was now testing equipment and training personnel along the Fife coast from Tentsmuir. On 13 April 1912, the new corps came into being as a recognised established military unit. (When the RAF was formed in 1918, it was just twelve days short of the RFC's sixth anniversary.) Furthermore, it was the RFC that originally held the motto *Per Ardua Ad Astra*—'Through hardship (or adversity) to the stars'. What was to become the RNAS—the Navy's counterpart to the RFC—began life as a part of the corps.

By the summer of 1914, with diplomacy losing its grip on events in the Balkans, the wider ambitions of Imperial Germany were spurred on.

At the time, with nothing much envisaged beyond artillery spotting and other reconnaissance duties, the future of military aviation in Britain did not look like it would amount to much, but by now fixed-winged, prop-driven, flimsy machines were operating off the beaches near the golf links at St Andrews at low tide.

This type of activity remained exploratory for now, but the impact and spread of airpower had come on in leaps and bounds by 1916, prompting demands for more land to provide the necessary maintenance and operating bases needed to launch, recover and house the growing fleets of aeroplanes. Against this backdrop, approval was given for work to begin on the establishment of an airfield in north-east Fife to provide air operations for the RNAS, the planned occupants, but before this could happen, several acres of fields, mostly belonging to Reres Farm, had to be cleared. (In 1983, a single stone farm cottage remained, surrounded by construction work for the present-day southern hardened aircraft shelter (HAS) complex on the north bank of the River Eden by Shelley Point.) Progress was not particularly fast, and by the Armistice in November 1918, when the RNAS as a naval arm was effectively transferred to the newly independent air force, the new aerodrome was not yet ready.

For all its rural surroundings, the air station is situated close to a particularly interesting neighbour. To the south, across the Eden Estuary, lies the rarefied small town of St Andrews, an historic royal burgh, with a ruined cathedral, dating from 1158. Construction continued over the next 150 years or so, which included the restoration of the two towers at the west end that suffered storm damage in 1272. The then bishop, William Wishart, oversaw the restoration, which was completed in 1279, the year of his death. The cathedral served as the house of God for a relatively short time, being ransacked in 1559 during the Protestant Reformation. What remained in the mid-sixteenth century is very much what you see today, and a similar fate befell St Andrews Castle, the home of the bishop. Following the Reformation and the abolition of the bishop's office, it also fell into ruin and remains largely unaltered.

In 1413, the world-famous St Andrews University was founded. As prestigious as its English counterparts, Oxford and Cambridge, it is the oldest university north of the border and attracts students from far beyond Scotland. Notable alumni include HRH Prince William and Kate Middleton; the writer and broadcaster, Dominic Sandbrook; the former leader of the Scottish National Party, Alex Salmond; BBC presenter, Louise Minchin; the author and playwright, Fay Weldon; and the Defence Secretary, Michael Fallon. The university's 600th anniversary celebrations in 2013 included a flypast by Typhoon aircraft, which at the time remained operational at Leuchars.

It is also worth mentioning the town's equally important status as the 'home of golf'. The Royal and Ancient Golf Club, with its exclusive if rather austere-looking clubhouse, sits to the north of the town with its links along the coast, and further west along the Eden Estuary is the no less exclusive St Andrews Golf Club. Among the town's most famous sons is Tom Morris (1821-1908), who is widely regarded as the 'father of professional golf' and is buried in the grounds of the ancient cathedral. His death is attributed to his falling down the steps of the then new St Andrews clubhouse, just shy of his 87th birthday. Between 1861 and 1867, he won the Open Championship no fewer than four times.

To the north of the RAF station is Comerton Farm and Tentsmuir Forest. Road and rail services run a short distance further north before reaching the Firth of Tay and the Tay Bridge, on the other side of which is Dundee. To the west is Balmullo Quarry, a distinctive landmark in the area, and where one of the base's Lightning aircraft buried itself in later years. To the east is the North Sea, and then Denmark. This, then, is where RNAS Leuchars—or Leuchars RFC Training Depot as official documentation of the time referred to it—was established, taking the name of the rural village just to the north-west of the station.

'Why was Leuchars chosen?' some people have asked. Why indeed? One of the little-known reasons for building an air base, for whatever purpose, here on the east coast of Scotland, despite its reputation for inclement weather, lies in the fact that this particular corner of Fife enjoys more sunshine and tranquil conditions than most parts of the UK by quite a wide mark. That is, apart from the infamous Leuchars haar that can engulf the area in a combination of low cloud and drizzle, sometimes for days. In a report that appeared in *Flight* magazine back in July 1938, when No. 1 Flying Training School (FTS) was coming to the end of its tenure there, Maj. F. A. de V. Robertson said:

> From the RAF point of view, the important facts are that there are more good flying days in the year at Montrose, Prestwick and Leuchars than at any other stations in the British Isles. Given the usual sun, Leuchars is a very pleasant place, with a large and good aerodrome. Its charm is enhanced by the proximity of St Andrews with its old-world university and its Royal and Ancient only a few miles across the Bay. It does not take long in the car to get into the Highlands.

Surely, after 'the war to end all wars' was over, the necessity of an independent air force had ended with it? The opposition to an air force was quite considerable, and the newly appointed Chief of the Air Staff, Air Marshal Sir Hugh Trenchard, had his work cut out trying to convince government and military chiefs of the merits of retaining the RAF in what were now leaner times. A memo on air power requirements from his predecessor (and successor), Maj.-Gen. Sir Frederick Sykes, dated 9 December 1918, asked:

> We wish to turn our swords into ploughshares, but is it in the best interests of the world that we should do so, especially in regard to the air force, not so fast as merely to shatter a wonderful machine, nor so slowly as to allow other nations to usurp our place? Highly specialised air forces are now essential.

The following year, and with Sir Hugh Trenchard back in position as Chief of the Air Staff, Winston Churchill in his estimates for the new air force included three separate schemes for the permanent maintenance of the RAF, seeking a decision from the Cabinet on what its general scale should be, depending on how the new 'junior' service was to fit into the overall defence strategy. As he saw it at the time, there was no guide for the Air Ministry to follow when deciding which of the residual airfields and other air force establishments remaining from the Great War would still be needed. A great many had already been done away with. Ultimately, it was considered that only one of two options could be taken regarding the long-term role of the service.

The first alternative was to regard the RAF as a means of transporting military and naval personnel—'a means of conveyance captained by chauffeurs'—as well as carrying out reconnaissance for these two services and, if necessary, dropping bombs at locations specified by and on the instructions of the Army and Navy in respect of their own operational priorities. The second, and of course preferred, alternative as far as the Chief of the Air Staff was concerned, was 'to make a real air service'. One that would encourage and develop airmanship and, more importantly, engender an 'air spirit' in a very much similar vein to that of the other two military services. It would be an air force capable of profoundly affecting future strategy, and there could be no room for compromise lest aviation be relegated to a minor role. Although not necessarily large, it should certainly be highly efficient.

Something that contrasts significantly with the situation today was the assertion at the time that the RAF needed to train its own experts. It had been suggested that the other two services should train RAF cadets and staff officers, but to do this would, according to Churchill, make the creation of an 'air spirit' impossible. Whatever the shape and form air power would take as a developing third-dimension military force, it was going to eat up resources constructing airfields, such that Navy and Army chiefs were in the lobby against their new sibling. Many of the current airfields had originally been naval and military assets but post-war were now air force assets.

The construction of the airfield at Leuchars necessitated some much needed repair work to the local infrastructure, one such being the upgrading of what was little more than a track from Reres Farm (which belonged to Mrs Mary Euphemia Elliot) to Comerton Farm. Reres Farm was situated at the south-east end of the current airfield, the road in question running due north about 960 yards to Comerton. This was authorised under Road Military Requisition Order No. 159, in order to replace an existing public road running across the proposed airfield site from Milton, near Guardbridge, direct to Reres Farm. At the time, Reres Farm sat outside the proposed aerodrome well to the east, but the construction of this short length of road was deemed necessary for the transportation of materials rather than using the established Newport–Guardbridge–St Andrews road that runs through the main base today. Comerton Farm would in turn be reached by a road running west to east, just north of the proposed aerodrome from the village of Leuchars. The Requisition Order met with no objection, save an initial complaint that the track was only going to be widened to 9 feet, but it was ultimately decided to widen the trackway between Comerton and Reres to 15 feet.

As late as August 1919, nearly a year after the Armistice, Scottish Command—which reported directly to the War Office rather than to the Air Ministry or Admiralty—was pursuing the need to repair the road leading from Leuchars railway junction to the village, as this had been damaged by 'horsed-vehicles as well as by motor vehicles'. The road was in such a poor condition that it was resulting in excessive wear and tear on the military transport used to transfer RAF personnel to and from the air base.

One possible option was for the War Office to issue a further Requisition Order to effect definitive repair work, but the favoured approach was to contact the North British Railway Company in light of the fact that it was benefiting from the recent substantial increase in fare revenue as a result of the number of military personnel now travelling to Leuchars. By November that year, the Railway Company had agreed to carry out all necessary repairs to the road without incurring any cost to the Air Ministry.

As with many such ventures, the construction of the air base at Leuchars remained a work in progress over the ensuing years. However, by 1921, when a further 175 acres of land was purchased by the Air Ministry for £15,000 to build married and other living quarters, the base was fully functioning.

2

Flying Training School

Owing to insufficient room for adequate training at East Fortune airfield, East Lothian, a conference was held at Leuchars, which had by now been established, albeit with only a limited base infrastructure. This led to the transfer of the Flying Training School to Leuchars, designed for a three-squadron TDS (Training and Development School), which was still in the process of being built. Essentially meeting the requirements of the RNAS, it was now decided that all pilots of fighter and two-seater reconnaissance aircraft for the Fleet should pass through this school on completion of their flying training, and that refresher courses would be held for pilots already serving at sea.

A recent successful launch of a two-seater aeroplane from the turret of HMS *Australia* was seen as a step towards the use of aircraft in the Fleet for gunnery purposes, but exactly why this made sense, given that carrier decks were already in use, is not explained in detail. However, Adml David Beatty suggested that a Grand Fleet committee should arrange and closely follow up experimental work regarding this development.

On 11 June 1918, the Admiralty contacted the Air Council (the management board, if you will, of the fledgling RAF), requesting extra personnel for Fleet artillery work. The Air Ministry also hosted a conference, this time concerning the training of pilots and observers of Navy co-operation units. It was agreed to press ahead with the forming of a Fleet Artillery Aircraft School at Leuchars, which pilots would attend either while serving with the Fleet or immediately on completion of flying training, or, as it was called, ab initio.

The official establishment of RAF Leuchars, as of 1 April 1920, stood at a total of 280 personnel, 114 of whom were part of the station's HQ strength. The largest active unit was 205 Fleet Reconnaissance Squadron, which had eighteen Parnall Panthers on strength and 102 personnel. The other established unit was 203 Squadron, which at this time had only a single Flight and twenty-nine personnel.

On 24 October 1921, Gp Capt. C. S. Burnett assumed command of the new group at Donibristle, taking over from Gp Capt. Clark Hall, with the RAF base at Leuchars being commanded by Wg Cdr R. Peel-Ross.

At this time the station's three squadrons were composed as follows: 3 Squadron equipped with Walruses; 205 Squadron equipped with Panthers; and 203 Squadron equipped with Camels. There was also a Training Flight flying Avro Mono 100s. Both 203 and 205 Squadrons were essentially operational for fleet requirements, 203 being a fighter squadron, and 205 a reconnaissance squadron. No. 3 Squadron had re-formed from 205 Squadron on 1 October 1921. No. 203 Squadron re-equipped with Nieuport Nightjars, while retaining some Sopwith Camels until 1922. These were to have trained for deck landing but instead were sent out to the Mediterranean. The Training Flight had its Avros supplemented by the arrival of two Sopwith Snipes, powered by Bentley BR.2 engines rated at 230 hp—the same engine that powered the Nightjars and Panthers. To give some idea of just how much of an improvement in power this was, the much more familiar First World War fighter, the Sopwith Camel, was powered by a BR.1 engine with an output of just 150 hp.

On 31 March 1922, 29 Group, which had formed the air element of the Grand Fleet, was disbanded and Gp Capt. Burnett took over as the Station Commander at Leuchars. He relinquished command of Leuchars later that year, on 15 November, handing over to Wg Cdr P. H. L. Playfair.

Parnell Panther of 205 Sqn photographed with personnel in 1921. (*MOD/Crown copyright*)

On an interesting historical note, in June 1929, the Prime Minister, Ramsay MacDonald, who had been returned to 10 Downing Street that month, made his first ever flight—not from Leuchars but from a recently prepared temporary landing ground at Lossiemouth. Mind you, Lossiemouth was the great man's home town.

The move towards the training of naval carrier-capable units came about on 1 April 1923, and 203 and 205 Squadrons were redesignated respectively as 402 and 401 Fleet Reconnaissance Squadrons, while 3 Squadron disbanded to re-form overseas. One year later, all air units assigned to the Fleet were given the grander-sounding title of Fleet Air Arm of the RAF, its roles and responsibilities continuing under the command of RAF Coastal Area. However, this element would return to the Navy's order of battle shortly before the outbreak of war in 1939.

As well as Coastal Area, the RAF's peacetime structure included Inland Area, the larger of the two UK-based elements. Everything else was overseas: Egyptian Area, Mesopotamian Area, RAF India, Mediterranean Group, and cadre establishments such as training schools and miscellaneous establishments such as supply stores etc. Leuchars naturally fell within Coastal Area due to its maritime remit and because at that stage it provided operational flying training—much as the later Operational Training Units (OTUs) and Operational Conversion Units (OCUs).

Leuchars was for now in the business of forming new carrier air units, and following carrier training and the departure of 401 and 402 Squadrons, the next two Flights (as they were now designated), Nos 403 and 441, were formed. The turnround was quite intense: Nos 443 and 444 Flights were formed on 1 December 1924 and 16 January 1925 respectively.

During 1925, Leuchars became a training base in every sense of the term. The next aircraft to arrive were Blackburn Blackburns and Avro Bisons, and a single dual-control Siskin. However, the change to a more recognisable flying training role did not dissipate the carrier conversion and FAA building role of the previous seven years, although 1925 saw the departure of more carrier flights—Nos 401, 405 and 406 to Donibristle, and No. 444 to Lee-on-Solent. This still left 404, 442 and 443 Flights at the end of the year, but the comings and goings of the carrier flights, both newly formed and those returning for refresher training, continued through to the end of the decade.

With few changes in 1926, life settled down somewhat. The training syllabus of pilots of any specialisation was not quite so complex or overwhelming, and while at first glance it is difficult to understand the prominence and importance of aerobatics in modern fighter aircraft from the layman's point of view, much store was set by this discipline during this early period. In more recent times it has often been regarded as little more than a frivolous activity for public entertainment at air shows in order to secure funds for service and other charities—seen by some as the only worthwhile and redeeming feature. It is, in fact, a skill that defines the capabilities of the pilot.

Looking through the log book of a typical flight commander of the day, one finds entries dominated by practice aerobatics and formation drills in equal or greater number alongside the engine tests and amphibian landings. Fg Off. John D'Arcy Keary, a pilot posted to 'A' Training Flight on 17 December 1926, recorded the following entries from 29 December 1926 to 11 January 1927:

29.12.26	Self	9869	15	Local Aerobatics
30.12.26	Self	9665	45	Local Aerobatics
31.12.26	Self	9869	35	Local Aerobatics
31.12.26	Self	9665	40	Local Aerobatics
03.01.27	Self	9869	55	Formation Aerobatics
04.01.27	Self	9869	35	Formation Aerobatics
04.01.27	Self	9869	20	Formation Aerobatics
04.01.27	Self	9869	15	Formation Aerobatics
06.01.27	Self	9867	30	Engine Test
07.01.27	Self	9867	50	Flight Formation X-Country Perth–Donibristle
07.01.27	Self	9867	50	Flight Formation X-Country Donibristle–Leuchars
10.01.27	Self	9665	05	X-Country Montrose–Perth
10.01.27	Self	9940	20	Engine and Rigging Test
11.01.27	Self	9940	20	Local Aerobatics

These types of entries were typical of the time. Other entries later include gun camera practice and the all-important amphibian and deck landings. The aircraft referred to in the entries are Fairey Flycatchers, but others operated at the time include Fairey IIIDs, while Gloster Grebes appear later.

The twelfth Fleet training course began on 1 October 1928, with four pupils, while the third RAF course completed. Up to and including the eleventh naval and the third RAF courses, a total of forty-seven students passed muster, bar one unfortunate naval student who was returned to his unit as unsuitable.

The aircraft now being flown included a number of new types. Aircraft design in all respects was moving ahead from the early days of the First World War, and it was commonplace for a single type to last no more than a couple of years before being superseded. In 1928, a range of new aircraft arrived at Leuchars as basic flying training was added to the syllabus, including Armstrong Siddeley Lynxes, Avro Bisons, Armstrong Whitworth Siskins and Blackburn Blackburns, as well as some of the earlier types such as Fairey IIIDs and Flycatchers. Training had now expanded to cover both finishing school and ab initio, and however intense and demanding training may have been, the output and transition from novice to operational pilot or observer was very short. In July, an RAF bomber squadron, No. 36, was formed with a Hawker Horsley biplane and commanded by Sqn Ldr A. W. Mylne. When ready, the unit was posted to Donibristle.

Among the naval units visiting was the former Leuchars 421 Flight. During the detachment, tragedy struck—but not in the air. Two of the Flight's members, Capt. R. W. Gordon of the Royal Marines and Lt E. J. E. Burt of the Royal Navy, were involved in a car accident just outside St Andrews in which Capt. Gordon was killed and Lt Burt seriously injured. Capt. Gordon was buried at sea from HMS *Tetrarch*, five miles east of May Island, at 1100 hours on 11 November.

The dangers of flying in less than perfect conditions with poor aids were demonstrated when a naval pilot, Lt Gibb of 461 Flight, was flying a Blackburn Dart during deck landing practices at night on HMS *Furious* on 28 October. Lt Gibb, not surprisingly under the circumstances, became lost and was left with no option but to attempt a forced landing near Aberdeen. His aircraft was completely destroyed by fire; he, however, managed to escape without injury.

The decade closed for Leuchars with 1929 notching up 3,370 hours of flying for the year, and in this last month ten RN officers and seven RAF officers passed out from training on their respective courses. From February 1930, the Fleet spotter reconnaissance training was now carried out entirely on the Fairey IIIF, and the Blackburn Darts that had been used previously were all stored at the station pending disposal.

Up until January 1932, RAF Donibristle had been administered by Leuchars but now became autonomous. For Leuchars, however, it was business as usual. Another FAA course commenced in January, but with only six pupils. The months ahead leading into summer saw a number of accidents, including fatalities. During February, an Avro 504 and a Fairey IIIF collided. The naval aircraft was being flown by an RAF crew— Fg Off. H. G. Hicks and AC1 Beattie—both of whom were killed, while S/Lt A. A. F. Talbot, flying the 504, was seriously injured. In August another Fairey IIIF crashed into Tentsmuir Forest, killing the two crew—Lt A. B. Kay of the Royal Navy and A. C. Foreman of the RAF.

September brought the carrier HMS *Furious* to the Firth of Forth, allowing two courses—No. 21 Fleet Air Arm and No. 17 Conversion—to carry out deck landing training. By 1933, the variety of aircraft types in use at Leuchars was at its greatest: Avro 504Ns, Fairey IIIFs, Flycatchers, Bulldogs (trainer version), Siskins, Moths, Hawker Nimrods and Ospreys. In January, an event looking to the future occurred when two Leuchars-

Fairey IIIF on a training sortie over the Tay Bridge, Dundee. This photo was taken on 6 October 1931. (*MOD/Crown copyright*)

7 October 1930, Fairy IIIFs overflying the Tay Bridge, Dundee. (*MOD/Crown copyright*)

based aircraft assisted in the search for two missing climbers in the Cairngorms, albeit unsuccessfully.

On 1 March 1935, the station identity (hitherto RAF Training Base Leuchars) was changed to No. 1 FTS. The school had disbanded four years earlier at RAF Netheravon due to the need (rather like today) to make economic savings. When re-formed at Leuchars, training courses began for air gunners and telegraphists—that is to say, for air gunners per se, and for naval personnel who had specifically trained as telegraphists. Curiously, many of these courses were terminated after only a month or so.

The following year, two similar courses were started in the same month as another little-known unit emerged—the Air Training Camp. Formed on 26 February 1936 under the command of Sqn Ldr B. K. D. Robertson, this unit did not operate any aircraft of its own but provided the necessary training, seemingly for bomber squadrons in particular, judging by its clientele at the time (Nos 15, 45 and 101 Squadrons) which typically pitched up with their aircraft and stayed for a month or two before heading off again, very similar to how matters had progressed over the previous decade.

A composite fighter command squadron turned up towards the end of the year, and then through the following year came a long list of mainly bomber but also fighter-bomber, maritime/coastal and FAA squadrons as well. The maritime/coastal squadron moored their flying boats nearby at Newport-on-Tay.

As busy as the station now was, the training era was coming to an end and the very circumstances that had kept it going were about to bring about a more visible change in its role. While Leuchars retained its link to maritime operations, the shift from training school to frontline station was just a couple of years away.

In 1937, the RAF Hendon air pageant—the first RAF organised air show—was staged for the last time. Until then, whatever the size, strength and available resources, the RAF had invited the public across the threshold of Hendon for one weekend each summer since 1920. Doubtless influenced by the desire to reach out to the wider public and hopefully create a positive effect on recruitment, it was now decided to hold several similar events across the country. This was clearly seen as a much more effective and profitable way of going about staging public air displays.

So, on 29 May 1937, several RAF stations opened their gates. Sponsored by the Air League but staged by the RAF, these events were to be held regularly from that year forward, in lieu of the Hendon pageant. Empire Air Day, like the Battle of Britain 'at home' days to come, was held once a year, with all participating stations open simultaneously. Thus RAF Leuchars held its first air show. On this occasion, the station took receipts

Vertical shot of RAF Leuchars, taken from 7,000 feet on 7 October 1936, the original Hangar complex made up of 7 Belfast Hangars is the most obvious segment of the station. Note also, the first married quarters, arching round from the admin area below and to the left. (*Royal Air Force Museum Archives*)

1935, Fairey IIIF with engine warming awaits a catapult launch. Note Bulmallo Quarry in the distance behind the framework support holding the aircraft, this is where years later Ed Rawcliffe's Lightning speared in. (*MOD/Crown copyright*)

of £571 12s, and 8,502 adults and 2,617 children were recorded as having attended, along with 1,099 cars and 216 motorcycles.

The aircraft which took part were largely locally sourced, to use a modern expression, or visiting from nearby, and the spectators at Leuchars in 1937 got to see Fairey IIIFs, which occupied about six of the twenty-seven display slots throughout the afternoon display. Being a fledgling affair, the organisation may have lacked a certain amount of imagination and creative thinking, so the six appearances by the Fairey IIIFs were each billed as 'One Fairey IIIF to be hoisted onto a catapult'. A seven-seater airliner was also made available for passenger flights at a charge of 7s 6d per head.

Before the end of the lull prior to the storm, an Air Ministry review took place during the early part of 1938, the upshot of which was that the flying training of Navy and Army pupils at Leuchars was to be brought into line with that of a normal flying training school, i.e. that the elementary training would be done by civil flying training schools, and that No. 1 FTS would be responsible for the intermediate and advanced training. However, this new instruction was short-lived, as Coastal Command took over the station and airfield and No. 1 FTS received its marching orders. It had returned to its old haunt at Netheravon by 26 August 1938, in one of the many moves hastened by the growing concern that conflict in Europe was once again inevitable. Changes elsewhere meant that No. 6 FTS moved from Netheravon to Little Rissington.

3

On the Front Line

RAF Leuchars transferred from Flying Training Command to Coastal Command on 1 August 1938, and Gp Capt. O. Grenfell was appointed as the new Station Commander. But it was to be a short appointment, as Gp Capt. B. E. Baker took over on 1 September. No. 1 FTS remained until the 26th of the month, when 233 and 224 squadrons, then equipped with Avro Ansons, arrived from their previous base at Thornaby in Yorkshire.

However, the changeover to an operational command and the ever-increasing likelihood of full-scale war with Germany did not prevent one more Empire Air Day being authorised. On 20 May 1939, Leuchars, along with many other RAF stations, including Montrose just up the road, opened its gates for the last time before the world went up in flames. On the outbreak of war, two more squadrons had arrived—Nos 220 and 612. All were now operating the Lockheed Electra Hudson, apart from 612 Squadron which was still equipped with Ansons. Leuchars was now operational, and patrols by the Hudsons were taking place across the North Sea, but with little to get excited about.

Just five days following the declaration of war, on 8 September 1939, a Hudson of 224 Squadron unsuccessfully attempted to engage a Heinkel He 111—not quite what it was meant to be doing. The Heinkel disappeared at speed into cloud. The typical sortie format usually involved two or three Hudsons carrying out a parallel track search of a quadrangle in the form of a continuous patrol. Take-offs were quite widely spaced, but for now there was little doing. This was the phoney war, and the expectation, as always, was that it would all fizzle out by Christmas. However, places like Leuchars were seeing whatever limited action there was. The British Expeditionary Force on the Continent were facing fewer challenges than perhaps the British Army of the Rhine (BAOR) did at any time during the Cold War.

The pre-war expansion, perhaps more visible elsewhere, had brought some additional infrastructure to the base at Leuchars throughout the 1920s and '30s. The hangar complex was extended to seven Belfast Truss hangars (a single and six linked in pairs) which, apart from the single and centre pair, sit to this day to the north of the main runway and just to the west of the cross-runway. They were arranged in a neat rectangular block until the 1970s, when the middle two were knocked down in order to build a new Technical and Supply HQ complex.

With the outbreak of the Second World War came the construction, further west of the Belfast Truss hangars, of four austerity-designated C-type hangars (so called due to the greater reliance on corrugated iron rather than brickwork and thus differentiating them from the regulation C-type hangars used on many Bomber and Coastal Command stations). The four C-type hangars sit in a kind of arrowhead arrangement, with one immediately behind the old control tower and two more on either side at an incline, while the fourth forms a stem to the rear of the centre.

On 29 January 1940, an aircraft from 233 Squadron reported trying to get a bearing from Leuchars from 1503 hours to 1600 hours without success, evidently due to BBC interference. Both the Hudson squadrons sent out daily patrols either singly, in pairs or three-ships to predetermined patrol areas identified with simple codes such as L1, L2 and so forth. Occasionally the weather, regardless of the operational circumstances, would intervene. Early in February operational flying was cancelled every day from the 2nd to the 8th, except for a window on the 3rd of the month.

At this early stage of the war, when aloft there was as much chance, if not more, of being shot at by armed trawlers and merchant vessels, who of course were the principal beneficiaries of the Hudson anti-ship and anti-submarine patrols. The Hudson crews continued to find themselves attacking Heinkels just as often as they found or engaged any surface threat. On 11 February, a detachment of Hurricanes for local air defence arrived from 605 Squadron, but their stay was temporary. To break the humdrum routine of returning empty-handed, save for having been shot at occasionally by friendly shipping, the end of the month was marked by Leuchars being beaten at both football and boxing by personnel from RAF Montrose up the coast. The scores were 5–3 and 21–19 respectively.

March 1940 brought a further increase in activity with the start of routine comings and goings by Avro Ansons of 608 Squadron, flying out from RAF Thornaby on 'police patrols'. Tragedy struck in the early part of the month when Fg Off. S. D. Slocum, flying Hudson N7334 on special duties, was shot down over Culverstone in Kent by 'our own forces', according to the Operations Record Book (ORB), which perhaps understandably does not identify which of our own forces were involved. At the time, Fg Off. Slocum's aircraft was seconded to the Photographic Development Unit based at RAF Heston.

The month brought some luck at last, when an aircraft from 224 Squadron spotted an oil discharge from what was believed to be an enemy submarine and ran in for the attack using the under-wing bomb distributor. Only one bomb released, but the Hudson, call sign G224, made a second attack, releasing the remaining two bombs on the point where the target was last seen submerging. A further two bombs were thrown at the edge of the oil discharge by an Anson that subsequently joined in. The oil on the surface was seen to increase substantially, and finally two Navy destroyers arrived to finish off the stricken vessel with a pattern of depth charges from each. The first was enough—a large round bubbling patch appeared and then no more. The squadron had further success a week later when one of its Hudsons engaged another U-boat. Again, three bombs were dropped, resulting in a large brown oil discharge directly over where the target was last seen diving.

A change in U-boat tactics came midway through the war, after U-333 remained on the surface to fight off an air attack by a Vickers Wellington on 2 May 1943, successfully bringing the Wimpy down. This seemed to influence thinking at higher level, and some U-boats were given heavier surface armament, although not with any great success. However, whether a submarine dived or stayed on the surface doubtless depended on the particular circumstances at the time. If all that was needed was for the captain to pull his head and binoculars inside the hatch and screw it shut, then diving would be the sensible option, but if half the crew were strung out along the deck taking advantage of the fresh air while battery recharging, then submerging was not a good idea. Better to loose off rounds at the attacking enemy aircraft.

Another aircraft of 224 Squadron came to grief on 14 March 1940 when N7212 crashed near the railway signalbox on the St Andrews to Cupar line.

As is the nature of war, casualties inevitably arose, unsurprisingly given the overwhelming odds presented by the Third Reich. On 12 April 1940, another Hudson and its crew of four were lost on operations. It is interesting to note the ranks of the four men in comparison with typical aircrew ranks of recent times: Plt Off. Yark (pilot); Flt Lt McLaren (navigator); Cpl Wilson (wireless operator); LAC Milne (air gunner).

Air Vice-Marshal C. D. Breese paid a visit around this time in order to decorate two sergeant pilots, L. T. Cargill and J. Hawken, with the Distinguished Flying Medal (DFM). Sadly, within the following four days Hawken was lost on a sortie, flying one of two Hudsons of 233 Squadron that failed to return alongside one from 224 Squadron. Less than a year later, Air Vice-Marshal Breese would be lost when flying from Leuchars to Sumburgh, while attempting a forced landing three-quarters of a mile south-west of Wick. The rest of his crew—Plt Off. R. N. Selley and Sgts S. L. J. Wright and W. F. Shaw—were also lost.

The Battle of Britain, a significant and unique aerial campaign, had demonstrated for the first time that Germany's military machine was not entirely impervious to resistance, but the victory had only bought time. The means of bringing absolute defeat to bear upon the Third Reich was not within the grasp of any single nation, and there was no immediate prospect of any kind of military proposition that would be able to bring about uncompromising victory.

Meanwhile, the war effort was increasingly developing to cover a broad and diverse spectrum of people and tasks. Personnel of the Women's Auxiliary Air Force (WAAF) played an important role particularly during the Battle of Britain (characterised by the image of fighter plotters), and the need for more female personnel brought about a recruitment drive. On 30 January 1941, a party of journalists arrived at Leuchars to obtain material for that very reason.

The Director of the WAAF had chosen Leuchars as the representative station, for no specified reason. In any event, the station's ORB, typical

Lockheed Hudson Torpedo Bomber of 224 Sqn, the crew are ready to board for another sortie, August 1940. (*MOD/Crown copyright*)

of the culture of the age, carried a reference—not entirely flattering by present-day standards—stating that 'photos were taken of the women at their various occupations, in the Mess etc'.

A recruitment film to encourage young women to join up was made in April, again at Leuchars. This appeared to expand upon the duties of WAAF personnel, covering such diverse roles as special duties clerks, telephonists, teleprinter operators, parachute packers, shorthand typists in the orderly room, and airwomen cleaning and testing spark plugs. Off-duty activities were filmed as well, fencing being chosen on this occasion.

On the evening of 11 February, 224 Squadron sent six Hudsons to attack the docks at Kristiansand. The mission involved steep dives, typically from about 12,000 feet, releasing four 250-lb bombs at about 6,000 feet, the aircraft attacking separate targets against what was described as heavy and accurate anti-aircraft return fire.

No. 233 Squadron had left the station at the end of 1940, and on 3 March 1941, Blenheims from 107 Squadron arrived at Leuchars, flying their first operational sortie two days later. Typical of the war period, the movement of units in and out was continuous, and it was unusual for any one squadron to remain in situ for more than a year. No. 42 Squadron arrived in 1941, equipped with Bristol Beaufort Is and IIs.

By 15 April, 224 Squadron had departed, leaving Nos 320 (Dutch), 42 and 107 Squadrons, which had been joined by Nos 86 and 114 Squadrons, operating Blenheim IVs and Vs. They were now being tasked with more ambitious sorties, specifically attacking U-boat pens and other docks, and Nos 320, 42 and 107 Squadrons were mainly engaged in convoy escorts throughout 1941.

An interesting fact about Leuchars during the war is that it was used for covert trips flown by BOAC to and from Sweden, on what has been described as an extensive scale. These flights carried Norwegians back from Sweden who had made it into the neutral country after escaping from the Gestapo. The aircraft were military types but with civilian markings on the airframes and flown by BOAC crews.

Reconnaissance Spitfires and Mosquitos arrived in 1942, as did 144 Squadron with more Blenheims on 24 April, while four days later, 455 (Royal Australian Air Force) Squadron arrived, equipped with Handley Page Hampdens initially but later receiving Bristol Beaufighter Xs. This same year, 42 Squadron carried out its famous attack on the *Scharnhorst* and *Gneisenau* in the English Channel as well as attacking the *Prinz Eugen* off Stavanger. Torpedo-carrying Handley Page Hampdens of 455 (RAAF) Squadron and 144 Squadron carried out anti-shipping strikes off the Norwegian coast, and 333 Squadron of the Royal Norwegian Air Force arrived with Catalinas at Woodhaven on the River Tay. Their crews were briefed at Leuchars for various tasks, which centred on anti-U-boat and escort patrols. Indeed, a number of aircraft squadrons parented at Leuchars operated from the Tay. Warwicks flew Search and Rescue (SAR) missions from there, operating in conjunction with high speed launches.

Early in 1942, Leuchars became home to one of the most impressive aircraft produced during the Second World War—the 'Wooden Wonder'—otherwise familiar as the de Havilland Mosquito. The aircraft were Mosquito BIVs of Bomber Command's 105 Squadron and were to launch from Leuchars specifically to attack a vital target inside the city of Oslo.

Some months after arriving, and led by Sqn Ldr Douglas Parry, four Mosquito BIVs got airborne at 1413 hours on 25 September and flew off on a north-east heading across the North Sea. The day of the attack was selected primarily because good weather was forecast, but it also coincided with a high-level conference in Oslo of senior Nazi Party figures, including the party's Norwegian leader Vidkun Quisling. Oslo, like so many European cities under German occupation, was home to some brutal goings-on in the form of Gestapo torture chambers and such like, and the Gestapo HQ in the city was one of 105 Squadron's primary targets. It is this very kind of raid that inspired the storylines for films such as *633 Squadron*. The raid was flown as a hi-lo-lo mission—that is to say, the formation flew out at higher altitude but, once past Drøbak, descended to 100 feet and headed up the Oslo Fjord. Reaching their target without much difficulty, they hit five buildings causing heavy losses among the Germans. Tragically, as was all too common at the time, collateral damage meant that eight Norwegians were also killed. The crews and aircraft were as follows: Sqn Ldr Parry and Plt Off. Robson in DK296-G; Plt Offs Rowland and Reilly in DK313-U; Plt Offs Bristow and Marshall in DK328-V; and FS Carter and Sgt Young in DK325-S.

Sadly, the mission was not without further casualties. The formation was intercepted on the return leg by a pair of Luftwaffe Fw 190s from Jagdgeschwader 1/JG 5 piloted by Unteroffiziere Klein and Fenten (The German rank of unteroffizier is equivalent to either sergeant or corporal!) The Fw 190s managed to hit two of the Mosquitos, DK313-U and DK325-S, the latter catching fire in the starboard engine and coming down while attempting to turn for the neutral territory of Sweden. Struggling to remain aloft, a wing clipped branches of a birch tree before the aircraft crashed into Lake Engervann, killing 26-year-old Carter and his 20-year-old navigator. Their bodies were recovered by two Norwegians in a rowing boat and were later buried in the British War Cemetery in Oslo.

One of the reasons for the mission being flown from Leuchars related to fears about the endurance of the Mosquito BIV. Although the reconnaissance PR1 version had demonstrated no concerns on this score,

Torpedo being loaded into a 42 Sqn Beaufort, March 1941. (*MOD/Crown copyright*)

Bristol Beaufort I N1172/AW-S of 42 Sqn based at Leuchars, photographed March 1941. (*MOD/Crown copyright*)

the BIV was a different matter altogether. Unlike its recce variant, called upon to carry only camera equipment and tasked mainly with operating at higher altitudes, including when over the target area, the BIV had to carry a bomb load of up to 2,000 lb. Moreover, a considerable chunk of the mission was to be flown at low level, which meant significantly greater fuel consumption. Therefore a 'launch pad' much closer to the target than 105 Squadron's home base in southern England was considered advisable. As it was, the remaining three Mosquitos managed to make it back as far as Sumburgh in Shetland, where they landed after having flown over 1,100 miles in a round trip lasting 4 hours and 45 minutes. They had fuel remaining in their tanks—exactly how much is unknown—and it had been proved that the 'Wooden Wonder' could strike with bombs against enemy targets over a considerable range. A further such raid on a greater scale took place in December 1944, on New Year's Eve.

In the fullness of time, Leuchars would become home to a volunteer Mountain Rescue Team (MRT) which remained until the RAF's withdrawal from Leuchars brought about the demise of the team in 2013. Like so many other innovations to arise from the Second World War, they owed their existence to the significant increase in military aircraft shot down. In 1942, a medical officer, Flt Lt George Desmond 'Doc' Graham stationed in Wales, seized the initiative to put together a team of servicemen for the specific purpose of rescuing downed aircrew across the inhospitable uplands of Britain's more remote and unpopulated (some might say uninhabitable) landscapes.

The remit of the MRTs that developed from Flt Lt Graham's first team has not changed much over the years, although retrieving rock climbers, hill walkers and misguided picnickers places a greater demand on their talents. The unit at RAF Leuchars came into being on a permanent basis in 1955, but it was formally established and recognised as part of the RAF Mountain Rescue Service in January 1944 (although they had sent out search parties earlier in the war).

Originally, ten teams were put together, including one at RAF Montrose. At the end of the war, the Montrose team moved to RAF Edzell, nearer the Highlands on the Angus border, but were there for only a short time before moving on again. Other teams in Scotland were established at RAF West Freugh and Kinloss, and by 1949 the team that had moved to Edzell was back at Montrose again, only to move back to Edzell the following year where they had their longest stay to date.

In 1955, the RAF moved out of Edzell, which later became a base for the US Navy, in keeping with the growing Cold War activities of the time, and the MRT moved to Leuchars where it was to remain. The Fife coast may not at first glance seem to be the ideal location for a mountain rescue team, but Leuchars has certainly worked well as a base for the MRT and perhaps has benefited from the often good weather experienced in the area. This has enabled the team to respond to any emergency when weather at the incident spot has been severe, allowing volunteers to react and prepare in a less hazardous atmosphere, take stock of the situation and deal with it accordingly. The helicopters of the SAR Flights based at Leuchars from the 1950s through to 1993 also provided obvious vital assistance with transportation as well as the rescue and evacuation of people stuck in otherwise inaccessible locations.

A Norwegian Mosquito squadron arrived in 1943 and operated as a fighter escort unit to torpedo-carrying Beauforts. As the conflict progressed, air warfare continued along the path of development that at the time looked set to provide optimum performance, range and capacity, together with the development of electronic aids. In the summer of 1944, two squadrons, Nos 206 and 547, arrived at Leuchars, both equipped with the B-24 Liberator. This was perhaps the largest and most technically advanced bomber to be based within the British Isles up until this point, but was still unable to carry a comparable bomb load to the Lancaster.

American built and with a tricycle undercarriage, the B-24 was quite advanced. Those at Leuchars were employed escorting Russian convoys, but later they carried out anti-shipping strikes in the Baltic and the Skagerrak, the latter being the channel between Denmark and Norway linking the North Sea with the Baltic Sea.

These sorties were flown at night using radar and Leigh lights. On 15 November 1943, a signal arrived from Air Officer Commanding (AOC) 18 Group confirming that Norwegian Lodestars were now permitted to operate from Leuchars under certain conditions, i.e. subject to arrangements being made with the Station Commander through BOAC, and also that permission to operate could be given only by the Station Commander and would be subject to RAF requirements. BOAC and the Norwegian Lodestar operators had a hangar assigned to them, while another of the new C-type hangars was placed at the disposal of the servicing wing under orders from the Chief Engineer at Coastal Command, three more station buildings being set aside for photographic processing in conjunction with a detachment from 540 Squadron.

AOC 18 Group, Air Vice-Marshal A. B. Ellwood, arrived shortly after, on 24 November, to present the DFC to Lt Cdr J. J. Ebbesen of 333 (Royal Norwegian Air Force) Squadron. A further signal was received during the month, congratulating one and all at Leuchars for their achievements during the previous month on anti-U-boat operations. The signal stated:

The brilliant success achieved in this vital field is the well-deserved result of tireless perseverance and devotion to duty and is, I am sure, a welcome reward for the aircrews and others who have spared no effort during long months of arduous operations and training. Now that you have obtained this remarkable advantage over the U-boats I know you will press it home with ever increasing vigour and determination, until in conjunction with the Royal Navy you have finally broken the enemy's morale.

St Andrews University lent its resources during the war. In addition to providing potential aircrew students to the University Air Squadron, Madras College was also made available to the station for training WAAF typists.

Not all the comings and goings at Leuchars were concerned with politicians, senior military officers and shady characters. The station did receive the odd celebrity as well, forces entertainment being a matter to be taken seriously in the climate of the times, and 7 November 1943 brought a pleasant surprise when Joe Loss and his orchestra performed at the station's theatre.

By January 1944, the Air Ministry was looking at further development of the airfield, one proposal relating to the east–west runway. It was recommended this should be extended by 1,600 yards to the east. There was even a plan to extend it to the west by 400 yards, which would have meant cutting through the mound or small hillock on which many an aircraft enthusiast over the decades has perched when photographing and filming the comings and goings during exercises and, of course, the annual air show. There was a great deal of enthusiasm for removing the hillock, as it was seen to pose a threat to aircraft operating from the main runway, but this would also have meant pushing the runway threshold through another potato field and placing the touchdown area just short of the railway station. Evidently, the proposals of the day did not progress all that far. The hillock is still very much there as of 2015, with the road from Dundee to Cupar and St Andrews running through it.

There was also a proposal to extend the cross-runway to the north-east, requiring the clearing away of some farm outbuildings, two bungalows and a cottage. The intended runways were to be 'ocean class strips', and the amount of work was considered negligible. However, a third runway was deemed necessary to accommodate the options for operating into wind, as all types of known aircraft at the time needed to be able to operate from the base under the least favourable conditions.

All this was with a view to commercial rather than military considerations, in order that Leuchars could be an emergency alternative with a terminal for use when other airfields might be 'out' due to bad weather. Throughout its existence since the start of the Second World War, the concept of the airfield as a commercial airport has continued, and is the case even now, as the RAF prepares to hand over all but the airside of the base to the Army, and is something that will be touched on again later in the book.

Meanwhile, BOAC had continued with its secretive air operations from Leuchars, collecting Norwegian refugees, the service having expanded considerably, with a significant amount of traffic to and from Stockholm employing a number of aircraft types, including Lodestars and Dakotas. Two of the resident squadrons, Nos 455 and 489, both prepared to move to RAF Langham in Norfolk, and four more Liberators arrived from Prestwick, having been flow over from America to continue the evacuation of refugees being carried out by BOAC. It would appear that the Liberators were better suited to this role as summer approached and the daylight hours increased. In a single day in early 1945, as many as nine or ten movements back and forth were recorded, while the station continued with more recognisable operations such as photo reconnaissance sorties and anti-shipping strikes by the Liberator squadrons.

The recce sorties were flown by Mosquitos of 544 Squadron. In addition, the station was home to 18 Group Communications Flight equipped with Airspeed Oxfords. The Mosquito PRs were mainly involved with reconnaissance sorties, as you would imagine, over the Norwegian and Danish coasts. These, like the BOAC flights, were lonely tasks. Typically a single aircraft would fly out—unarmed and reliant on speed, height and stealth to reach the designated target—and then try to make it back before the Luftwaffe could respond.

What is rarely considered about this period of the war is how much flying and ammunition was used simply for training. During a week of air-to-air training for the crews of 455 and 489 Squadrons, the amount expended included 26,332 rounds of 20 mm. When this statistic is considered—just a snapshot of not even the entire usage by all the combat elements of a single Coastal Command station—it rather places in perspective the overall cost of prosecuting the war on the much wider scale.

In April 1944, an extension of the north-east to south-west runway was agreed. The work also included the widening of a section of the perimeter track and involved the relocation of the Watch Office. This period, of course, was the run-up to D-Day—albeit most people were unaware—and it may well have been disappointing as well as puzzling when instructions were received from HQ Coastal Command that all leave was to be cancelled except on compassionate grounds.

While the bulk of Allied armed forces concentrated in the UK ready to land on the Normandy coast on 6 June 1944, the element making up RAF

Leuchars faced a rather quiet period, with no enemy aircraft or shipping encountered. The only activity recorded concerned Mosquitos from 333 Squadron carrying out live training with depth charges, while another BOAC Mosquito left for Stockholm, returning the next day as three more headed out.

It would appear that the final attempt by aircraft based at Leuchars to engage any enemy shipping came on 5 May 1945, when Liberators of 206 and 547 Squadrons sighted U-boats on the surface with a small number of escort vessels, which opened fire as they were attacked with depth charges. Twelve were dropped from one aircraft and all turret guns engaged, with hits scored. The first vessel in this encounter, with 547 Squadron aircraft attacking, is described as lifting by the stern 45 degrees out of the water before sinking stern-first. Bodies and wreckage were seen on the surface five minutes later. A second U-boat began to submerge and was attacked, according to the ORB, by an unidentified Liberator, while another aircraft of 547 Squadron attacked a 500-ton coaster with six 250-lb depth charges. At 2156 hours, one of 206 Squadron's aircraft attacked a U-boat that had just surfaced, the front gunner opening up first, followed up by six more 250-lb depth charges. The vessel was seen to submerge, with a swirling oil patch and possible debris evident. Elsewhere, forty U-boat survivors were seen in dinghies, rafts and rowing boats on an oil patch. One aircraft of 547 Squadron failed to return, with no signal received, and is probably the last loss of a Leuchars-based aircraft to enemy action or simply lost while on patrol.

As late as 20 May 1945, three Liberators from 206 Squadron reached Gossen airfield where nine Me 109s and six Me 110s were found on a single dispersal at 0830 hours, while six more Me 110s were found dispersed around the perimeter at Ørlandet, and twelve Me 110s at Trondheim. Just a few days earlier, this kind of operation would not have been possible without drawing a hostile reaction, but now RAF aircraft were roaming over enemy air and naval bases while all was on view with no response.

One of the most remarkable aspects of the Second World War was the readiness with which both principal Axis powers surrendered and accepted the change in circumstances when ordered by their High Commands to do so. We have all seen images of German and Japanese officers behaving not just agreeably but with near subservience before men against whom they had had fought ruthlessly in war, yet their acceptance of the situation was absolute.

Another Liberator from the same sortie on 20 May sighted six stationary U-boats at Stavanger and ten more at Oslo. The third aircraft in the sortie overflew Bergen and counted twenty U-boats in the harbour together with a County-class cruiser standing by. Each of the aircraft carried the usual load of depth charges just in case, although now unlikely to engage, but despite expectations, these sorties still listed German shipping and aircraft as enemy. The scenes they saw represented the remnants of the defeated Third Reich.

These curious sorties, with Liberators flying out over the Norwegian coast and seeing plenty but not engaging other than to take snaps, was the order of things up until as late as 25 May, when, at 1827 hours, Liberators from the two squadrons intercepted and circled the German pocket battleships *Prinz Eugen* and *Nürnberg*, together with an escort of two cruisers and two destroyers, all on a heading of 183 degrees and travelling at 14 kts. They were picked up at position 57°10'N and 06°55'E, their course from there clearly taking them towards Germany where the reception party awaiting them would be from the recently installed new 'management team', to use a present-day corporate term. As was now the norm, there was no exchange of fire, the Liberators from Leuchars merely taking a few photos before heading home.

This appears to have been the conclusion to all Second World War enemy encounters for Leuchars-based aircraft. From here on, anti-ship and anti-submarine patrols would continue to be mounted by 206 and 547 Squadrons, but without finding any vessels classed as enemy. However, Leuchars did suffer two casualties during May 1945, when Mosquito RF605 from 248 Squadron crashed a short distance north-east of the station on the 18th. The two airmen on board, FS A. W. Porter and LAC R. W. Chalmers, were both killed.

But with the war still raging towards its climax in the Far East, Britain was now faced with the imperative demands of the immediate impact of peace, radical changes to the international order and to the country's position in the world, and its long-term future.

4

Peace and Tranquillity

As far as the RAF was concerned, the first priority after the war had ended was to take the opportunity to celebrate the moment that the common, unregarded airman had held the fate of the world in his sweaty palms and had not let it drop. The Battle of Britain was considered to have been the principal turning point in the fortunes not only of Fighter Command but of the free and civilised world, and it was less than two weeks after the Japanese surrender on 2 September 1945 that the battle's fifth official anniversary was marked. With 15 September falling on a Saturday that year, it could not have been more appropriate for staging a number of public 'at homes' at RAF stations.

Across the UK, one hundred RAF stations opened their gates to the general public, and Leuchars was one of them. What could never have been predicted at the time was that fifty years on, of all RAF stations it would be Leuchars, ever faithful to tradition, not Biggin Hill or Hornchurch or Tangmere, that would become the sole location at which this event would continue to be held annually, the southern stations having long since been abandoned by the junior service. Nor perhaps could it have been imagined that almost three-quarters of a century later, not a single RAF station could be made available to hold the event commemorating such a significant moment in RAF history, resources having been so severely reduced and stretched, if not having disappeared altogether.

The Battle of Britain 'at home' event, first held in 1945 and to become an annual extravaganza, was a radically different affair to any of the service-organised air shows seen in recent times. For a start, entry was free and private cameras were banned. The flying had a more spontaneous feel about it and was not subject to quite the degree of control and management that has become so pervasive today. The local paper carried the headline 'RAF "AT HOME"; Leuchars Station reveals war-time secrets', and the article went on to review the day:

In common with numerous other stations up and down the country, the Coastal Command RAF aerodrome at Leuchars was open for public inspection last Saturday and to the thousands of visitors the veil which had been pulled over the station in 1939 was lifted almost entirely. The event was reminiscent of those Empire Air Days of pre-war, but the attendance, though large, did not equal the big turn-outs of earlier years, principally due to the fact that road and rail transport are not yet on a real peace-time footing.

Group Captain C. R. Taylor OBE and his staff of officers, NCOs and men had everything in splendid order for their guests from all over Fife, Perth and Angus. And the thousands who attended were given free access to almost every portion of the station.

Visitors to previous pageants [a reference to the Empire Air Days, sponsored by the Air League and staged by the RAF in the immediate years before the war] were amazed how the drome had developed in size, and this gave one a feeling of timidity at daring to trespass into a community which for six years contained so many war secrets. But the personnel, who guided visitors, explained intricacies and answered innumerable questions, did everything in their power to make the visitors feel at home.

Mosquito, Beaufighter, Avro Anson, Typhoon, Spitfire, Mustang, Buckmaster, Dakota, Lancaster, Liberator, Wellington and Halifax were all there and very much made up the flying display. The commentator, Sqn Ldr Hart, is described as having given a racy description of each as they lined up and left. The star attraction was a Gloster Meteor, an eyewitness describing its departing climb after a high-speed run: 'It went up in an almost vertical climb of thousands of feet in a matter of seconds.' Nobody knew then just how relevant the Meteor would be as far as Leuchars was concerned. That said, with such a large and varied amount of display flying—largely by pilots with little or no training, rehearsal or set parameters—it is perhaps more of a wonder that the annual event was not marred by more fatalities than there were.

Leuchars saw tragedy during one of the early displays. At the 1948 show, a Spitfire of the then home-based 237 OCU crashed, killing the pilot. But this was not all: a fatal display flying accident occurred at no fewer than four other stations, three involving a de Havilland Mosquito, the worst of which claimed the lives of ten members of the public, including a small child. At the time, this was the worst air show accident in the UK.

It took some time for the approach to display flying in the early post-war years to be thoroughly shaken up, despite such experiences. As late as 1959, during the Leuchars show that year, an RN Scimitar (a large carrier-borne all-weather jet fighter) while displaying in low cloud had a fire warning light for one of its two engines illuminate. The pilot completed his display with the troubled engine shut down before returning to his home base at Lossiemouth, but I rather fancy that if the same thing were to happen now, the pilot of the stricken aircraft would cease his display and follow procedures for an emergency landing somewhere else where the danger to the public would be minimised.

Leuchars was still operational within the control of 18 Group Coastal Command through to the end of the 1940s, as it had been at the outbreak of war. The units based there in 1949 were 120/220 Squadron, equipped with the Avro Lancaster GR3, and 237 (PR) OCU, flying a mix of DH Mosquito PR34s and T3s, Airspeed Oxfords, Spitfire PR XIXs and Harvard IIBs. In addition was the HQ 18 Group Communications Flight, flying the Avro Anson XIX, the Percival Proctor IV and the Tiger Moth.

For the time being, Leuchars continued on a peacetime operational footing, but with nothing to place much of a demand on the units based there, although 237 OCU's Spitfires and Mosquitos had their work cut out providing photo reconnaissance training for aircrew going on to such units. As for the rest, the Lancasters of 120 and 122 Squadrons had nothing much to go scanning the North Sea for, as the dawn of the Red Banner Atlantic Fleet was yet to appear over the horizon, although it would not be long in coming. At the time what was of greater concern for serving military personnel was how far the post-war rationalisation would go.

In the meantime, other concerns were being addressed, including what to do in the event of the breakdown of civil order. This was something that seemed to exercise the minds of those in government in the early post-war years, when rationing was set to continue and, of all things, to get even worse, and industrial unrest was on the increase. In December 1949, Operation 'Homeland' was drawn up. It envisaged that the total resources of the RAF in the UK would assist civil ministries during industrial disputes and national emergencies. To facilitate this, all UK-based commands were divided into Emergency Transport Units (ETUs) and Emergency Labour Units (ELUs), both transport and labour being overseen by a number of emergency headquarters each controlling four units. Leuchars was now the base for No. 5 Emergency Transport Force HQ, including ELU No. 21 complete with advance party.

5

Cold North, Cold War

On 29 March 1950, as part of the proposed changes to the air defence network, Leuchars was transferred to Fighter Command. The station could expect to receive new hard-standings at either end of its lengthened runway, cross-bar approach lighting to replace straight-line approach, and ground-controlled approach radar. The first five stations to receive this would be Coltishall, Linton-on-Ouse, Leeming, Wattisham and Biggin Hill, the upgrades being due for implementation in 1950/51, with further upgrades planned for Duxford, Leuchars, Odiham, Tangmere and Waterbeach in 1951/52. The proposed standardisation plans included a dual runway layout with war-readiness platforms sited within 400 yards of any runway.

But before this could get under way, objections were politely raised by 90 Signals Group, which was responsible for the new Instrument Landing System (ILS). Specifically, among the many ambitious plans not to come to fruition as a result of the objections, or rather concerns, raised was the idea of building blast walls around the operational readiness platforms (ORPs) at each runway end. This was ditched because it would interfere with the ILS, as would the parking of aircraft at the upwind end of the active runway. The idea of parallel runways, measuring 2,000 yards by 50 yards with 100 yards spacing (to allow simultaneous scrambles and recoveries), also failed to materialise. Anyone familiar with the present-day Heathrow Airport will have noticed the simultaneous approaches there, which was the proposal for the RAF's fighter bases.

These recommendations had come from the Central Fighter Establishment (CFE), which also advocated dispensing with existing hangars such as the four austerity C-types at Leuchars. The idea was to have a series of small hangars, which were supposed to be self-contained, this concept in many ways being applied several years later with the introduction of HAS (hardened aircraft shelter) complexes.

However, much of what had been recommended would not go forward for reasons of cost alone. The idea of parallel runways was very ambitious, but had it been implemented it might have made a difference to the efficiency of launching all fighters in a survival scramble. Whether it would have meant the difference between defeat and victory when faced with the prospect of Armageddon is, however, open to debate. Further requirements were for sufficient hard-standings for all aircraft of the Unit Establishment (UE), which would need to be based on the maximum possible capacity, and a wing operations room, which would be well protected and sunk into the ground.

While the Meteor was an aircraft considered by the CFE as requiring elaborate reconstruction across the approved range of airfields, attention was turning to the next generation of fighters—the Swift, Hunter and Javelin. In all likelihood it was the wingspan of the latter (52 feet) that determined the wing spacing on dispersals. The QRA dispersals to be located at each end would need to be able to hold twelve aircraft each, and the operational turnround on such aircraft was expected to be complete in seven minutes. This time was based on the expectation that a blockage in the new 30-mm Aden cannon would require a complete gun change in the wing as far as the Meteor NF and Javelin were concerned. However, this problem did not arise with the Hunter, as its four 30-mm Aden guns would be fitted in a package unit allowing the whole component to be removed and a new one fitted regardless of how many guns were in need of repair. Thought had also been given to the location of fuel storage facilities, with at least four installations planned on each airfield in order to minimise the impact of a single well-aimed attack.

Meanwhile, even though an official transfer from Coastal to Fighter Command had taken place, Leuchars remained to all intents and purposes a maritime station, and the home base of the Avro Lancaster ASR/GR3s of 120 Squadron until the end of 1950. But as the transition from maritime patrol base to fighter base neared completion, the first fighter unit arrived in May, 222 Squadron, equipped with the latest day fighter type, the Gloster Meteor, and in the process of replacing its Mk 4s with the Mk 8.

The next to arrive, in November, was 43 Squadron—a unit which by all accounts was not keen on moving from its long-established home at RAF Tangmere in West Sussex, despite having formed in Scotland, at Stirling, in 1916. The squadron's diarist even recorded, following the final dining-in night at Tangmere at which AOC in C Fighter Command, Sir Basil Embry, was present: 'The less said about our feelings on arrival at Leuchars the better.' If only he had known just how much the 'Fighting Cocks' would become synonymous with north-east Fife. It was to become the longest-serving squadron at Leuchars.

No. 120 Squadron remained at Leuchars until June 1950, and 237 OCU stayed with its Mosquito PR34s and Spitfire XVIs and XIXs until October 1951, so a varied mix of units was at hand when Leuchars was involved in a major exercise to stage a land/air warfare offensive support demonstration. The exercise, jointly co-ordinated between 12 Group Fighter Command, 18 Group Coastal Command, RAF Leuchars and Scottish Command (Army), took place on 3 June, the principal aim being for the benefit of Army units based in Scotland. For this, other RAF aircraft were detached to Leuchars from 31 May to 4 June, including four Mosquito B35s from 14 Squadron, then based at RAF Celle in Germany, and six Vampire Vs from 26 Squadron at Wunstorf. The home team included seven Meteors of 222 Squadron, and there were eight Spitfire Mk 22s of 603 Squadron from Turnhouse. All demonstrated their air-to-ground capabilities over the Tentsmuir range. Two attacks were carried out by each of three sections of Spitfires, demonstrating the use of 20-mm cannon in close air support, the Meteors following with a similar profile, and then the Mosquitos formation bombing at medium level using smoke bombs. The Vampire Vs demonstrated rocket firing and medium dive bombing using individual rounds.

Later in the month, 222 Squadron carried out the first of what was to become a quite routine post-war requirement of units based at Leuchars, with deployments across the UK and overseas. All of the squadron were attached to Acklington from 8 June to 8 July for an armament practice camp

On 2 January 1951, both 43 and 222 Squadrons, now settled at Leuchars, set about training in the local area, having had New Year's Day off. No. 222 Squadron attempted to get airborne to make use of the Tentsmuir range, but poor weather meant that only four managed it. Conditions the next day were largely the same, so the afternoon was devoted to sports. Two weeks later, both squadrons were tasked with intercepting a formation of American B-36 Peacemakers—enormous aircraft with a 230-foot wingspan and ten engines! Six were rear-facing props and four were turbojets fitted at the end of non-jettisonable wing pylons, commonly referred to as six turning and four burning. Having flown non-stop from America, they were to tour Scotland before heading off to Lakenheath.

Their courses and times were far removed from the pattern of their intended flight plan and timings. Therefore only one Meteor from 43 Squadron successfully intercepted the B-36s, whilst two of four Meteors from 222 Squadron, when running short on fuel, managed a single cine attack on one B-36 while returning home. A type of intercept referred to as a 'C.3' was one of three attempts made to intercept the formation, which entailed carrying out a vertical dive attack from above. However, the gun-camera film was ruined owing to a technical fault. Tragedy struck three days later, when Fg Off. Danton of 43 Squadron was killed following an air-to-ground firing sortie. His body was recovered from the sea a week later. In February, the squadron achieved a record by exceeding 400 flying hours. This was all the more remarkable because it was short of both pilots and aircraft at the time.

On Sunday 3 June, three of Leuchars' squadrons—Nos 43, 222 and 602—participated in good weather in a Royal Observer Corps (ROC) exercise, and four days later 43 Squadron provided aircraft for King George VI's birthday flypast, the salute on this occasion being taken by HRH Princess Elizabeth. Later that month, 43 and 222 Squadrons were called upon to take part in an aerial firepower demonstration over the tank ranges at Stobs Camp near Hawick and were joined by six de Havilland Vampires from 3 Squadron flown specially from BAFO (British Air Forces of Occupation) in Germany. The idea was to demonstrate the firepower of modern aircraft to the Army. Despite bad weather, all planned sorties were flown, perhaps motivated to a degree by the need to impress the Army. Princess Elizabeth, being an Honorary Air Commodore, also presented the commanding officer of 603 Auxiliary Squadron, Sqn Ldr P. J. Anson, with the Esher Trophy.

The summer of 1951 at one stage saw no fewer than six RAF fighter squadrons crammed onto the station: 43 (Meteor F4s and F8s), 222 (Meteor F4s and F8s), 602 (Vampire FB5s), 603 (Vampire FB5s), 608 (Vampire F1s and F3s) and 612 (Spitfire XVIs). They were joined in September by a further regular unit, 151 Squadron, which had originally formed in Essex during the First World War and was a night fighter unit equipped with the de Havilland Vampire NF10.

When 151 Squadron, under the command of Sqn Ldr A. D. Boyle, arrived or rather re-formed at Leuchars on 15 September, it adopted the saltire of St Andrew as the standard marking on its aircraft and continued the night fighter role it had routinely held throughout the war. During the Battle of Britain, the squadron had flown Hawker Hurricanes, as had 43 Squadron, but thereafter the paths of the two had diverged, with 43 Squadron remaining an essentially tactical/day fighter unit while 151 Squadron moved on to re-equip first with Boulton Paul Defiants and then Mosquito NFs. In 1946, the squadron had disbanded, like so many, but now seemed to have a new future mapped out.

In the early 1950s, air combat profiles still assumed the big battle characteristics of the fighter escort to large bomber formations, similar to those of the Second World War. Shortly after the Fighter Wing formed at Leuchars, the Meteors of 43 and 222 Squadrons were involved in an

Meteor F8 of 43 Sqn, 1951. (*Barry G. Mayner*)

exercise, on 5 July 1951, which required them to act as bomber escorts down to Linton-on-Ouse. The bombers on this occasion were played by eight Meteors from 43 Squadron, while the Meteors of 222 Squadron acted as fighter escort. The formation was intercepted before it reached its target, or as the operational record says:

> The formation was intercepted successfully before the target was reached and effective attacks were made by the intercepting forces on the bombers. The escorting fighters found difficulty in preventing the interceptors from getting through as it was difficult to accelerate to the attackers' speed in time to catch them before they reached the bombers.

The return of peace had encouraged a renewed effort towards display flying, which with the significant number of squadrons was evident at Leuchars in 1951, By September the aerobatic team of 43 Squadron had re-formed, and since the spring had in fact been working up their sequence of manoeuvres on top of everything else. Led by Flt Lt Eric Wingham and now fully operational with the Gloster Meteor F8, the squadron had previously gained something of a reputation for formation aerobatics during the inter-war period at Hendon.

The new team's most prestigious moment came that month when invited to represent the RAF at the International Air Display in Cannes. Further displays marking the Battle of Britain followed at RAF stations at Dalcross, Kinloss and the homestead at Leuchars. This year, counting the involvement of Leuchars units alone, there was also a formation from 151 Squadron, and pilots from 222 Squadron provided solo aerobatics at RAF Dalcross, including Plt Off. Duncan Simpson (who later became something of a household name as chief test pilot at Hawker Siddeley), while Fg Off. George Gunn flew a similar display at Kinloss.

In the morning a practice squadron formation was flown in preparation for the afternoon display, which took place in good weather without a hitch. Sgt Stuart Chalmers of 222 Squadron also flew a solo aerobatic display at Leuchars, while Flt Lt Morris took the squadron's T-bird Meteor T7 to first place in the afternoon air race. In the evening, parties were held in the various messes. Less than a week before, 222 Squadron had said farewell to Fg Off. D. G. Elliott, its first National Service pilot, who was released from service on 10 September. He had left in order to resume his civilian career at Glasgow University, but would continue flying with 602 (City of Glasgow) Auxiliary Squadron and met up with his old friends whenever the squadron returned to Leuchars for exercises.

October 1952 brought a significant air defence exercise, when Exercise 'Ardent' took place in three separate phases, allocating a two-day period for each phase but at different times, the idea being to assess the ability of aircrew to intercept and engage at both day and night, as follows:

1.   0001 hours on 4 October to 1700 hours on 5 October;
2.   2230 hours on 9 October to 0330 hours on 10 October;
3.   0900 hours on 11 October to 2200 hours on 12 October.

Five squadrons participated in making interceptions, claims and kills. These were 43 and 222 Squadrons, with Meteor F8s, 151 Squadron flying Vampire NF10s, and two detached units—264 Squadron with Meteor NF11s, and 809 Squadron of the FAA with Sea Hornet F21s. Interestingly, the naval squadron, which happened to be flying single-seat, twin prop engined fighters, had the second highest kill rate. The best attained was by the Vampires of 151 Squadron. Total claims and kills were as follows: 43 Squadron—21 claims; 222 Squadron—21 claims; 151 Squadron—31 kills; 809 Squadron—22 kills; and 264 Squadron—10 kills. The exercise involved a degree of moving about during Phase Two, 151 Squadron deploying to Acklington, while all squadrons deployed to West Raynham during Phase Three at 1530 hours on 11 October.

Leuchars was now undergoing its long-awaited transformation into a more realistic fighter station. Hard-standings and ORPs were all under construction, meaning large parts of the airfield were out of use. March 1953 brought an upgrade of sorts for 151 Squadron, when it swapped its

Vampires for the bigger and heavier Meteor night fighters. Just as it was getting used to twin-seat Meteors, the other two squadrons were preparing to get rid of their single-seaters the following year.

Ceremonial, as you will gather from these pages, has always placed a great demand on the RAF, just as with the two more senior services, and 1953 was perhaps the most significant post-war year in this respect. The coronation of HM Queen Elizabeth II is arguably among the most significant events for the UK since the war, and all three squadrons at Leuchars deployed in full to take part in the flypast over RAF Odiham in Hampshire as part of the Royal Review. The day fighter squadrons were led by Wg Cdr P. G. H. Matthews, while 151 Squadron was led by Sqn Ldr A. D. Boyle. A further eight officers from the station were employed in the static display.

At the other end of the month, 43 & 222 Squadrons were involved from the 27th to the 30th in Exercise 'Coronet', which required them to deploy to Duxford. The aim of this exercise was to provide training for AAFCE (Allied Air Forces Central Europe) in their offensive and defensive roles, and for anti-aircraft artillery. The Leuchars Wing had the role of simulating high-level bombers once again, which amounted to a sortie being flown daily to the Continent, refuelling at Wunstorf (an RAF station that incidentally was portrayed by Leuchars in the film *High Flight*), and landing and refuelling

A Brace of 151 sqn Meteor NF crews shortly after taking on their new mount in 1953. (*Barry G. Mayner*)

before returning to carry out a further sortie. They took what was seen as a golden opportunity to practise their high-level 'sweep formations'. The interceptions of the defending aircraft were considered to be poor quality, and as a result the profile used was deemed to be successful.

By 1953, 43 Squadron had increased its aerobatic team to a five-ship, and 19 September should have brought the curtain down on another successful year. However, the weather intervened on the day, and while the flying display went ahead in marginal conditions, the only ones to miss their slot as a result were the 'Fighting Cocks' and a billed supersonic dive over the airfield by a visiting F-86 Sabre. Post-summer, the squadrons were able to address the matter of air-to-air firing practice that had suffered earlier in the year as a result of all the other engagements and exercises such as 'Coronet'. By the end of September, the air-to-air gunnery results were the highest yet achieved by the day squadrons, but because 151 Squadron was still getting the hang of the Meteor NF, its scores in both air-to-air and air-to-ground firing were determined to be in the low average range.

The idea of having to intercept low raiders, which were seen as an increasingly likely threat, was gaining currency in addition to that of high-altitude bombers, and exercises instigated to practise countering the low-flying enemy air strike now entered the peacetime syllabus. Exercise

A mixed bag, 151 representative formation of all types and marks on charge as of April 1953, a Meteor NF11 (just taken on), Vampire NF10 (just going), Meteor T7 (sqn hack) and a Meteor F8 (possibly also accrued for the purpose DACT or indeed another hack) all overflying the station. (*Barry G. Mayner*)

'Premraf', on 15/16 September 1953, was intended to give the Home Fleet a chance to test their response to such low and fast targets, and again the Leuchars Wing obliged by playing the bad guys. Despite bad weather yet again, they carried out strikes alongside four Canberras from RAF Coningsby. Being the era that this was, both the Meteor and the Vampire were already viewed as approaching obsolescence after less than a decade of operational service, and various home-grown aerospace companies had been hard at work developing the 'second generation of jet fighter'.

On 29 July 1954, 43 Squadron received its first Hawker Hunter F1 fighter, WW599, and by 15 December, 222 Squadron had received three. The first appeared on the flightline two days later, when it was utilised by the ground crew for familiarisation. The Mk 1 Hunter marked a radical jump forward, certainly visually. Along with another type, perhaps the only post-war fighter not to be stationed at Leuchars, the Supermarine Swift, there were many obvious changes. Engines were no longer mounted on wings, which in turn were designed with a pronounced sweep-back, as was the fin and tail section. Although the power of the single engine was not much more than the combined thrust of the Meteor's two Derwent engines, it was of a more efficient and slender axial-flow design rather than the bulbous centrifugal layout of the early engines, and the airframe of the Hunter, while bigger and heavier, was sleek and thin.

For the remainder of 1954, however, 222 Squadron pressed on operationally with its Meteor F8s, and 43 Squadron soldiered on until September when it was declared non-operational and its Meteors were flown out to other units while more Hunters flew in. On the eve of that year's Battle of Britain display, a Hunter of 43 Squadron made its first recorded flight to appear in the authorisation book. Familiarity with the new jet fighter was still limited when the commanding officer, Sqn Ldr Roy Lelong, flew a handling display during which he created a sonic boom (then still perfectly legal), which was evidently quite entertaining.

Even so, progression onto the Hunters still had some way to go, and ground lectures for the bulk of the squadron's pilots were only just complete when intensive flying trials were scheduled to begin. Given that the work-up was only just starting, the aerobatics commitment usually borne by the 'Fighting Cocks' was this year taken by 222 Squadron, putting together a twelve-aircraft flypast and an aerobatic team that had been beaten into second place during a Group aerobatics competition at Leuchars in May by 43 Squadron. A hefty degree of flying time had to be allocated to this during the month, yet the squadron still achieved its target number of training hours. (The target for a Phantom squadron in the early 1970s was about 300 hours; the target number of hours for 222 Squadron in September 1954, flying the Meteor F8, was 600.)

By March 1955, the squadrons were seeing more usage of the Hunter than the Meteor, which was gradually being phased out. It was around this time that the proliferation of aerobatic teams across the RAF Commands reached its zenith. Fighter Command, above all, had enough resources allocated to create another Command in its own right. Having built a reputation for formation aerobatics either side of the war, 43 Squadron wasted no time in putting together the first Hunter team, although this is an arguable point, as the four-ship 'Black Knights' of 54 Squadron, based at Odiham in Hampshire, were in direct competition with the three-ship 'Fighting Cocks'.

This all fostered a healthy sense of rivalry, an esprit de corps, and more importantly a level of confidence and professionalism that has always been difficult to quantify when explaining the value of such activities to some—and not just the bean counters either. In the lead-up to their appearance at this year's Farnborough air show, the 'Fighting Cocks' were selected to give a display before the Secretary of State for Air on 1 July. Apart from those assigned to the aerobatic team, the squadron was stood down on leave for the next ten days—a well-earned rest following intensive 'Phase B' flying trials.

The Leuchars wing represented as it was during the period 1955 to 1957; 151 Sqn Venom NF3, a 222 Sqn Hunter to the right of the formation, but no unit markings and a 43 Sqn Hunter to the left. (*MOD/Crown copyright*)

Operational flying continued for the other two squadrons, as indeed it did for the 'Fighting Cocks' as well. They were involved with a significant amount of night flying during the month, although this was severely curtailed on numerous occasions due to low cloud and fog. However, from 19 July the weather allowed a limited programme to be flown at night. Following the night flying exercise, 43 Squadron was involved with Exercise 'Kingpin', an air defence exercise held on 21 July, in which the squadron's Hunters succeeded in intercepting aircraft at between 45,000 feet and 50,000 feet—possibly a record for RAF intercepts at high altitude—while the night fighter squadron, No. 151, underwent preparatory training prior to re-equipping with the de Havilland Venom NF3. For this, three Bristol Brigands were detached from RAF Colerne in Wiltshire to assist in the conversion training of the navigators onto the AI (Airborne Interception) Mk 21 radar.

This same month saw a new innovation with the arrival of 'C' Flight of 275 Squadron, equipped with Sycamore HR14 helicopters. It was among the early units fulfilling a function that had been sadly lacking during the Second World War, that of Search and Rescue. Formed in 1941, the squadron had a maritime origin, its crest being the head of a walrus, and it managed SAR then with Westland Lysanders adapted for amphibious use. Its tenure at Leuchars was at an end in 1959, when it took on the more able Westland Whirlwind, but rather than handing over to a replacement unit the identity simply transferred between squadrons. A total of four such SAR Flights operated from Leuchars between July 1955 and March 1993, working in conjunction much of the time with the MRT. Many people, not just aircrew, owe their lives to the SAR squadrons. In 1993, the last SAR Flight to operate from Leuchars departed, leaving the Scottish Region covered by 'D' Flight of 202 Squadron at Lossiemouth and, from the RN, by the 771 Squadron detachment at Prestwick.

July brought the re-equipping of 151 Squadron with Venom NF3s, and in September they were successful during Exercise 'Beware' when pitted against Valiants for the first time. However, it must be said that the success enjoyed was achieved only due to the effectiveness of the intercept radar and with a degree of allowance for the Venoms to close in on the targets. The Venom was already an outdated airframe.

By October the air show commitment was usually over until the following year, but the 'Fighting Cocks' were now on their way to Scandinavia, which meant preparation for almost the entire month. Training as such was afforded a low-level priority, but some was accrued as a by-product of the flying associated with the detachment. Altogether, sixteen Hunters of 43 Squadron left Leuchars for what would be a tour of Norway and Sweden during which flying displays were given at both Oslo

151's Venom NF3s being turned round on the flightline in front of the old Belfast Hangars. Note the clam shell style canopies, *c.* 1956. (*Barry G. Mayner*)

and Stockholm and all aircraft remained serviceable. Everything went well, and excellent hospitality was extended to one and all. Upon return to the homestead, the squadron had a five-day stand down before preparing for gun trials.

As 1956 arrived, the two Hunter squadrons operated a mix of aircraft—a situation that was not too unusual on any squadron at the time. Apart from the stable of Hunters on charge, also included was a Vampire T11 and a Meteor T7, and 43 Squadron also had a Meteor F3. In February, the first Mk 4 Hunters began to arrive, and the following month 43 Squadron's new commanding officer, Maj. R. O. Roberts (USAF), declared that 'completely normal training on the Hunter has begun', meaning the trials were complete.

Much of this at the time involved firing the 30-mm cannons at towed flags. There was also an arrangement with the neighbours, 222 Squadron, to make best use of available aircraft. No. 43 Squadron had received seven Mk 4 Hunters, and these were being used most of the time. The Hunter F4 brought fully powered elevators and additional fuel capacity, all of which was much appreciated. On 15 March, six of them deployed to Church Fenton as part of Exercise 'Formulate', a reinforcement exercise.

The 'Fighting Cocks' team also had a new leader, Flt Lt Peter Bairsto. As they now represented No. 13 Group officially, they were selected as the principal aerobatic display team at the 1956 Farnborough air show.

The 'Fighting Cocks' aerobatics team from 43 led by Flt Lt Peter Bairsto in a work up for the 1956 Display season. (*MOD/Crown copyright*)

As of March, they were ready enough to present their sequence with four aircraft, the first opportunity arriving that month in the form of Maj.-Gen. Odd Bull, Commander of the Northern Sector, Royal Norwegian Air Force. However, the weather precluded the team from showing the good commander what they could do, so he was invited to launch a scramble of four Hunters on his signal instead. Once airborne, they all promptly diverted to Prestwick. Such was the impetus on gaining currency on type at the time that two RAAF (Royal Auxiliary Air Force) pilots were sent from 602 Squadron at RAF Turnhouse to convert onto the Hunter up to operational standard. The two flying officers—J. D. A. Henshaw and F. H. Mycroft—would then put that training to use by reinforcing the squadron in an emergency, maintaining currency through frequent visits.

April afforded the 'Fighting Cocks' another chance to demonstrate their prepared display, and this time the honoured guests in the audience at RAF Marham were Marshal Nikolai Bulganin and Nikita Khrushchev. The team arrived at Marham early enough to fit in three practices in order to ensure they were ready. Evidently impressed, the radio and press were 'quite gushing' in their appreciation of the display on 23 April, the BBC describing it as 'probably the best formation aerobatics show ever seen in this country', which is praise indeed. This was also the first time that the team used smoke canisters under the tailpipes, it being hoped to repeat this in all forthcoming engagements.

It was announced on 2 June that the Leuchars Pipe Band would wear the kilt and plaids of the MacGregor tartan, influenced in no small part by Air Vice-Marshal Andrew MacGregor, a senior member of the clan who had served in Fighter Command during his final active service appointment and happened to live nearby at St Andrews. He personally approached the then clan chief, Sir Malcolm MacGregor, to obtain permission for the tartan to be worn, and once his permission had been given all that remained was official service approval.

One year on since their arrival, one of the 275 Squadron SAR helicopters had to be rescued itself. It had flown out to Bell Rock lighthouse to pick up Cpl J R. Eckford, a radio technician who had been servicing equipment there. On the return journey the chopper ditched in the sea. Flt Lt George Hartman, the captain, later said simply that something went wrong with the aircraft and they were forced to land in the water, three miles from the lighthouse. Together with his navigator, FS R. W. R. Griggs, and Cpl Eckford, he was rescued by a sea rescue launch based at Tayport, a fishing boat also responding. All three had managed to get out and into their Mae Wests before the launch arrived.

September was now established as the annual 'silly season', routinely incorporating the Farnborough air show in the first week of the month.

The show was now very well supported by the armed forces, with, of course, always a particularly strong contribution from the RAF. The month also included the annual Battle of Britain display, which usually followed a week or two later. But for RAF Leuchars, there was no display in 1956 due to the main runway being resurfaced. That said, some aircraft continued to operate from the station using the 1,650-yard cross-runway during Exercise 'Stronghold', which employed the use of the newfangled telebrief scrambler. This reconstruction work on the airfield was prompted by the pending arrival of Javelins. During the period between 15 June and 15 August, the runway was strengthened and the Leuchars-based squadrons were deployed elsewhere, 43 Squadron being detached to RAF Turnhouse, while 222 and 151 Squadrons were sent further afield to RAF Acklington.

This was now the age of the RAF jet aerobatic teams, which arrived with the Hawker Hunter in particular. The teams proliferated across the Commands at home and abroad like school football teams. Nine Hunters from 43 Squadron were deployed to RAF Odiham, from where they took part once again in the Farnborough SBAC show, this time with smoke canisters fitted and streaking coloured plumes in their wake. Bad weather during most of the week meant a few flat performances, but improvements in conditions did allow three full displays to be performed.

As the Battle of Britain was commemorated once again, 222 Squadron provided an aerobatic team of four Hunters and two solo aerobatics pilots to match the effort from 43 Squadron, while 151 Squadron provided eight Venoms to perform flypasts at various airfields, as well as a single aircraft for aerobatics. All these different display teams and soloists had to be signed off as competent by the AOC 13 Group but without the need for any higher authority. Unlike 43 Squadron, 222 did not carry quite the same recognition or official status, but the standard of flying was certainly not inferior within the confines of rehearsal time.

The team had disbanded at short notice back in April, with most of the assigned pilots being posted away, but the commitment to forthcoming events was resumed with the formation of another team, led by the commanding officer, Sqn Ldr Ken Cooke, together with Fg Offs Ed Durham and Geoff Timms, and FS Reid. Given their chequered existence in 1956, they displayed mostly around the North East of England, including Acklington and Newcastle, finishing with formation aerobatic displays at two Battle of Britain shows at RAF Ouston and RAF Thornaby. Across the way, 43 Squadron's team, led by Flt Lt Peter Bairsto, included Fg Offs Marcus Wilde and Ron Smith, and Sgt Peter Lampitt. They also had a fifth pilot, Lt Alistair Campbell, RN, and various machines were provided as static aircraft, again mostly local—Turnhouse,

Ouston, Dyce and Kinloss—but also Wellesbourne Mountford in Warwickshire.

The status of the 'Fighting Cocks' as the 13 Group team brought a wider-ranging number of commitments throughout the year. In addition to Farnborough and Battle of Britain commitments, they were sent earlier in the year to Rome's Fiumicino Airport where they displayed alongside many of their NATO contemporaries, flying their national teams for the most part. La Patrouille de France were flying Mystère IVs, the Diables Rouges from Belgium had Meteors, a team from the Spanish Air Force were flying F-86 Sabres, the Italian Frecce Tricolori had F-84 Thunderjets, the USAF Acrojets flew T-33 Shooting Stars, and the Skyblazers of the USAF European Command were flying the most advanced mount of all, the F-100 Super Sabre.

The 'Fighting Cocks' team were hoping for continued centre-stage success the following year, but were overshadowed on that occasion by none other than their future Leuchars partners down the road, 111 Squadron, who were selected in 1957 as the first 'official Fighter Command aerobatic team', an unprecedented nine-aircraft formation, for which resources for practice and so on were afforded to the picked unit, naturally.

No. 111 Squadron took the name the 'Black Arrows', and unlike the 'Fighting Cocks' and other Hunter teams of the day, were given permission to respray their aircraft semi-gloss black. In 1958, they were authorised to display a formation of sixteen.

Following Battle of Britain week, all three squadrons were immersed in Exercise 'Stronghold', which included deployments to Coltishall, Horsham St Faith and West Raynham in Norfolk after the deployments to Acklington and Turnhouse. Personnel of 151 Squadron had to contend with the minimum facilities at Turnhouse, which meant living in tents, accommodation for the officers being among the most limiting due to overcrowding. That said, those who deployed to the three stations in the Eastern Sector commented favourably on the facilities and the reception they received. All of the Leuchars squadrons claimed a total of fifty-three successful interceptions during the exercise, which included RAF Canberras, Meteor F8s and Valiants, as well as USAF B-45 Tornados, B-47 Stratojets and B-57 Canberras. At the completion of 'Stronghold', all were to have been flown back to Leuchars using three Handley Page Hastings aircraft, but the weather at Leuchars was bad enough to force the majority to return by road and rail.

Following the extra-curricular activities of September 1956, the Warwick Film Company was expected at Leuchars to capture 43 Squadron going about its business for the film *High Flight*. They arrived at the beginning of October and stayed well into November, during which time they filmed the aerobatic team air-to-air firing and low-level work. Two incidents occurred during this period, the first when a Hunter flown by Fg Off. R. G. Scott collected a bird in the engine on take-off and ended up in the Eden Estuary. (To give some idea of the basic feel of the time, the aircraft was retrieved by a traction engine from a local garage.) The second incident involved the loss of the radio bay doors during a high-speed run by Fg Off. D. T. Hamilton, causing Category-3 damage. The lack of strong sunlight at this time of year then forced the film company to pack up until the following summer, leaving on 23 November. As Flt Lt Peter Bairsto noted, they 'departed to their plush studios to fit some "faces" to our efforts', but he also stated that the squadron 'should feel honoured to have been associated with a film about the Royal Air Force which should receive worldwide publicity'.

At the end of his October report, Maj. Ray Roberts (USAF) noted that there had not been a single month of normal flying for 43 Squadron, in particular since it had received its first Mk 1 Hunter in 1954. Writing in the ORB, he noted:

> This has been another 'abnormal' month for operations. In fact, this squadron seems to find itself doing 'abnormal' or unusual jobs as a routine matter. Since receipt of the first Hunter aircraft nearly two years ago, there has not been a 'normal' month as far as combat training is concerned. In spite of the additional commitments such as Hunter field service trials, intensive flying trials, low-velocity ammunition firing trials, goodwill trip to Norway and Sweden, high-velocity ammunition firing trials, fuel dipping modification to Mk 1 Hunters, providing the 13 Group aerobatic team whose programme included two trips abroad, the SBAC show and the latest, which is flying sequences for a feature film about RAF life, we have managed to do a reasonable amount of training and certainly to keep the standards of flying in this unit at a high level of perfection.

On top of everything else, 43 and 222 Squadrons had the commitment to maintain an aircraft at cockpit readiness, often rotated, and at the time involving a fair amount of detachment from one unit to another. This was what in later times became QRA (Quick Reaction Alert), then IAF (Interceptor Alert Force) in more recent times, and then reverted to QRA again. Readiness was actually maintained at a higher state in the Hunter era, as Ed Durham recollects:

> When I was on 222 we just used the term Battle Flight in the North. Exercise 'Fabulous' was a Southern thing and we, 222, went down to

Horsham St Faith (aka Norwich Airport) to do the duty for about a week, returning home to Leuchars on 6 October 1956. The QRA business then became Flinders briefly, before becoming Halyard. In the former we kept aircraft on a two-minute state, crews in the cockpit, all the time. The duty was shared between day and night fighters. I was on Javelins by this time and did my fair share of time in the cockpit throughout the night.

No. 43 Squadron now took delivery of four of the new upgraded Hunter F6. With its 200-series Avon engine taking static thrust from 7,550 lb to 10,000 lb, performance was markedly improved. Notably, 222 Squadron soldiered on for now with its Mk 4s, while 151 Squadron could look forward later in 1957 to getting the next generation all-weather fighter and the first designed from the drawing board as such—the Gloster Javelin.

On 9 November, due to the short runway still being in use since the resurfacing on the main runway began in 1956, 43 Squadron's re-equipment with the Mk 6 Hunter was temporarily suspended. This was due to a CFE report that the new Hunters needed at least 2,000 yards of runway to operate safely. Incidentally, fifty years later when the main runway was being resurfaced again in preparation for the arrival of Typhoons, the then resident fighters, bigger and heavier Tornados, were not prevented from using the same cross-runway despite the latter type's reputation for lacking the energy for short-field performance. After operations were suspended, the Mk 6 Hunters so far issued were withdrawn, much to the disappointment of pilots and ground crew alike.

Changes were afoot at the start of 1957, but the more dramatic changes waiting around the corner were not to come about until April. In the meantime, the year began with the harmonising of guns on the Hunters for air-to-air firing, which started on 7 January for the 'Fighting Cocks'. However, after a good start, fuel shortages as a result of the unfolding Suez Crisis limited flying for all. By May, all operational flying was virtually suspended for the Wing, and time was being devoted to practising flypasts, aerobatics and parades in preparation for the visit of HM Queen Elizabeth II on 4 June.

April brought a dramatic change to the RAF's frontline inventory, which in relative terms put subsequent Defence Reviews, certainly as far as air power is concerned, firmly in the shade. The Defence Minister, Duncan Sandys, a not entirely objective minister (was there ever such a character?), announced to the House of Commons the findings of the most radical review of air power since the end of the First World War when a force of 188 squadrons was reduced to twelve inside a year. This time only the fighter element would be predominantly affected, and not to quite the same extent, but the reductions would be severe and driven by faith in the 'all-missile' future. Less than a year earlier, in July 1956, the Air Defence Committee had recommended that the number of RAF fighter aircraft should not drop below a figure of 480:

> Although the country as a whole cannot be protected against nuclear attack, the defence of the very much smaller target presented by an airfield is a feasible task. A manned fighter force, smaller than at present but of adequate size for this limited purpose, will therefore be maintained and will progressively be equipped with air-to-air guided missiles. These fighter aircraft will gradually be replaced by a ground-to-air guided missile system.

The answer from Fighter Command was to ground certain pilots on short-service commissions, which would largely put paid to the remaining National Service pilots. On the day that 222 Squadron flew their last bread-and-butter sortie, Leuchars' commanding officer, Gp Capt. Beardon, announced that a total of fifteen officers at the station would be affected.

On the other hand, the pending arrival of ever more potent fighter designs was being addressed expectantly. A concrete extension to the main runway was complete with new approach lights, and resurfacing work was also proceeding on part of the taxiway and aircraft servicing platforms. Some more good news at this time was the introduction of the five-day working week. This, however, meant the end of Wednesday sports afternoons, which were instead replaced by regular periods of PT following morning Met briefs for all aircrew.

The film company arrived back at Leuchars on 5 July to finish off, and despite their efforts being bedevilled by bad weather, more air-to-air footage was gained. They departed two weeks later, followed shortly after by 43 Squadron's aerobatic team, who headed out to Odiham to prepare once again for the year's Farnborough air show. This was necessary for no other reason than the main runway 09/27 was back under maintenance, meaning that for the second year running the station would again be closed to the public in September. The squadron's aerobatic team still flew their well-polished display sequence at Kinloss and Turnhouse, even though their commitment to Farnborough had been cancelled in favour of the new Fighter Command representative team from 111 Squadron, the 'Black Arrows'. However, the station remained open and effective for operational flying using the cross-runway.

The end of the year saw a return to a more substantial operational footing for the station, with tactical flying involving practice interceptions and more exercises. Many other aircraft acted as targets, including B-47s and Canberras, which the Leuchars squadrons were quite used to, but these were now being joined by aircraft of the new V-force—Valiants, Vulcans and Victors. It was realised that the performance of the new V bombers was such that the need for good interceptions was becoming imperative, the new long-range jets already highlighting the Hunter's shortcomings in this regard. What would otherwise have been seen as a significant step forward was the arrival, or better still return, of the first three of 43 Squadron's new Mk 6 Hunters in January 1958. This, however, now looked rather inadequate in light of experience.

The 43 Sqn Hunter pilot here is unidentified, but 'Cocky II' the squadron mascot is instantly recognisable. (*MOD/Crown copyright*)

6

All Weathers, All Night

The Gloster Javelin was the first RAF fighter designed from the start to carry the pilot and navigator/radar operator and all the necessary equipment for all-weather interceptions in a cockpit and airframe intended for that very purpose. It was the biggest, heaviest and most powerful and heavily armed interceptor up to this point. What it was not was manoeuvrable, nor was it complete on arrival. Never before had an aircraft (apart from some Second World War designs) had so much development applied over such a short space of time. Between 1956 and 1959, no fewer than nine marks of Javelin were delivered to the RAF, and there was a running option as well—which type of AIR (Airborne Interception Radar) to use.

Leuchars-based 151 Squadron received its first Javelins the year after the first squadron formed on Mk 1s at Odiham. The squadron's first two jets were received on 3 May. These were Mk 5s, which was an indication of just how rapid the development towards a definitive model had been. The Javelin was very much suited to the requirements of Leuchars. The need was for something that had not existed before—a fighter type possessing an endurance more akin to a much bigger multi-engine long-range patrol aircraft but with fighter performance and the ability to respond to a scramble order within a very short space of time, typically five to ten minutes.

An awful lot of bad press dogged the Javelin throughout its service, and its agility was never fully trusted by the RAF. Certainly, its poor public reputation was never challenged. When the Mk 8s and 9s were first delivered in 1959, the addition of an afterburner did little if anything to improve performance. Inexplicably, it even had an adverse effect if used below an altitude of 20,000 feet by causing a reduction in fuel flow. That said, it was the best answer to meeting any projected threat from long-range aircraft sneaking into the North Atlantic.

Early in 1957, everyone was preparing for the visit of HM Queen Elizabeth II, and despite the recent knocking from its aerobatics perch by 111 Squadron it was decided that 43 Squadron should still provide the aerobatic display on 4 June rather than the premier choice from down south. On the day, the full flying schedule went ahead, but the display by 43 Squadron had to be flat owing to heavy cloud.

The Queen and Prince Philip arrived in a de Havilland Comet and were accompanied by the Rt Hon. George Ward MP, Secretary of State for Air; Air Chief Marshal Sir Dermot Boyle, Chief of the Air Staff; and Air Vice-Marshal Alfred Earle, AOC in C 13 Group. The royal party met aircrew from 151 Squadron, who were still flying their de Havilland Venoms, while in the hangar stood a single example of the brand-new Gloster Javelin bearing the squadron's markings, which was ironic given the recent Sandys review. Pride of place on the day went to the famous 43 Squadron, which received a new standard from The Queen—the first time a squadron standard had been presented by a reigning monarch.

As the royal visit also heralded the re-equipment of 151 Squadron with the Javelin, a formation flypast by sixteen of them from 46 Squadron based at Odiham and 141 Squadron from Coltishall roared overhead. Just three days after the royal visit, a memorial stone presented by the Royal Norwegian Air Force to RAF Leuchars was the subject of an unveiling ceremony in the presence of Maj.-Gen. H. M. H. Jorgensen, who delivered a short address before unveiling the stone. The RAF senior party included Air Marshal Sir Brian Reynolds, Air Marshal Sir Thomas Pike, AOC in C Coastal Command and AOC in C Fighter Command respectively. The stone, best described as a small obelisk, about 10 feet tall, still sits just inside the main gate of the technical and operational site near the guard room today.

As more runway repair work was about to begin this month, and given the Javelin's far from adequate short-field performance, it was decided that it would be best for 151 Squadron to be deployed away to Turnhouse rather than rely on the cross-runway, the deployment beginning on 17 June. Prior to this, the squadron was required to ferry its Venom aircraft away for disposal to other units. Still at Turnhouse later in the year, getting to grips with its significantly more challenging new mount, the squadron was detached away between 16 and 24 September on Operation 'Strikeback' at Sola in Norway, taking eight Javelin FAW5s with it.

The airfield at Sola had four active runways, the main one running from north to south being 3,000 yards long but twice the regulation width of a British runway. Conversely, the ORP at either end was narrower than the UK specification. The Javelin crews would also be dealing with civilian air traffic controllers. One aspect of Norwegian military life that could prove a little embarrassing and, given the right circumstances, amusing, was that the custom of separate messing facilities for officers, senior NCOs and junior ranks had long since been abandoned. Maintained by HM forces to this day, the custom is something which everyone accepts as part and parcel of the perks and benefits of career progression. Considering that being accepted for a commission for any junior rank or NCO is always a possibility, then that career progression has no limits. But, of course, for any element of Britain's armed forces in the rather more deferential era of the 1950s, with National Service to boot, to suggest that the set-up in Norway posed any inconvenience and to regard any resentment as petty concern would be to misunderstand the British service culture completely.

So it was that British tastes (at least the more rarefied ones) were accommodated. Even so, due to the deployment taking more officers than NCOs, the officers were crammed in. In most cases, three officers shared a single room, and one bunch certainly collectively drew the short straw when nine of them were bunked in a single room. The squadron's airmen were billeted with the ground crew from an FAA squadron that was also participating in the same exercise. These chaps were all crammed into a disused dining room. Double-tiered bunks were placed in blocks of four with little space between them, while the latrines and ablutions were under canvas. Eventually, a small billet was found on 17 September, which together with a small classroom alleviated matters just a tad.

These were not the only problems encountered. Norway, like many other Scandinavian countries, then as now, had a particularly high cost of living, and while everyone was paid LOA (local overseas allowance), this was found to be wholly inadequate. But messing arrangements aside, apart from the only two air wireless fitters on the detachment and one navigator becoming ill, the operational side of the exercise was quite successful. No. 151 Squadron impressed all with its efficient handling of the new aircraft, and the operation commander, Maj.-Gen. Norman D. Sillin (USAF), expressed surprise at the speed at which the Javelins got airborne and managed to intercept Bomber Command's Vickers Valiants at 48,000 feet, especially using the GCI (Ground Control Interception) equipment available!

On 22 July 1958, Nos 151 and 43 Squadrons, now equipped respectively with the Javelin Mk 5 and the Hunter Mk 6, were joined by 29 Squadron. The new guys had vacated their former homestead, RAF Acklington, as it was to be handed over to Flying Training Command in 1960, at which point their old stablemates, 66 Squadron, were disbanded. The arrival of 29 Squadron at Leuchars emphasised the ability to provide long-range interception in all weathers, while 43 Squadron's Hunters provided a point-defence/day fighter force. The Javelins of 151 Squadron carried a

British AI.17 intercept radar, the Mk 6 aircraft of 29 Squadron carrying an American AI.22 AIR fit, otherwise known as the APQ-43. All these fighters also carried the same standard armament of four 30-mm Aden cannons.

Before all the changes set in motion by the Sandys White Paper, the existing units continued to prepare for the worst-case scenario in terms of the Cold War. In October 1958, an exercise was held, called Operation 'Sunbeam', the aim of which was to obtain the maximum level of practice of the UK air defence assets 'under the conditions anticipated in the initial stages of a global nuclear war'.

This scenario was played out assuming several large air raids. These were concentrated into three periods, one during the night and two during daytime on 16, 17 and 18 October. There appears to have been a degree of assumption involved, as the time between each raid was specified and allowed each of the squadrons involved to turn round and build up to the maximum of all available aircraft and crews so that each raid was met with the heaviest possible response. All three squadrons were assigned to the GCI sector control: 29 Squadron to the radar station at Boulmer near Alnwick in Northumberland; and 43 and 151 Squadrons to the station at Buchan near Peterhead in Aberdeenshire. Recent modifications to the operations room and the ATC included new telebrief scramblers and radio receivers, which apparently resulted in an unexpectedly high level of noise in ATC when all were in use at the same time.

Ten raids were mounted throughout the exercise, with a high level of successful interceptions, but this was put down largely to the good weather and the fact that electronic jamming aircraft accompanying each raid seemed effective only above 45,000 feet. Ferranti operated two Canberras during eight of the raids in order to trial the AI.23 radar system, to be used in the forthcoming English Electric Lightning all-weather interceptor. The following month, ten Hunters of 43 Squadron were sent to Wattisham to meet what was now termed the 'Halyard' commitment (later known as QRA) from 111 Squadron, while its aircraft were sent to Leuchars in order to practise air-to-air firing over the Inverbervie high-altitude range.

During April 1959, with the Wing now settled again following the recent application of the Treasury axe, more of the myriad exercises began on 17 April. This time there were two. The first of these, 'Groupex', affected all three units, with 43 Squadron scrambling twelve of its Hunters to intercept the Javelins of both 29 and 151 Squadrons which were returning from an earlier deployment. No. 151 Squadron had been sent to Geilenkirchen on 9 April, whilst 29 Squadron had headed out to Ørland in Norway on 10 April, both to participate in Exercise 'Top Weight'. This required the two all-weather squadrons at their respective locations

OC B Flight, 151 Squadron, Sqn Ldr Sledgmere briefing sqn crews during preparation for exercise sunbeam. (*Royal Air Force Museum Archives*)

151 Sqn Javelin crews relax before a sortie, *c.* 1958. (*Royal Air Force Museum Archives*)

to intercept formations of other NATO aircraft including V bombers, Canberras, F-84F Thunderstreaks, and F-100 Super Sabres. Given the reputation of the Javelin, they did well, but the disparity in scores, perhaps only relative, was quite stark, with the crews of 29 Squadron notching up 94 kills to 151 Squadron's 191. On their return to Leuchars on 17 April, 43 Squadron's Hunters claimed splashes (simulated downings) of nine Javelins.

The Mountain Rescue Team were getting regular trade, and were called out on 10 November to look for a Navy Scimitar pilot who had had ejected in the Kingussie area. After searching for the Scimitar and its pilot for two days, the wreckage was found by the SAR helicopter. The pilot, meanwhile, had managed to reach a farmhouse and had been returned to Lossiemouth by car. A happy ending, at least on this occasion, save perhaps for the inevitable Board of Inquiry!

The 1960 'at home' day was held on 17 September. This year, the total number of RAF stations across the UK opening to the public with displays

The Leuchars Fighter Wing *c.* 1959, aircrew grouped in their respective squadrons, from the left; 29 Sqn, 43 Sqn (with Leuchars CO sat centre) and 151 Sqn. (*Royal Air Force Museum Archives*)

was twenty-five, a reduction of 75 per cent since the first one fifteen years earlier. While some stations managed under changeable weather conditions, Leuchars was a virtual wash-out. A Chipmunk light trainer from the University Air Squadron and a helicopter were all that could manage to get aloft from the airfield. Otherwise, two Valiants made a single flypast each, and an Argus twice attempted a flypast using a ground-controlled approach to overshoot but each time was not seen due to low cloud. So sparse was the activity that the commentator was left trying to make the most of the prospect of anything flying at all. Each time he felt confident enough to pick up the microphone, he alerted the crowd to something, anything, approaching or starting up. Some Hunters of 43 Squadron did also manage to get airborne.

Before September was out, two airmen from Leuchars had to be plucked from the sea by one of the home-based helicopters of what was now 'C' Flight of 228 Squadron, after their dinghy capsized out on the Eden Estuary. They were dumped on terra firma none the worse for wear,

Ready for a flypast over Dundee, 1961, Major Hancock and the flypast crews; Fg Off
Henwood, Fg Off Reed, Flt Lt Pomfret, Flt Lt McGann and Flt Lt Daniels. Kneeling
is Flt Sgt J Dunnington, who received the BEM previous year, and Fg Off O'Connor
(J Eng o). (*Royal Air Force Museum Archives*)

their slightly damaged dinghy, the property of the Leuchars Yachting
Club, being collected the next day after having made its way alongside the
Guardbridge paper mill.

A further change in the operational focus at Leuchars came about in
1961 when the Hunters of 43 Squadron were deployed permanently to
Nicosia in Cyprus. They departed on 20 June to become the resident air
defence fighter unit for the island. This left the two Javelin squadrons,
Nos 29 and 151, concentrating operations entirely on long-range, all-
weather interception.

With 151 Squadron effectively disbanded from 19 September, having started moving aircraft to St Athan for final disposal six days before, it was not too long before another unit took its place, 25 Squadron arriving from Waterbeach with Mk 9 Javelins in November. The squadron had re-equipped at the beginning of the year, having previously operated the Mk 7. Its outgoing commanding officer, prior to arriving at Leuchars, had not spoken highly of the move, any more than 43 Squadron's commander had when eleven years earlier it had made the move north of the border. Wg Cdr J. Walton simply noted, 'The squadron regrettably had to re-deploy to Leuchars following the Cyprus detachment.' He did not make clear quite what his cause for regret was, but in any case, on arrival the squadron was already under the command of his successor, Wg Cdr P. G. K. Wilkinson. They flew more or less directly from Cyprus to Leuchars, all arriving by 28 November after a brief four-day stop at Waterbeach en route. The day after their arrival they were engaged in intercepting V bombers in Exercise 'Spellbound'. The new commanding officer had a more constructive comment to make about Leuchars, noting that 'the new home station of the squadron has done everything possible to help us to settle down, both domestically and operationally, and by the end of the month full flying had re-commenced'.

In December, the Leuchars Wing was tasked quite separately. No. 25 Squadron was to remain at the station, where snow and ice had prevented fourteen working days of flying. As a result, the aircrew attended no fewer than twenty-one lectures and demonstrations. The subjects included, of all things, ejector seat training, intelligence on the Iraqi Air Force, aircraft recognition, and the tactics and operation of Firestreak, while other officers were detached away on various courses including SAR at Mountbatten and AWFLS (All-Weather Flying Leaders Squadron) at West Raynham. Meanwhile, they entertained the press and Scottish Television on 5 December, even though the weather prevented any kind of flying.

However, 29 Squadron was off again, this time to Geilenkirchen, taking all seventeen of its Javelins: sixteen FAW9s and the T-bird T3. It was planned that the squadron would be over in Germany from 4 December 1961 until 1 February 1962. The transit route for the flight was under the control of the RAF radar stations at Boulmer in Northumberland and Patrington on the north bank of the Humber. Flying a course of 136 degrees, the still-air travelling time over the distance of 455 nm at 42,000 feet would be 57 minutes. From Patrington's control they would pass to the Amsterdam FIR (Flight Information Region) under the call sign 'Stovepipe'.

Trouble had arisen as a result of Soviet attempts to close the land routes along the established corridors into West Berlin some twelve years earlier,

20 June 1961, Hunters of 43 Sqn ready for departing Leuchars for Nicosia in Cyprus where they provided local air defence and tactical air support before the emergency move to Aden in 1963. (*Barry G. Mayner*)

and now fighter escorts were required to be on hand for transport flights leaving and entering the corridor following another increase in tension that resulted in the building of the inner Berlin Wall. The Soviet and East German authorities were doing all they could to physically prevent West Berliners from leaving the city to travel west, but the one thing that they had not attempted to block was the movement of aircraft to and from West Berlin.

Barry Mayner served as a navigator with 29 Squadron back in 1961 and was involved with the deployment to Geilenkirchen to fly escort for flights in and out:

I was detached with 29 to Geilenkirchen in December 1961 for two months for the escorting of Comet II sorties, if the Soviets tried to close the corridors, as well as the land/rail routes. We deployed on 5 December. The wind at Geilenkirchen was gusting to 55 knots at 90 degrees across. EGPG, our boss, phoned FC [Fighter Command] and queried the conditions. He was told to deploy the squadron without delay!!! I was adj [adjutant] listening to the conversation. My pilot was Mike Russell, and we touched down at Geilers in 55 knots of Xwind with 20 degrees of drift (I was looking down the runway). As the ac weather-cocked, the right wing rose about eight feet in the air and I was still looking down the runway. I said, 'Mike have you got it?' The reply, amongst four letter words, was full aileron and full rudder into it. After a few lurches and swings we straightened up.

All ten aircraft landed in similar conditions. That night the armourers had to download all the Firestreaks onto sandbags in the revetments as no handling equipment was available. Three missiles were damaged and Bill Hyland had to do a Unit Inquiry. I think 5 & 11 were a bit peeved that they had been usurped by us [they were still flying Mk 5s].

We had four aircraft (missile armed) on state for eight weeks and very few training sorties. I sent on Xmas Eve, without anyone knowing, a telegram to the C in C Fighter Command via German telephone (!) wishing him and his Staff a Merry Xmas and Happy New Year, at midnight on 31 December. He replied to EGPG. He handed the signal to me and said, 'I think this is for you, Barry.' It read, 'TO 29 SQUADRON, WISHING YOU AND YOUR FAMILIES A HAPPY NEW YEAR AND HOPE YOU ARE NOT TOO DOWNHEARTED.'

As January 1962 arrived, 25 Squadron was able to make some inroads in the weather, which showed little sign of improving, managing to take part in three exercises with the V-force and to co-operate with a number of 'Bomber Affiliations' whereby the V bombers made themselves available as targets during their own training sorties for the Javelins to intercept. Having got rid of the snow and ice, the runway was now bedevilled by strong cross-winds and rain which prohibited night flying, but the squadron did get airborne on occasion at night to intercept some 'embellished' targets, again V bombers, available for practice intercepts.

To demonstrate the importance of good working personal equipment, the squadron's crews were involved in Exercise 'Kingpin', an air defence exercise, on 18 January. It was found that their pressure jerkins would not fit over their immersion suits and, as a result, most of the squadron were limited to 42,000 feet. Therefore many targets that they should have intercepted were allowed through because they were up at 43,000 feet or more. On 29 January, five of 25 Squadron's jets had to divert to Lossiemouth following Exercise 'Spellbound' on account of the runway at Leuchars being blocked by eight Javelins visiting from 85 Squadron. No. 25 Squadron was also involved with trials for V bomber tail warning radars, requiring it to carry out a number of sorties for that purpose.

While the weather remained bad, the commanding officer took advantage of the situation to imbue a sense of worth in all squadron personnel with a lecture on their specific role in the event of hostilities. This included all technical and administration staff as well as aircrew. Everyone, especially the ground crew, appeared to appreciate this greater insight into just how important their own individual role was and how vital a contribution they would be making to the country should the balloon go up or, to use a more contemporary phrase, should the shit hit the fan.

With improving weather in March, 25 Squadron was again involved with intercepting V bombers high and fast, engaging with Victors and Vulcans in particular. 'Ciano' exercises with jamming aircraft also consumed a chunk of the operational training schedule. Some ECM (electronic countermeasures) Valiants just off the coast were thrown into the mix here. Also included was AIR training involving tail-chases against violently evading targets, and the renewed emphasis on this was seen as a considerable improvement.

April 1962 was a month in which a radical change took place in Fighter Command's commitment to provide aircraft at readiness for interception and investigation purposes. Essentially this concerned the integration of Fighter Command as an assigned unit and component part of the air defence force of SACEUR (Supreme Allied Commander Europe), and a reappraisal of the readiness commitment. It was decided that a total of 3½ per cent of the Command's fighter force should be at constant readiness. This was to be split between the two remaining groups, 11 and 12, who would each maintain their share, 11 Group covering the northern half of the country and 12 Group the south. This involved two aircraft at ten minutes' readiness instead of just one at two minutes'. In the north, 25 and 29 Squadrons shared this commitment at Leuchars. Up until then, they had been detaching aircraft and crews to Middleton St George, with crews sitting in the cockpit for quite long periods, as Ed Durham described earlier. This was the much dreaded Flodden commitment. The new procedure went by the codename Flinders.

As the year progressed, the focus shifted to 25 Squadron countering ECM. Six aircraft deployed to Middleton St George for another 'Ciano' exercise from 13 to 16 April, and on this occasion the problem of too many fighters to targets was encountered, attempts to avoid this backfiring when scramble orders were staggered. The new Flinders commitment had an adverse effect on the availability of air and ground crew and aircraft alike, as now two jets were tied up in preparation to launch at the drop of a hat, 24 hours a day, for the duration that the responsibility was held. From the following month, 25 Squadron was expected to be away from Leuchars for a period of about twelve weeks on deployment to Gütersloh in West Germany.

Because of the length of the detachment, many decided to take their wives with them, even though this would have an impact on personal finances as the RAF would not pay an allowance for married quarters for those involved. Even so, the Station Commander and his staff at Gütersloh did what they could to help by making available as many spare married quarters as possible.

In order to find out what was going on, the commanding officer of 25 Squadron evidently had to fly out to Gütersloh in advance to spy out the lie of the land, as it were. On his return he briefed the squadron to expect to be maintained at a very high readiness state or 'state of preparedness', and although it was not confirmed or made clear, the presumption was that the Berlin Corridor was again concentrating everyone's minds.

On 26 May, seventeen Javelins of 25 Squadron arrived at Gütersloh and, sure enough, the next eleven weeks were spent training and being on hand to reinforce the RAF fighter force in West Germany for an expected renewal of tension over the Berlin Corridor. Training for this moved away from high-level interception to medium- and low-level patrols, a radical change in circumstances to those at Leuchars. While in Germany, the squadron operated from a dispersal position on the airfield.

In 1962, 29 Squadron spent nearly half the year overseas on various deployments. In March, four aircraft were also deployed to Middleton St George as part of what was still the Halyard commitment. Four months later, the highlight of July's flying effort was an operation mounted by the squadron in concert with ex-Leuchars 43 Squadron, now based at Akrotiri, together with some of the Canberras from the Strike Wing there. This involved interception and monitoring, in order to obtain information concerning movements, of twelve Tu-16 Badger long-range reconnaissance bombers from Bulgaria to the United Arab Republic.

Barry Mayner was still with 29 Squadron and was among those scrambled to make the intercept:

My first Russian was a Badger being delivered to Egypt on 16 July 1962. No. 29 Sqn, we were on detachment from Leuchars to Akrotiri. Four of our Javelins were scrambled to intercept on information provided by telephone calls from Sofia to London to Cyprus when the Badgers got airborne. We intercepted the stream of aircraft nearly 350 miles west of Akrotiri. Two of us managed to catch a Badger and take pictures.

Barry has quite a long association with Leuchars, having served a number of tours there, first on Javelins with 29 Squadron and later on Phantoms with 43 Squadron. In recent times he and his family have run a Bed & Breakfast in the area, catering for many of those travelling from near and far to attend the air show each year.

No. 25 Squadron had a week's stand down on return from Gütersloh

Whisky Four, the Dutch aerobatics team of the 1960s made their debut appearance at Leuchars in 1962, this year saw the first appearance at RAF Battle of Britain at home displays by NATO air arms other than those of the USA and Canada. (*Koniglicht Lucht Historiche*)

before the Battle of Britain display on 15 September, for which it provided a nine-ship flypast at Aldergrove as well as for the home crowd. That year's see-what-your-taxes-pay-for extravaganza brought a milestone in terms of participation by foreign military aircraft. Hitherto, only aircraft from the USAF and RCAF had made regular appearances. Along with the majority of the other fifteen RAF stations welcoming the public through the gates, NATO air arms were also evident. Visitors to Leuchars got to see a display by the Royal Dutch Air Force aerobatic team 'Whisky-4', flying four Lockheed T-33 Shooting Stars, the two-seat trainer version of the first American-built jet fighter. In its operational configuration it was known originally as the P-80, which was later changed to the F-80. Indeed, that year's display was regarded as the best yet.

Only weeks later, the polarised stand-off between East and West deteriorated. US Intelligence had detected an attempt by the USSR to station medium-range ballistic missiles in its most prominent client state in the western hemisphere—Cuba. This came to light when a Lockheed U-2 high-altitude reconnaissance aircraft photographed what was identified as launch site preparations on 14 October 1962. The next two weeks brought the planet closer to Armageddon than it has ever been, and while the world went about its business, the drama took place largely shielded from the press, which reported what snippets it could.

An opening phase attack may well have been directed against UK airspace. Defence against the threat was essentially in the hands of twelve manned interceptor fighter squadrons and twelve surface-to-air missile (SAM) squadrons, as follows:

Base	Sqn	Type	Sector Control (GCI)	UE
Leuchars	25	Javelin FAW9	Boulmer	16
Leuchars	29	Javelin FAW9	Boulmer	16
Middleton St George	33	Javelin FAW9 withdrawn on 22/10/1962	XXXXX	16
Leconfield	19	Hunter F6	Patrington	16
Leconfield	92	Hunter F6	Patrington	12
Binbrook	64	Javelin FAW9	Patrington	12
Coltishall	23	Javelin FAW9	Neatishead	16
Coltishall	74	Lightning F1	Neatishead	12
Wattisham	41	Javelin FAW8	Bawdsey	16
Wattisham	56	Lightning F1A	Bawdsey	12
Wattisham	111	Lightning F1A	Bawdsey	12
West Raynham	85	Javelin FAW8	Patrington	16

SAM Wing 148 (Church Fenton)		
Base	Sqn	Type
North Coates	264	Bloodhound Mk 1
Dunholme Lodge	141	Bloodhound Mk 1
Woodhall Spa	222	Bloodhound Mk 1
Misson	94	Bloodhound Mk 1
Breighton	112	Bloodhound Mk 1
Carnaby	247	Bloodhound Mk 1
SAM Wing 24 (Watton)		
Base	Sqn	Type
Watton	263	Bloodhound Mk 1
Marham	242	Bloodhound Mk 1
Rattlesden	266	Bloodhound Mk 1
North Luffenham	151	Bloodhound Mk 1
Woolfox Lodge	62	Bloodhound Mk 1
Warboys	257	Bloodhound Mk 1

All were intended as a shield for the V bomber and Thor intermediate-range ballistic missile bases, yet despite the now much publicised rise in tensions during this period, life continued without any perceptible change, for the Leuchars Wing at least.

The Cuban missile crisis occurred over the period from 15 to 28 October. However, to put matters into perspective, regarding both military reaction and public perception, on 16 October, OC 25 Squadron led a formation of six Javelins on a flypast over Leith Docks and Princes Street in Edinburgh on the occasion of the state visit to Scotland by King Olav V of Norway. The following day, 29 Squadron flew twelve Javelins to Wattisham as part of the first leg of its deployment to Akrotiri for Exercise 'Cypex'. But apart from a QRA scramble in the afternoon on 23 October, with nothing of interest to report back, the month presented no change to the otherwise busy pattern of flying, mainly in connection with 'Bomber Affiliation' exercises. It all appeared to be business as usual for Fighter Command, whereas Bomber Command and that element of Transport Command detailed to support them by ferrying crews to and from the dispersal airfields were preparing for Armageddon. No. 25 Squadron was essentially non-effective by November, but was kept on at Leuchars prior to being officially disbanded and its aircraft sent to join 11 Squadron in Germany, which was re-equipping with Mk 9s at the time.

The CO remarked:

> From a historical point of view it is most unfortunate that the decision had to be made to disband this squadron which has a considerably longer record of unbroken service than many of the all-weather squadrons still remaining in service. With regard to general efficiency, the squadron has flown more hours than any other Mk 9 Javelin squadron in the service over the past two years. In fact, with the exception of one in-flight refuelling equipped Javelin squadron, we have flown over a thousand hours more than our nearest rivals. One is left with the impression that perhaps the reason for disbanding this squadron rather than another was to save as much money as possible on aircraft hours and fuel bills! However, we cannot help but feel, as Cordelia in Shakespeare's *King Lear*, 'We have seen the best of our time: machinations, hollowness, treachery and all ruinous disorders follow us disquietly to our graves.'

As 1963 began, there was much in the way of change for the operational units at Leuchars. Following the disbandment of 25 Squadron as part of the further 'rationalisation' of the fighter force, 29 Squadron was officially notified on 11 January that it was to replace 43 Squadron in Cyprus. This was expected to bring about a number of aircrew changes to the squadron, as indeed it did. The contraction of the Javelin force at this time, and the need to shuffle people around and find staff for other vacant posts, may have precipitated an unusual number of moves and, sure enough, no fewer than fifteen of 29 Squadron's aircrew were posted prior to departure. A USAF exchange officer, Lt Col. G. W. Eagle, was posted to fly the Mk 8 Javelin with 41 Squadron at Wattisham, and Sqn Ldr George Beaton, 'A' Flight Commander, was to stay at Leuchars and would in due course become the commanding officer of the re-formed Javelin OCU, following which he was to be posted to Kelsas in Oslo as Squadron Leader Air Ops. Three were to stay on to join 23 Squadron, and one officer, Flt Lt Brian Carroll, would return to 23 Squadron flying the Lightning, an aircraft in which he later established a record ceiling in the order of 87,300 feet in a Mk 53 over Saudi Arabia. No. 29 Squadron's two by now rare-breed master navigators* were to be sent to Bahrain and Aden. The places vacated were taken by a large chunk of aircrew from the former 85 Squadron, which had just disbanded.

Master navigator, as master pilot, was a now defunct aircrew-only rank equivalent to that of warrant officer. The equivalent ranks in the Army would be company and regimental sergeant-major. Other aircrew warrant officer ranks were all titled in the same generic fashion: master air gunner, master bomb-aimer, master air electronics operator, master flight engineer, master air loadmaster and master signaller.

At the end of February 1963, with 25 Squadron already disbanded, 29 Squadron was preparing to replace the Hunters of 43 Squadron as the resident air defence unit based at RAF Nicosia in Cyprus. Its place at Leuchars would be taken by the Javelin Mk 9s of 23 Squadron, the 'Red Eagles', who were to move from Coltishall. Meanwhile, 29 Squadron was declared non-operational as of 1 February. Flying continued, the majority of which was devoted to air tests and to the training of new aircrew members.

On 26 February, five aircraft left as an advance party for Cyprus, led by the squadron's commander, Wg Cdr E. G. P. Jeffery. The squadron was to be declared fully operational with the QRA commitment for Air Forces Middle East by 1 March. Much of the ground training during the month was, not unexpectedly, given over to desert survival, and one of the squadron's own, Flt Lt Bill Shields, was able to expand on the topic by relating his own personal experience.

During February, severe weather at Coltishall had curtailed the operational flying programme of 23 Squadron, which was alleviated slightly by a window of improved conditions on the 14th. Thereafter it was back to the odd occasion when the runway was clear and available diversion airfields made getting aloft possible. Towards the end of the month the weather began to improve noticeably, but now time was taken up with preparations for the move north.

The first move came on 24 February, when two Javelins arrived permanently at Leuchars and immediately took over the QRA commitment from 29 Squadron, which was getting ready for the more agreeable climate of the Mediterranean. As well as now being solely responsible for the Northern 'Q' (Flinders), 23 Squadron was still tasked with providing the Southern 'Q' at Coltishall (shared out among a considerable number of squadrons, from Middleton St George in County Durham to Wattisham in Suffolk). The squadron had taken over the duty from 8 February until the end of the month, despite already getting ready to move.

By 1 March, 23 Squadron was still only partially transferred, further moves on the 15th and 18th bringing a further nine jets, with a five-ship led by the commanding officer, Wg Cdr A. J. Owen, on the latter date. The transfer was complete on 21 March, with a number of Beverleys and Valettas from Transport Command doing the honours, airlifting the rest of the squadron's equipment and stores. At the time, QRA scrambles, even for the more prominently positioned Northern 'Q', were few and far between compared with the high number that developed in the late 1960s and would remain through to the collapse of the Berlin Wall. By the end of March, the squadron's Javelins had been scrambled only twice, one of which was to assist an aircraft in distress, but otherwise it was a busy month. The regular flying programme got under way in earnest, with eighty-seven daytime practice intercepts and sixty-four at night. In addition, two exercises, 'Barrage' and 'Top Hat', took place on 23 March and 27/28 March respectively.

The tempo of routine flying increased in April to a total of 248 hours and 20 minutes, during which there was an emphasis on low-level interceptions between 500 feet and 2,500 feet. Wg Cdr Owen recorded that the month was 'socially a quiet one but the rest was doing us good'. May, however, was a different matter on that score. The squadron hosted a number of visitors, including foreign students from nearby St Andrews University, Dundee Salvation Army, City of Edinburgh Police and, on 22 May, eighteen pupils and two teachers from the Sacred Heart Girls' School in Edinburgh. All manner of visitors descended on the station throughout its RAF existence, as with most bases I suppose, but Leuchars certainly seemed to prove a particularly attractive destination.

In May, live firing of Firestreak missiles took place during a detachment to Valley, and a demonstration of air-to-air refuelling was laid on for HRH Princess Margaret, followed by a trip to Sola in Norway, a base often in receipt of Leuchars aircraft. For the remainder of 1963, 23 Squadron had

A 23 Squadron Javelin FAW9 at the Lossiemouth air day, July 1963. (*Richard Freail*)

the run of the place, save for the SAR 'C' Flight of 228 Squadron with its Whirlwind HAR10 helicopters and the University Air Squadron providing further diversity in the air with its de Havilland Chipmunk T10 elementary trainers. Having got their feet under the table, they were kept busy with the usual balance of exercises, one of the pilots, Flt Lt Tug Wilson, earning the nickname 'St Peter' as he had spent some time repairing a fishing net. Eventually it got thrown into the lagoon off the end of the runway and when dragged back ashore contained no fewer than sixty-nine fish!

June brought royal escort duty, live firing, an alert exercise and demonstration flying for the annual AOC's visit, and on 12 June the commanding officer led six Javelins to intercept and escort a Boeing 707 carrying the President of India from the USA to Heathrow Airport. This was carried out sixty miles north-west of Prestwick, over which location the Javelins parted from the 707.

Just two days later, four Javelins were involved in Exercise 'Ciane' which involved intercepting Canberras at 40,000 feet, but the big operation of the year came on 26 September with Exercise 'Triplex West' when ten aircraft were air-refuelled to Malta. The next day, eight of those flew on to El Adem in Libya, while five more flew out and were air-refuelled from Leuchars to Malta, which pretty well accounted for the entire squadron. By the end of the month, the training exercises had yielded a total of 355 successful interceptions and five unsuccessful ones.

The month of November was not quite so fruitful. Restrictions on flying in cloud had been imposed due to the effect on the engines caused by the sudden change in temperature, but more about that later. However, flying was conducted whenever possible, and to give an idea of the contrast with the more active month of September, November accrued a total of 249 hours and 50 minutes of airborne time. No. 23 Squadron continued with the Javelin at Leuchars until the latter end of 1964, when conversion to the Lightning Mk 3 was at hand.

7

QRA and Lightning Response

Quick Reaction Alert came into its own with the arrival of the English Electric Lightning. At the time of its introduction into service, the Lightning represented the kind of quantum leap in sheer physical performance over its immediate predecessors that is simply not experienced today. Even with the arrival of the American F-22, the margin in performance between it and the nearest existing type was relatively wide. The Lightning doubled the speed of the Hunter and the Javelin, trebled the rate of climb of the former and quadrupled that of the latter. Its ceiling performance also left the earlier two behind by quite a margin. These were the Lightning's good points, but it also had some bad points. It carried half the armament of the Javelin and desperately depended on airborne tanker support; it also presented a very high cockpit workload. Indeed, the pilots who made it through the Lightning OCU could be regarded as the most exceptional among the exceptional.

The aircraft was already more than three years into its operational career by the time the first jets arrived on posting to Leuchars on 28 February 1964. They belonged to 74 Squadron, which had the honour of being the first to form on Lightnings, arriving at Leuchars with the original Mk 1 aircraft it had received in 1960. However, the Mk 1s were less than ideal; in fact, they were practically unsuitable for the long-range endurance sorties that faced them. What was much sought-after here was in-flight refuelling, but the Mk 1 Lightning did not possess the capability for this. Given the Lightning's short legs and raging thirst, the Javelin presented a much better prospect in this regard. Nevertheless, the arrival of the Lightning at Leuchars took place in a blaze of publicity.

Commanded at the time by Sqn Ldr Peter Botterill, they were operational within five hours of arriving. Two new pilots had also just joined, determining the flying programme for the month ahead. This was to be made up largely of radar conversion, even though the Lightning OCU, whence the two newcomers had arrived, had recently started giving trainees a larger number of radar training sorties than had previously been the case. The need to get to grips with this required some considerable concentration to begin with. In the meantime, the pilots of 74 Squadron were doing a good deal of overnight travelling to and from Wattisham in order to familiarise themselves with the brand-new Mk 3 Lightning, which would make the squadron the first with Mk 1s and Mk 3s. The Mk 3 Lightnings were the first version to be officially cleared to Mach 2 operationally. Earlier versions—whatever speed they could actually reach—were restricted to Mach 1.7. The standard round-the-clock readiness state was ten minutes.

In April, the first of the new uprated Mk 3s were delivered, the first example arriving on the 14th, thus allowing one of the Mk 1s to be promptly dispatched back to Coltishall for use by the OCU. The next arrived on 29 April. The Mk 3 remedied the range and endurance problems of the Mk 1 in so far as it was fitted with an in-flight refuelling probe, which meant that with the promise of tanker support, Lightnings launched from Leuchars could reach quite some distance out if needed. To give some idea of the situation for the crew, Ed Durham described being 600 miles north of Lossiemouth at night looking for the tanker as not being the most comfortable set of circumstances for any young man, even one with a large amount of confidence.

The arrival of this thoroughbred interceptor, even in its Mk 1 configuration, was none the less a considerable step forward as far as the RAF was concerned, but the month was rounded off on a lacklustre note. Scarcely any flying took place in the last week due to the presence over the station of the infamous Leuchars haar.

By June 1964, 74 Squadron was still to make significant progress in the process of converting to the Lightning Mk 3, with ten pilots beginning the Mk 3 ground school. This was the third and largest course so far. The squadron had been relieved of its QRA duty on 8 June, and all but one pilot selected to train on the new model completed the basic conversion.

The earlier Mk 1s had been used extensively for formation aerobatics, mostly in 1961 and 1962, and the wear and tear was becoming increasingly apparent. Peter Botterill noted:

> The age and hard usage of the Mark 1 Lightning is beginning to be very noticeable in terms of serviceability. Many faults occur with monotonous regularity in all aircraft systems, there being no general trend. Despite many hours of rectification put in by the long-suffering ground crew, the flying hours achieved continue to be very low.

The number of defects and the rectification time required continue to increase. It is therefore with some relief that the Mk 3 aircraft are being accepted. The early results are promising, forty sorties being flown with only two Mk 3 aircraft during the month.

The month referred to was May, and in June four more Mk 3s were delivered and three Mk 1s were removed.

Towards the latter half of 1964, 23 Squadron's aircrew had not yet been told whether they would be converting to the Lightning, and this was the cause of some concern among the pilots. Their concerns on this occasion were justified. The reason was that all Javelin aircrew would be required for the squadrons that would retain the aircraft beyond 1964 in Cyprus and Malaya. The ground crew, however, were seeing a number of them convert to the new type. Come August, the aircrew were going to be largely preoccupied with flying their old jets to Shawbury Maintenance Unit. Most of the 'flat iron' folk had received their posting notices by early July and, as expected, in the main they were going to 29 Squadron at Akrotiri in Cyprus and 60 Squadron at Tengah in Singapore, with seemingly most being sent to the latter.

In August, 23 Squadron received its first three factory-fresh Lightning Mk 3s direct from BAC Warton, while two Javelin FAW9s were delivered to RAF Shawbury, one for inspection and the other for a double engine change in order to conform to new modification requirements. Two more Javelins were lost at Leuchars, an FAW9 and a T3, both of which caught fire, the former on a take-off run and the latter during an engine run. Both were complete write-offs, but fortunately nobody was injured.

With the transfer of crews and aircraft to the Mediterranean and Far East still to take effect in the main, much of August was taken up with air-to-air refuelling, navigation and formation flying. The latter was more to do with the squadron's last public showing, planning for which included the RNAS Lossiemouth and ROC open days, a flypast for the opening of the Forth Road Bridge by HM The Queen and the RAF Battle of Britain open days. In addition, twenty-seven tactical formation practices were flown.

August brought tragedy to the station, and to 74 Squadron in particular, when Flt Lt Glyn Owen was working up an aerobatic sequence for the forthcoming Battle of Britain displays at Leuchars and Acklington. He had been advised prior to his rehearsal on 28 August of cloud-base limitations and had accordingly elected to fly a limited or rolling display. All had gone well and as the planned manoeuvre was complete it may have been the case that the cloud base had lifted somewhat because he called ATC to advise that he was going to finish with a loop and then turn in to land. He ran in from the east, heading across the airfield from the sea, then pulled up to commence the loop, stalled and entered a spin. He ejected but the sequence did not complete, resulting in tragedy. The outcome had been watched by many people on the station, which compounded the situation.

Just over ten years earlier, Flt Lt Owen had ejected from an F-86 Sabre while serving on 66 Squadron, then based at Linton-on-Ouse. On that particular occasion he was singularly lucky. His squadron had lost three aircraft, two in the same incident in which both pilots died, but he had been involved in an unrelated event, flying at 45,000 feet, when he detected a lack of oxygen and descended to a lower level. Three minutes later both fire warning lights illuminated and, with nowhere suitable to land, he ejected safely. He married the following week.

September brought the delivery of two more Lightning F3s and a T4. Operation 'Heavenly', referring to the transfer of the remaining Javelins to Akrotiri, commenced on the 25th of the month, with three flown out that day and arriving in Cyprus at 1330 GMT on the 28th.

No. 23 Squadron officially re-formed at Leuchars on 1 October, on which date QRA responsibilities for the 'Red Eagles' terminated. The 'Red Eagles' had taken delivery of a total of eight Lightnings by the end of September, seven F3s and one T4, the jets having all been flown up to Leuchars from Warton by pilots from the OCU at Coltishall. The first six squadron pilots had begun conversion on 21 September. Meanwhile, 23 Squadron got to grips with its new mounts and command passed from Wg Cdr A. J. Owen to Sqn Ldr John McLeod. Lightnings from RAF Leconfield arrived during November to take on the Northern QRA duty while 23 and 74 Squadrons were completing their work-up to operational readiness.

As January 1965 arrived, 74 Squadron was looking forward to its first direct posting-in (post-F3 conversion) from the OCU, even though it would be some time before it became operationally effective. As was noted, 'The Coffee Bar was in urgent need of a J.P. [Junior Pilot] to run it enthusiastically!'

In June, HRH Princess Margaret visited the station to present a new standard to 74 Squadron, while 23 Squadron was involved in mounting the flypast, preparation for which soaked up the bulk of the first week's flying. No. 74 Squadron had worked up a four-ship formation drill/display team for the princess's visit, led by Sqn Ldr Bill Maish, with Flt Lts Dave Liggitt, Henry Ploszek and Tim Cohu, together with Terry Maddern in reserve. Flt Lt Dave Mitchell was working up his solo aerobatic sequence at the time.

By now, the new QRA sheds were being used to accommodate the 'Q' aircraft up at the west end of the airfield, and 23 Squadron had seven

Group Captain Harbison assists HRH Princess Margaret with the presentation to 74 Squadron of their new Standard, 3 June 1965. (*The National Archives*)

scrambles during the month. In three cases, the contact descended to low level and disappeared from radar cover, another was a Navy Scimitar, and three turned out to be Russian Badgers—perhaps the very first Soviet Air Force aircraft to be intercepted by the Leuchars Wing. They were shadowed until they withdrew out of range. The Badger idents gave a renewed sense of purpose, although it would not have been understood at that time just how much the tempo would build. Sqn Ldr McLeod noted, 'For once, the QRA commitment became attractive and rewarding, and the sorties themselves had much operational value.'

Owing to runway repairs in July, the QRA was mounted from RNAS Lossiemouth by 74 Squadron from 2 to 5 July. Three aircraft, six pilots and a small party of ground crew went up there, but nothing doing, as they say.

As 1965 was the year in which the 25th anniversary of the Battle of Britain fell, this naturally meant an extra special effort was made for the annual September displays, and twelve stations were open on the day. The Leuchars-based units had a busy time in this respect, with 18 September being the climax. The two Lightning squadrons had each trained up a solo aerobatics pilot, the chap from 74 Squadron being detached to RAF Lyneham from where he could operate on the day, flying his display at

Blast Off! A Lightning F mk 3 of 74 (Tiger) Sqn getting off runway 09 quite smartish *c.* 1964–65, possibly on QRA launch. (*MOD/Crown copyright*)

two stations—Colerne and St Mawgan. The Javelin OCU provided two individual demonstration crews, one taking a T3 (T-bird) Javelin to Finningley, while a Meteor Mk 9 was flown at Acklington. No. 23 Squadron's solo man remained at the homestead to impress the local crowd, and all three units put together a four-ship formation drill team, which became a three-ship flypast in the case of 74 Squadron due to unforeseen technical problems.

All the base's flying units did something. The SAR 'C' Flight of 202 Squadron, demonstrated rescuing someone from the perils of the airfield grass, while the University Air Squadron put up a solo Chipmunk trainer, and a glider and tug ensemble came down from RNAS Arbroath. As the RAF, indeed HM forces, were about to be downsized yet again, this would be the last time that as many as twelve RAF stations would open their gates simultaneously to the general public across the UK. The number of such events continued to be gradually eroded over the years, and the list was down to four by 1975.

The beginning of 1966 brought about a series of changes elsewhere. As the growing number of Lightnings available were being issued to operational units, the disposition of some of those units changed as well. At Geilenkirchen in Germany, 11 Squadron was seeing its crews run down rapidly. Equipped at the time with the Javelin Mk 9, they were already handing over to 19 Squadron, recently arrived from Leconfield. As the commanding officer of No. 11 remarked, the squadron took every opportunity to remain fully proficient in the use of its Javelins as weapons systems until its disbandment. It also stood QRA at Geilenkirchen during the first week of January.

During the rest of the month, all of the squadron's aircrew were posted out, including two sergeants and a master pilot. The RAF had once seen many NCO aircrew, and the Javelin was perhaps as modern and sophisticated an aircraft as those fliers, with chevrons instead of braid, got to fly before the stage was reached when officer pilots and navigators filled all the slots. Nine of their aircraft were ferried to Shawbury where it is likely some could have lived a while longer in the hands of the newly re-formed OCU. Indeed if they had, they would have been born again with the crest of 11 Squadron on their fins, as in keeping with the growing RAF custom of assigning disbanded squadron numbers to other, non-operationally declared, active units as shadow numbers, 228 OCU was allocated 11 Squadron as its shadow/reserve identity in 1966. This meant that if push came to shove, some or all of 228 OCU would be called upon to deploy on a war footing, resurrected as 11 Squadron in this case, of course. It would not have to wait too long before regaining full operational status once again—April 1967, in fact.

The end of March also brought Exercise 'Windmill' during which Leuchars prepared to mount an operation at short notice, designed to intercept Soviet Tu-95 Bears flying north of the Shetlands en route to the South Atlantic. This involved two Victor tanker aircraft from RAF Marham. Combining this and the exploits of a young pilot, Fg Off. Mike Donaldson, 23 Squadron broke all records for sorties flown by a Lightning squadron to date. At this particular time, preparations were under way to base a Target Facilities Flight (TFF) at each of the operational UK Lightning bases. Each was to receive typically three Mk 1 Lightnings.

March 1966 brought particularly good weather to north-east Fife, and the Leuchars units were not slow to take advantage of the unexpectedly favourable conditions. Both 23 and 74 Squadrons carried out a number of supersonic intercepts, sorties lasting for about half an hour, the bulk of which were done without in-flight refuelling which was unavailable until 25 March. Meanwhile, this was the month when 228 OCU received verbal instructions that it was to formally adopt the shadow identity of 11 Squadron.

As the weather improved, each of the Leuchars units began working up a solo display pilot/crew as was the established routine. The amount of

Montage of 23 Sqn Lightnings, *c.* 1965. Note the 228 OCU Javelin in the background on lower two frames, and the Hunter in training scheme. The Lightnings are fitted with Firesteak missiles. (*Bob Offord*)

effort afforded to display flying by RAF aircrew, while a mere shadow of what it had been just ten years earlier, was still considerable at home and overseas, such was the importance placed on the consequent sharpening of flying skill and increase in public prestige. Flt Lt Al Turley of 23 Squadron and Flt Lt Dave Liggitt of 74 Squadron, together with a solo Javelin crew from 228 OCU, began working on their display sequences, 23 Squadron also putting together a four-ship display team. The Station Commander noted that 'while this was good for the morale of those involved, it wasn't quite so for those upon whose shoulders fell the added strain of additional night flying and QRA duties'. No. 23 Squadron took over QRA on 22 April (the squadron on QRA normally held the mantle for about six weeks). This month also saw the arrival of the first two of three Lightning Mk 1s for the new Leuchars TFF—XM145 and XM139—arriving on 26 and 28 April respectively.

Neil Clark, a young married corporal serving on 74 Squadron and living in St Andrews at the time, recalls the day (21 April 1966) when Javelin XH883 with a student crew approached from the sea. An emergency having developed, they needed to jettison the ventral fuel tanks, but when the pilot went to release them he instead operated the 'clear wing' switch, releasing the drill/acquisition Firestreak rounds, which of course were carried under-wing. The trajectory of the aircraft at the time brought it over the Jubilee golf course, and one missile glided across the Eden Estuary and embedded itself on the 16th green. It was found by a party unaware of its origins, and as this was the middle of Student Rag Week, it was thought at first that it was a cunning scheme by the Charities Commission to promote their campaign. Indeed, the Officer Commanding the OCU, Sqn Ldr George Beaton, received a letter from the Students' Union, the content of which was apparently quite interesting but has since sadly gone missing.

Beaton was a typical middle-to-senior-ranking officer of the era. He originally joined the Army during the Second World War and thereafter joined the Glider/Parachute Regiment in 1944, being trained as a glider pilot. However, he missed the D-Day drops and was a standby for Operation 'Market Garden'. At the end of the war he transferred to the RAF and was trained as a fixed-wing pilot, joining 29 Squadron in 1961. He took over 'A' Flight from Sqn Ldr Peter Harding, who himself went on to become Chief of the Air Staff and subsequently Chief of the Defence Staff and, interestingly, was the first Chief of the Air Staff to have operational experience of flying helicopters. Having left 29 Squadron just before the move to Cyprus, Beaton had been Acting CO for the long detachment to Malta/Cyprus in 1962. When the Javelin OCU was re-formed at Leuchars, he was the CO for the whole period until final disbandment. Beaton was promoted to wing commander before leaving the service some years later.

This was now an era in which aircraft noise had become a significant problem. The transition from prop engines to jets brought a harsher, more intense noise and an inevitable increase in decibels. However, by the time the second-generation fighter aircraft or, more specifically, Hunters and Javelins arrived from 1955 onwards, the increase in noise was unmistakable and was for some a blight on the local tranquillity. Ever since then, the resonating roar and low-register thunder of high-performance jet engines has been a routine characteristic of the environs of Leuchars.

The town of St Andrews has lived with this feature since the days when American cars had bigger wings than some of the new fighters entering service, seemingly with understanding and tolerance, and for perhaps longer than any other similar community. That said, not everyone sees the need or justification, and once in a while the pot boils over. In September 1966, a petition was put together (admittedly with only seventy-five signatures) by inhabitants of the Milton Bank, Toll Road and Motray Crescent areas complaining of the 'highly unsatisfactory housing conditions caused by the noise from the RAF station nearby'. This had in part been prompted by local plans to build new houses in the villages of Guardbridge and Leuchars. The petition placed before the Planning Committee expressed concern about the health and well-being of everyone, and went on:

> While we appreciate that the station must operate, we are now convinced that the modern operational activities of such an important defence unit are totally incompatible with the normal life of inhabitants of the community.

While not responding to this petition, the then Station Commander, Gp Capt. Arthur Strudwick, had some months earlier written an open letter to the *St Andrews Citizen*, clearly conscious of the growing disquiet among local inhabitants at a time when the volume of jet noise had probably reached a peak. The letter, dated 3 March, aimed to prepare the base's neighbours for the coming summer season and the expected jet noise level, which was going to be exacerbated by display practices:

> Sir,
> Certain Royal Air Force stations are now starting preparations for this year's flying display season which begins with the smaller displays in various parts of the country and culminates in the Battle of Britain 'at home' day in September. In addition to these national events, RAF aircraft will be performing before international audiences at NATO functions and bases where it is equally essential for reasons of national prestige that the displays are of the highest possible calibre.

Nos 23 and 74 Squadrons and 228 OCU, all based at Royal Air Force Leuchars, will be participating in a series of displays in Scotland, England and abroad during 1966. The precision, high standard of flying and the split-second timing demanded for these aerobatic and formation displays make it essential that our pilots practise regularly and conform as closely as possible with the conditions under which their actual displays will be carried out.

Nearly all our aerobatic and display practices are carried out over or in the vicinity of RAF Leuchars so that the progress and performance of our pilots can be closely supervised and the pattern of the display related to the focal point at the airfield.

Although pilots take precautions to avoid causing unnecessary noise, flight at low level by high-performance aircraft inevitably creates some aerial disturbance. Every effort is made to keep this noise to a minimum and to restrict it to reasonable hours, and I hope that local residents will accept the inconvenience for several days during the next few months.

On 16 May, Wg Cdr Keith Williamson took over command of 23 Squadron. The fact that a wing commander was taking command of a single-seat squadron as recently as 1966 shows just how long the rank structure of Fighter Command units had taken to catch up with those of Bomber Command, which was appointing wing commanders as squadron commanders during the war. The Javelin squadrons had long since had the rank of wing commander appointed to this level, almost certainly in recognition of the complexity and performance of the new fighter. Wg Cdr Williamson himself had a quite successful career ahead of him, although he may not have known it at the time. He was destined to become Chief of the Air Staff in 1982.

With 74 Squadron now based at Leuchars, there came the honour for the squadron to host the annual Tiger Meet, this being the opportunity to compare tactics and engage in various sortie profiles involving fighters (or, rather, aircraft from across NATO with the tiger as a common squadron crest). This year's Tiger Meet, from 5 to 9 July 1966, included the following:

31st Sqn Belgian FAB	3 × Lockheed F-104G Starfighter
439th Recce Sqn RCAF	4 × Lockheed RF-104G Starfighter
53rd TFS USAF	2 × McDonnell Douglas F-4C Phantom II
79th TFS USAF	3 × North American F-100D Super Sabre
Escadron de Chasse Adl	3 × Dassault Super Mystère B2
52nd AKG T-33 Luftwaffe	2 × Lockheed T-33 Shooting Star
2nd JBG F-86 Luftwaffe	4 × North American F-86 Sabre

On the eve of proceedings, 74 Squadron was on QRA (as it was throughout the meet) and seven of its aircraft were scrambled on 4 July to intercept three Bisons. This represented another defining indication of future operations, and on this occasion the Russians came within 140 miles of Leuchars itself. Using a borrowed colour-film camera, Fg Off. Richard Rhodes took some shots which, as was very much now the norm, were sent off to HQ Fighter Command. The Tigers had one more operational scramble this month, against a de Havilland Comet Mk 2.

Meanwhile, the focus of the month was the Tiger Meet. Not all managed to make the first day, 2nd JBG joining later in the week and sending four aircraft. Together with 52nd AKG, this made the Germans the largest visiting contingent. As well as the serious aspect to the event, it was also a social convention, with trips to various locations and mess functions, and many of the visitors were billeted in the homes of squadron personnel, something of a tradition at the Tiger Meet. There was also the chance to gain experience of other aircraft, each of the pilots/crew getting to fly in each other's hardware. One Phantom pilot was overheard saying that he would offer one Phantom trip for twelve T-33 rides—evidently a bargain, as the Germans readily agreed. The co-operation (what NATO is all about) extended to the ground crew, of course, and was epitomised by the scene of a Canadian instructor supervising an RAF fitter on the correct way to service a fault with the hydraulics of a German F-86. The F-86 pilots from the Luftwaffe were actually in the process of converting to the F-104 at the time, but were reportedly keen to attend. Everyone played to their strengths: the F-100s and Belgian F-104s practised low-level attack profiles through the Highlands; the Canadians photographed everyone and everything, their mission being tactical reconnaissance (as determined by the 'R' prefix designation on their F-104s); and the host unit, 74 Squadron, mixed it with the F-4s and French Super Mystères and found the latter to be quite able, despite the limits of the French jet compared to the Lightning Mk 3.

On the last day of the meet, the participants engaged in demonstrating their charges over the airfield. One of the French pilots, Capt. Joel Dancel, got airborne at about 1000 hours to rehearse a solo aerobatic display prior to the afternoon's proceedings in which he was to provide the finale, but shortly after getting airborne, his Super Mystère crashed into a nearby field and he was killed instantly. It was decided that as a tribute to Capt. Dancel—a consummate professional and someone imbued with the spirit of aviation—the afternoon ceremony and flying should still go ahead, with the flags of the participating nations lowered to half-mast as a mark of respect.

The afternoon's proceedings began with a review of the line-up of visiting aircraft by the AOC in C Fighter Command, Air Marshal Sir

Flt Lt Ian McBride of 74 Squadron and Paul Kimminau of the USAF 79th TFS Squadron prepare for a flight in one of 74's T5s during the Tiger Meet, July 1966. (*Ian McBride*)

Frederick Rosier, and two visiting generals from the USAF, Gen. Robert Lee, Air Deputy to SACEUR, and Gen. John Hardy, C in C US 3rd Air Force. This was followed by representatives of each of the squadrons getting airborne, plus a Spitfire and Hurricane from the Battle of Britain Flight at Coltishall and five Lightnings of 74 Squadron, led by Sqn Ldr Bill Maish with Flt Lts Terry Maddern, Henry Ploszek (former Firebird and later Red Arrows team manager), Don Brown and Dave Liggitt. The latter flew a solo aerobatic display. All got airborne in customary Lightning fashion, rotating through nearly 90 degrees on take-off to climb almost vertically in full reheat.

The main composite formation, including a Lightning T5 flown by Capt. Jim Throgmorton of the US Marine Corps, flew past following a formation display and bomb-burst manoeuvre by the Lightnings.

As of August 1966, the commander of 74 Squadron noted that QRA interceptions over the high seas against Soviet aircraft were ensuring that all personnel viewed QRA with more interest and enthusiasm than was usually the case. His squadron had also recently received its first Mk 6 Lightning and was looking forward to the greater range its bigger ventral fuel tank would bring. In the meantime, the single Mk 6 was in the hangar going nowhere until some technical issues were resolved. Earlier in the year, the squadron had sent a detachment out to Creil in France where

The rather more formal side of the 1966 Tiger meet, USAF F-4s and French Super Mysteres. (*The National Archives*)

they were the guests of 10 Squadron of the Armée de l'air (the French Air Force), and early in September, 74 Squadron reciprocated by hosting four Super Mystère B2s from the Creil-based EC1/10 'Valois'. Accompanied by some ground crew and an ATC officer, they were entertained with a visit to the Edinburgh Military Tattoo.

That same month, on 24 August, Flt Lt Al Turley of 23 Squadron had to eject from Lightning F3 XP760 when flying as one of a pair tasked with intercepting four Hawker Hunters at 35,000 feet. In order to save fuel, and in a wholly accepted practice, the Lightnings flew with one engine shut down. This way, naturally, the ever-thirsty aircraft would have a substantial amount of fuel left for the intercept, when, given the quarry, a pattern of dogfighting was almost certain to ensue. So when the targets were approached, both pilots attempted to relight the No. 2 engine. Flt Lt Turley made three attempts without success before the audio warning sounded and the Reheat Fire 1 and 2 warning displays lit up. To deal with this the pilot throttled back the one engine he had, which resulted in a pitch up to a nose-high attitude of 70 degrees. With the loss of speed and momentum, and the aircraft sinking rearwards, coupled with the loss of hydraulics, the Lightning entered into a spin. The pilot ejected successfully at 5,000 feet and was rescued 40 minutes later while adrift in his dinghy off the Fife coast.

During the summer all Mk 3 Lightnings were subject to temporary operating restrictions, including minimum flying below 3,000 feet and aerobatics prohibited as a result of problems diagnosed earlier with the tail fin torque convertor. This needed to be modified on all Mk 3s before the restrictions could be lifted. (The modifications had already begun with the aircraft based down south at Wattisham.) Meanwhile, the TFF received its third Mk 1 Lightning during September, and just in time, as Dave Liggitt and Al Turley needed to use the Mk 1s for their aerobatic displays, the Mk 3s at Leuchars still being under restriction at the time.

The squadrons would go ahead with their usual four-ship formations for the September air show but restricted to flypasts only. On the day, the weather simply was not having it, with cloud at 300 feet and complete cover at 600 feet. Sqn Ldr Bill Maish wrote in the ORB, '17 September proved to be the OCWF's nightmare. It is commendable that any flying programme at all materialised.' Flt Lt Dave Liggitt from 74 Squadron did manage to fly two solo displays, one earlier in the day at Finningley, and the squadron's formation also managed to get aloft, but their neighbours, 23 Squadron, could not get airborne at all. Furthermore, Flt Lt Al Turley, 23 Squadron's only authorised display pilot, was still out of action following his mishap the previous month so was unable to match Dave Liggitt with his own solo sequence.

However, the Javelin OCU, against the odds, had a much better day. Out of a unit strength of eleven FAW9 jets, four T3s and three Canberra T11s, nine of the Mk 9s were utilised, with two deployed to Coltishall and Finningley as static aircraft and two more on show at Leuchars. Five more were able to fly a four-ship formation and solo display as planned—the last public appearance of RAF Javelins. At least one T3 and one of the Canberras were parked up for public perusal. It was a fair contribution from 74 and 228 at least, given the weather, which was nearly a repeat of 1960.

Because 228 OCU was heading toward disbandment at the end of the year, a good deal of repair and modifications was not carried out and an earlier plan to fit the Mk 9 Javelins with radio compass/DME (distance measuring equipment) was not expected to proceed. In any case, no more new student courses were planned, and the three Canberras were likely to be the first to go, either to 85 Squadron for target facilities purposes or to No. 60 Maintenance Unit at Leconfield.

As the Javelin's time was drawing to a close, many serving on 228 OCU could have been forgiven any amount of apprehension about just what the future in or out of the RAF held for them. They need not have worried, as flying jobs were found for most of the aircrew, the pilots for the most part being posted at the end of the year to the Central Flying School, while several of the navigators hit the jackpot and were going to form the initial cadre of F-4 Phantom qualified navigator/weapons systems officers.

October 1966 represented something of a milestone for Leuchars. It was about to become the first Fighter Command station to be tested by Tactical Evaluation (originally planned for 18 October but postponed to the following day due to the weather). This first evaluation was considered as a practice run; there was a degree of notice afforded and time given to walk the station personnel through the proceedings in order to get an idea of what would be expected in the future. However, when that time came, there would be no notice and no prompting.

The Tactical Evaluation, or TACEVAL, came about as a need to test NATO air bases on the Continent to ensure that personnel understood that they were in a situation where being placed on a war footing at very short notice was an ever-increasing likelihood and were aware of the requirement to react instantaneously to the klaxon whenever it sounded. The exercise at Leuchars was planned around three phases. The first was anti-intruder, this being a test of base security during the initial transition to war; the second phase was general war, which of course speaks for itself; and the final phase was a more straightforward intense operational training phase for the squadrons, but all the same, the station's technical and administrative support of the flying effort was every bit a part of the

Representative aircraft of 228 OCU flying over Fife, probably the Firth of Tay in the background *c.* 1966. The aircraft from nearest camera are; Canberra T11, Javelin FAW9 and Javelin T3. (*MOD/Crown copyright*)

exercise and evaluation of readiness. Hot on the heels of the station's first TACEVAL came a further realisation that Leuchars as an interceptor base was at the spearhead.

The period from 20 to 25 October was marked by a heavy period of QRA activity in which many interceptions of Bison aircraft were made and photos taken of Leuchars-based Lightnings shadowing the Russians. The stories hit the national press and attracted television coverage. The demands of this particular period were way above what two jets sitting at ten minutes' readiness could cope with alone, and at one stage ten Lightnings with pilots were available if required. On top of this, on 25 October, four of 23 Squadron's aircraft were air-refuelled out to Akrotiri where they were to remain until relieved by aircraft from 74 Squadron on 13 December. The month accounted for fourteen live scrambles, and on one occasion, on 11 October, a Lightning from 23 Squadron encountered 'Window', also known as 'Chaff', being issued from the target aircraft. This consists of small tin foil strips which play havoc with radar displays. The pilot was ordered not to close to any more than 3 nm from the target

Perhaps the earliest photo of RAF Fighters shadowing a Soviet Military Aircraft, two Lightnings of 74 Squadron with a TU-16 Badger, note the nearest Lightning is a mark 3, the more distant aircraft with the larger fuel blister, is a mark 6. (*Ian McBride*)

and on his return was personally summoned to HQ Fighter Command for debrief. This was another first for Leuchars with the deployment of electronic countermeasures against the station's aircraft.

Among the many official and VIP guests in and out of the station this year were the Duke and Duchess of Gloucester, who landed on 28 October en route to an official engagement in Dundee and departed from the station two days later.

By November, 74 Squadron's progress in acquiring Mk 6 Lightnings was going well, but the rundown of the Mk 3s was overtaking the arrival of the new jets. However, by the end of the month, seven Mk 6s had been delivered, while just three of the older Mk 3s remained. On the upside, the pilots were quite impressed with their new mount, finding it more pleasant to fly than the Mk 3. Best of all, of course, was the greater unrefuelled endurance that resulted in greater range and flexibility and perhaps a smidgen (but only that) less time nervously glancing at the fuel gauges. Of course, the Mk 6 also brought the advantage of the return of the two 30-mm Aden cannons that had been removed from the Mk 3 in the mistaken belief that dogfighting and strafing were features not likely to be relied upon in the operational future of the quick-response interceptor. It was now determined that guns gave the pilot the opportunity of a warning shot and an immediate attack capability during vis-ident (visual identity). The guns went together with the infrared (IR) missiles and provided the

HRH the Duke of Gloucester with Gp Capt Arthur Strudwick before flying out on 30 October 1966 following a visit with the Duchess of Gloucester to attend a function in Dundee. (*The National Archives*)

aforementioned flexibility for warning-shot attacks from all angles and further weapons once the missile 'bolt' had been shot.

As early as December 1966, the long-term future of the Lightning force was abundantly clear. It was expected that the F-4M Phantom would begin to replace the Lightning from around 1972/73, it in turn being released from the ground attack role at the same time by the arrival of the first of the Jaguar aircraft. Not that any of this would have been obvious to the outsider, for whom the future direction of the deployment of aircraft in these roles had more the appearance of a piecemeal response forced by unexpected economic developments. The truth is that the plan that actually took shape was largely in hand, although other plans were to be thwarted, such as the proposed introduction of F-111s. Also recommended at this time was a £2 million upgrade to sixty-one of the new Mk 6 Lightnings to carry 30-mm cannons in the forward section of the ventral fuel pack.

Many proposals were made during the 1960s to improve the Lightning's capability. Among these, some that might come as something of a surprise to those who have always regarded this classic supersonic interceptor as a peerless machine included a proposed increased 'g' clearance. This was to increase the 'g' limit at combat weight to 7 g. Yes, just 7 g. It was proposed to give the British fighter manoeuvrability comparable with the Soviet MiG-21c, which at the time was likely to be used as a bomber escort. However, the proposal was ditched because it would have required a long period of research and development and might have resulted in a need for the airframe to be redesigned. Another vetoed idea was to fit the Lightning with the American Sparrow missile for all-round attack capability at longer range. This was dismissed because 'it is not considered practicable to develop a completely new weapon system for the Lightning'.

The times ahead were tight for pilot instruction, with an expected increase in the number of new Lightning pilots being trained from late 1968 to early 1969 in order to make good a likely shortfall among the current pool who were retraining on the Phantom, all of which needed to be balanced out to ensure that a minimum level of experience was maintained. A rather worrying problem also loomed on the horizon, again placing Leuchars in the spotlight, as the level of Soviet long-range military reconnaissance flights increased whilst the number of successful interceptions by the RAF's Lightnings decreased. This was put down to the Russians using a more northerly route, placing them beyond range. That said, the response of the early warning radar stations at Saxa Vord on the tip of the Shetlands and the control coverage provided by the MRS (Master Radar Station) at Buchan in Aberdeenshire did not let anyone down. Many of the interceptions were made by the F-102 fighters of the USAF 57th Interceptor Squadron based at Keflavik in Iceland, and many of these sorties were controlled by the Buchan station, which meant an increase in intercepts for the American squadron.

In March 1967, 74 Squadron completed ninety-six hours of trials on Mk 6 Lightnings with over-wing tanks. While this was completed satisfactorily, one aircraft burst both tyres on landing from one of the sorties, but otherwise there were no major concerns. The following year, Leuchars Lightnings, although not from 74 Squadron, would be putting the over-wing tanks to very good use, but problems would be encountered along the way. No live QRA scrambles occurred in March, which might have indicated that the recent phenomenal change in operational tempo due to the sudden rise in Soviet long-range air activity was over. No. 74 Squadron was ordered on five practice scrambles, so it seemed like a brief return to the old days.

There was a considerable degree of change at Leuchars in 1967. When 74 Squadron left for sunnier climes, specifically the Far East and RAF Tengah, its place was taken by 11 Squadron, which the previous year had been assigned as the shadow squadron to 228 OCU. The squadron re-formed in August with the Lightning Mk 6 under the command of Wg Cdr David Blucke. 'The Eagles' were to re-form as an operational fighter squadron once again, as had been hoped by their last operational

Royal Norwegian Air Force Officers' wreath laying ceremony at the Norwegian War memorial on 27 April 1967, Gp Capt Strudwick also present. (*The National Archives*)

CO, but much had to be done, as Sqn Ldr Peter Collins, the new 'A' Flight commander, acknowledged. He also noted that this marked the first time that 'The Eagles' had been active in the UK for thirty-eight years. As of 1 April, only Peter Collins and one other officer, Flt Lt J. N. Anders, had been posted to the fledgling No. 11, with four more following from 10 April, and by 21 April the new unit's personnel strength stood at six pilots, two ground crew officers, one warrant officer, thirty-seven NCOs and thirty-seven junior ranks. They were therefore ready to go, and with two more pilots joining them from specialist Lightning courses at Warton in Lancashire, the squadron, such as it was, was thrown into a short-notice exercise followed by a no-notice one.

Exercise 'Springtime', a 24-hour NATO air defence exercise, got seven sorties out of 11 Squadron's handful of people. This was followed by the no-notice TACEVAL, another one of those seriously minded drills for all NATO units to get everyone in the frame of mind to jump to it and prove that they knew what they were about. The HQ Fighter Command team who instigated the TACEVAL did take the new squadron's circumstances into consideration, officially exempting it this time around, but there was a good response just the same from air and ground personnel. This contributed to the overall high marks awarded to the station. At the start of the proceedings, 11 Squadron still had no aircraft, taking delivery of its first Mk 6 Lightning during the exercise and managing to get it air tested.

Other pilots flew with the resident 23 and 74 Squadrons to gain some experience and carried out a fair share of interceptions. As they were to replace 74 Squadron, they were billeted in the old OCU premises until June, by which time No. 74 was to have left and the new squadron should have received its full complement of twelve Lightnings. Interestingly, with a view of things to come, although perhaps not necessarily something that Lightning pilots would expect to continue on, the squadron was invited to Warton during May, where as well as being shown various aspects of Lightning production, a 'very interesting presentation' was given on the Anglo-French Jaguar fighter/trainer.

May saw 23 Squadron back on QRA, with 74 Squadron non-effective and 11 Squadron yet to become fully operational. This was a relatively quiet QRA period, evidenced by the increased number of practice scrambles—fourteen by day and two at night. There was also the odd live launch. At 0441 hours on 19 May, one Lightning set off to intercept what turned out to be a KLM Boeing 707 bound for Amsterdam; then at 0933 hours on 24 May, another was scrambled to intercept what was described as an 'x' raid north of Lossiemouth, which turned out to be, of all things, a Douglas A-1 Skyraider.

Mrs Elizabeth Dacre visited 23 Sqn, on 11 May 1967, to present the Squadron with the Dacre Trophy, here Wg Cdr Keith Williamson explains the paraphernalia of a Lightning Pilot's flying and survival kit. Keith Williamson's career finished with his appointment as Chief of the Air Staff in 1982 and promotion to Marshal of the RAF on retirement. (*The National Archives*)

An official handover ceremony was staged on 15 May to mark the departure of 74 Squadron and the formation of 11 Squadron in its place, now equipped with four brand-new Lightning F6s. The Under-Secretary of State for Defence for the RAF, Merlyn Rees MP, was present to take the salute and address the parade, and a small flying display was laid on during the afternoon in which all three squadrons took part. This included a Victor tanker demonstrating air-to-air refuelling with two Lightnings, while 23 Squadron's Flt Lt Al Turley flew a solo aerobatic display. No. 74 Squadron was dined out that evening.

The squadron's departure for Singapore began on 1 June, it taking twelve days to move all its aircraft out, while Gp Capt. J. M. Nicholls took over from Gp Capt. A. Strudwick as Station Commander on 9 June. The latter was promoted to air commodore and posted to HQ Southern Command, which formed part of the Army's structure. On 30 June, 11 Squadron took over the QRA commitment as planned and equipped with the Red Top missile, giving the Lightning a collision-course fire capability. Before this, on 15 June, Flt Lt Kevin Mace, one of 11 Squadron's new pilots, while holding QRA with 23 Squadron, had intercepted two Badgers.

Towards the end of August, the squadron had quite a busy schedule, including Exercise 'Fawn' which involved the Royal Danish Air Force, and a survival scramble as part of Exercise 'Kingpin'. It was also given a display commitment at very short notice, being tasked with working up a flying drill formation, not just a flypast, and a full solo aerobatic sequence for the forthcoming September displays. The solo requirement was almost certainly due to the long-term hospitalisation of solo pilot Flt Lt Al Turley, who had recovered from his ejection over the North Sea but had since been involved in a more serious accident in which he and his wife were badly injured when their private aircraft caught fire in mid-air. The pilot afforded the honour of standing in was Fg Off. Richard Rhodes, who had transferred from 74 Squadron after ferrying one of its Lightnings to Singapore before returning, but not before consuming a copious amount of beer, according to Ian McBride.

The new squadron commanding officer, Wg Cdr David Blucke, made a particular note in the ORB detailing the number of formation and solo practice sorties flown between 16 August and the *moment critique* on 16 September. Flg Off. Rhodes was able to fit in just seven display rehearsals before the Battle of Britain display, when he was the curtain-raiser for the air show at Acklington, followed by a second display at Leuchars less than

Tigers out, Eagles in, 74 and 11 Squadron standards are paraded passed the CO Gp Capt Strudwick and Mr Merlyn Rees MP, 15 May 1967. (*The National Archives*)

two hours later. For both displays he flew XS918, an aircraft that was lost in the Firth of Forth nearly three years later. According to squadron records, the display four were Wg Cdr Blucke himself, with Flt Lts Dave Trick, Harry Drew and Lofty Lance, with Flg Off. Geoff Fish as spare. They managed just three practice display sequences between 8 and 15 September before displaying at the same locations, being airborne for 43 minutes to cover Acklington and 41 minutes for Leuchars, with 56 minutes between landing and take-off again. This was quite a demand on unrefuelled time for any Lightning—even the Mk 6 with its extra fuel capacity. As Harry Drew recalls, rather modestly:

> We worked up a four-ship consisting of OC 11 Sqn as leader, myself as 2, Lofty Lance as 3 and Dave Trick as 4. Sadly, I am the only one still alive! There were probably about five or six practices before performing at various air shows and finishing up with the Open Day at Leuchars on 16 Sep 1967. Many of us were new to the Lightning [although experienced on other types] so Rich [Rhodes] was one of the more experienced.

This all took place without a hitch in less than perfect weather conditions—but the show must go on! It was this kind of extra commitment beyond the primary purpose of continually sharpening operational skill and reliability that made the RAF of the day the household name worldwide that it still is. It is certainly quite remarkable how the level of expectation of that era contrasts with the present day. If the same demand was now made of a newly forming Typhoon squadron, just three or four months into working up to operational status, and with such a limited time to rehearse, someone's head would roll.

Meanwhile, 23 Squadron also began replacing its own Mk 3 Lightnings with the Mk 6 towards the end of the year. This was a tricky time for the squadron as it had lost many of the experienced pilots it started the year with. One of the flight commanders, Sqn Ldr Ron Blackburn, had been posted to Coltishall with no replacement, and Flt Lt Al Turley was still on the sick list and was not expected to return before his due retirement date the following March, which left the Squadron Commander, Wg Cdr Williamson, one flight commander and a US Marine Corps exchange officer, Capt. F. L. Pieri, as the only pilots who had completed a full first operational tour.

When the re-equipment was largely complete, the 'Red Eagles' deployed five pilots and four of the new Lightnings to Sola air base in Norway on 25 October. The detachment was commanded by Sqn Ldr Norman McEwen and its twenty-one personnel included two officers, apart from

The Norwegians were among early overseas visitors to the airshow, a couple of their F-5s are seen here alongside Lightning of the home team and a USAF RF-4C Phantom II, 16 September 1967. (*Colin Lourie*)

Dutch F-104 display team from the Dutch Starfighter training unit "The Dutch Masters" a name also adopted by the team, 16 September 1967, they made a return visit the following year. (*Colin Lourie*)

the five pilots, and mostly aircraft and avionics technicians, as one would expect, together with two safety equipment fitters and one clerk. While there, the usual pattern of intercepts were carried out—mainly supersonic against targets at altitudes up to 53,000 feet and speeds up to Mach 1.4— along with some lower-speed intercepts, 300-400 kts, at 500 feet. The high and fast targets were played by Lightnings, while the low-flying ones were a pair of Norwegian F-5 Freedom Fighters, the intercepts being controlled by the Norwegian radar base at Randaberg while ATC was controlled by Stavanger and Sola.

On the second day of the deployment, Lightning XR725 was taxiing along one of the runways in a howling gale and heavy rain when its port main wheel sank three feet into the concrete. It transpired that this runway had been sabotaged during the war and since then only the centre section had been in use. However, none of this had been mentioned during the initial airfield briefing, and ATC had allowed the pilot to taxi down the runway without further comment! Lifting gear was flown out from Leuchars, and under the supervision of the OC Engineering Wing the aircraft was lifted out and was able to return to base under its own propulsion, albeit at low speed. On its return it was declared Category 3 (meaning repairable damage). For its part, the Royal Norwegian Air Force provided an airlift bag, which prevented the aircraft sustaining considerably more damage. The runway in question ran from 110 to 290 degrees, with the 110 threshold less than 100 yards from the sea. The bit in the middle that was maintained was rough and uneven, prompting Sqn Ldr McEwen to allow its use by the Lightnings for taxiing only.

In early March 1968, a story surfaced in the local papers claiming that the construction of a civilian air terminal at Leuchars had been approved. Fife County Council had proposed to contribute the princely sum of £1,000 towards the project, the total sum required being £20,000, which seems rather a paltry amount even for 1968. But despite the eager optimism of the reports, the project had yet to take off and of course never did get off the ground, to use a shameless pun or two. That said, half an acre of land to the west was earmarked for the parking of fifteen cars and, while it remained merely a speculative venture, the press were reporting that work had already begun on the site. What was also needed was a further £2,000 to £3,000 to build new access roads, as the existing roads around the area were considered substandard.

Various events, both public and VIP, were arranged that year to mark the Golden Jubilee of the RAF. The focus was to be HM The Queen's review of the RAF at Abingdon, followed the next day by a public open day. For this, Leuchars was tasked with providing a single Lightning with over-wing tanks and missiles for the static display, the official stipulation, as issued to all units commanded to participate, being that the aircraft should be in immaculate condition. In addition, 11 and 23 Squadrons were each to provide four Lightnings for a flypast involving forty aircraft in total. Four more Lightnings were to come from 5 Squadron at Binbrook, twelve from Coltishall and four from 111 Squadron at Wattisham. The latter station was also to be the deployment airfield for Leuchars aircraft. Twelve Hunters from 229 OCU at Chivenor would make up the rest of the formation.

A particular honour was bestowed upon the four-ship of 23 Squadron, led by Wg Cdr Williamson together with Flt Lt J. H. Fawcett and Fg Offs H. W. Oliver and A. J. H. Alcock. Subject to the weather and all else being well, they were to form the fourth formation in the slot behind the Hunters, which would trail the rest of the Lightnings overhead RAF Halton en route. The overall formation leader was to make the decision to go/no go, depending on cloud base, for a reheat climb demonstration by the four from 23 Squadron. If the order was given, they were to drop back 3 nm and space out into a finger-four formation in preparation for their great moment before Her Majesty. On arrival overhead, behind everyone else, they would initiate a rotation climb in full reheat to 36,000 feet and then recover to Wattisham from altitude, with the whole lot repeated on the public day, together with a solo demonstration by a Coltishall Lightning in addition. What fun!

The formation layout was as follows:

1. First Vic of twelve Lightnings from 226 OCU;
2. Second Vic led by four Lightnings of 111 Squadron, with four from 5 Squadron on the right-hand side and four from 11 Squadron on the left;
3. Third Vic of twelve Hunters from 229 OCU;
4. Four Lightnings of 23 Squadron bringing up the rear, with a reheat climb if weather permitted.

Perhaps the most significant event of the year, certainly as far as 23 Squadron was concerned, was when Sqn Ldr Ed Durham and Flg Off. Geoff Brindle flew two Lightnings with over-wing tanks all the way from Leuchars to Toronto to take part in the city's air show in August. One of the aircraft was XR725, which was back in circulation after the incident at Sola. This was the first time that such a crossing had been made, and to achieve it required a reserve of two more Lightnings and six Victor tankers.

Ed Durham, now a flight commander on 23 Squadron, was on his third tour of duty at Leuchars. His first time was back in 1956/57, when he was a young flying officer with Hunters on 222 Squadron, and he had returned in 1964 with 74 Squadron and the Lightnings. Two other pilots, Flt Lt Tony Craig and Flg Off. Cliff Robinson, made the trip to Toronto in a VC10 of Air Support Command. Flt Lt Craig was to fly a solo display sequence, with Flg Off. Robinson as the reserve. The formation flew out on 27 August, taking off from Leuchars at 1040Z, the two Lightnings landing as a pair at Toronto at 1802Z. Having been greeted by a large throng of people, including the press and the air show organisers, the two pilots went off to their hotel for a well-earned rest after being strapped into their Martin-Baker seats for 7½ hours. As the original departure date of 26 August had been missed, there was no time to complete a reconnaissance of the local area, which put a bit of a squeeze on the itinerary for the next few days. Ed Durham wrote in his report:

> Because the aircraft were a day late in arriving it was not possible to carry out the sector recce. Consequently the first time the Lightning pilots saw the show area was on the practice day. This created no difficulties but it meant that there was very little time in which to co-ordinate the RAF display. It would have been advantageous to have worked out and practised a full RAF display before the detachment left UK.

On the return flight to the UK, the detachment was intercepted 120 nm out from Leuchars by four more of the 'Red Eagles' as a welcome-home escort. Ed Durham noted that none of the pilots experienced any fatigue on either the outward or inbound flights, which was put down to the cockpit workload remaining at a constant level. The pilots sustained themselves during the trip with bite-size chicken sandwiches, glucose sweets, chewing gum and orange squash, but because the food containers were awkward and bulky to handle, nobody ate much. To sum up, the whole thing had been a great success and very well received, Ed Durham's conclusion being that if the Lightnings were to take part in future Canadian international air shows, as their 1968 success suggested they should, the number of aircraft deployed should be increased.

It was proving to be quite a hectic year for all, and regardless of the further increase in live QRA activity, the demands of ceremony remained heavy. Following on from the royal review of the RAF on the occasion of the service's 50th anniversary, and just prior to the trip to Canada, RAF Leuchars was afforded the Freedom of St Andrews. To accompany the parade through the town there was to be a flypast consisting of sixteen Lightnings together with four Chipmunks from two University Air Squadrons. Whirlwind helicopters from 202 Squadron were also to take part. All units were involved in contributing, including the TFF, and were drawn up as follows:

1. Two Whirlwinds of 'C' Flight, 202 Squadron;
2. Four Chipmunks of St Andrews and Dundee University Air Squadrons;
3. Eight Lightnings (and one spare) of 23 Squadron;
4. Six Lightnings (and one spare) of 11 Squadron;
5. Two Lightnings of Target Facilities Flight (TFF).

The entire formation was commanded by David Blucke, whose No. 11 Squadron was stretched to the limits to make it all happen. It provided eight Mk 6 Lightnings for the actual flypast, as well as the squadron T5 (T-bird) to act as an airborne spare, while having two more Lightnings on QRA with just one more aircraft available, which was undergoing reheat runs. Flt Lt G. I. Reynolds, the compiling officer for the August entries in the ORB, remarked, 'A commendable achievement by the squadron engineering team.' The event was treated as an auspicious occasion by the RAF, who invited all the former Leuchars station commanders they could muster. Invitations went out to twenty of them, including three retired air marshals.

The Freedom of St Andrews parade was the penultimate major public event for the station that year, the final one being at home, literally, for the air show on 14 September. It celebrated both the 28th anniversary of the Battle of Britain and the 50th anniversary of the RAF, and an additional effort was made across the country, given the added sense of occasion.

On 29 November, XM174, a Mk 1A Lightning of the TFF, was being flown by Flt Lt Ted Rawcliffe when control was lost and the aircraft finished up plummeting towards Balmullo Quarry at the top of Lucklaw Hill, a prominent landmark in the area. While not breaking any records as the oldest pilot to fly the Lightning, Flt Lt Rawcliffe was certainly on the older side of average at the age of 43. His aircraft had suffered an engine fire and descended towards the quarry at an angle of about 60 degrees and a bank to port of about 30 degrees.

The problem had started, as was so often the case with crashes involving aircraft with pneumatic power controls, with the hydraulics behaving not quite as they should. Flt Lt Rawcliffe, who had lost contact with Leuchars ATC, tried to restart the No. 1 engine and jettison the ventral tank, and in an effort to prepare to make some kind of landing he lowered the flaps and undercarriage despite the problems he was experiencing and attempted to turn onto final approach. However, the controls 'seemed soft' when rolling the aircraft into the turn and he ejected as it pitched sharply, leaving the aircraft to spear almost literally into the side of the quarry. The men who were working there at the time, four at the foot of the quarry, managed to get clear just in time, one suffering burns to both hands. This was Flt Lt Rawcliffe's second successful ejection. The previous incident

Mr T. T. Fordyce, Provost of St Andrews, inspects the Queen's Colour Squadron during the Freedom of St Andrews ceremonial parade, 22 August 1968. (*The National Archives*)

Diamond 16 of Lightnings flypast as part of the freedom of St Andrews ceremony on 22 August 1968, Station Commander, Gp Capt John Nicholls and Mr T. T. Fosdyke, Provost of St Andrews reviewed the parade. (*The National Archives*)

Taxiing out from the cross-runway, 23 Squadron Battle of Britain four-ship taxi out, 14 September 1968. (*Colin Lourie*)

Close up of 23 Squadron pilot taxiing, 14 September 1968. (*Colin Lourie*)

happened back in April 1966, while he was serving with 60 Squadron at RAF Tengah, flying a Javelin on that occasion. He and his navigator, Flt Lt A. L. Vasloo, ejected following an engine fire.

Accidents involving high-performance aircraft were frighteningly regular during this era, with fatalities occurring far too often. The most notorious reputation was carried by the Lockheed F-104 Starfighter, which peppered the air arms of Europe during the 1960s and '70s. However, the accident rate of this aircraft can be mitigated by the simple fact that it was so widespread in military service within most NATO air forces, not to mention the Bundesmarineflieger (Federal German Naval Air Arm). Had the Lightning been in similarly common use, there is no doubt that it would have been the leading candidate for such a dark reputation.

On 5 March 1970, a pilot of 11 Squadron, the Qualified Weapons Instructor (QWI) in fact, was lost only nine miles north-east of Leuchars. As with so many Lightning losses, he was faced with the much dreaded engine fire. First Reheat 1 and then a few seconds later Reheat 2 illuminated in the cockpit following a series of gentle manoeuvres with another Lightning. The pilot of the second aircraft confirmed that Lightning XS918

On 7 November 1968, this USAF F-4C Phantom II had made several go around attempts to land with wheels up. Eventually Captains Barr and Nelson held their breaths and placed the Fighter down on runway 09 sustaining only light fire damage. The aircraft was flown out again on 3 December 1968. (*The National Archives*)

was indeed on fire and the pilot ejected successfully, although he was not picked up immediately.

Everything conspired against him from the start. The search took place at night, for six hours. His aircraft had gone down at 1900Z on 4 March, but his body was not discovered until 0100Z the next day. On top of this, the official accident investigation found that he was not wearing the authorised pattern immersion suit. The report further described 'many errors in the state of the survival kit' and 'the poor standard of the pilot's own kit', also finding that the survival kit had not been attached correctly. It was far from clear how this could have come about, but that it took six hours to find the pilot after ejecting and that he was separated from his dinghy would be sufficient under any circumstances for the incident to end in the tragic way it did. The pilot was highly experienced—he was, after all, the squadron's QWI—and had previously flown Hunters with 208 Squadron in the Middle East where he was a member of the squadron's aerobatic team chosen to represent Air Forces Middle East in 1962. Steve Gyles was a pilot on 11 Squadron at that time:

There was a lot said at the time; equally a lot that was not made hugely public. He did indeed modify his immersion suit. He had the rubber boots cut off, to be replaced by wrist seals. We all thought it was a good modification as it allowed the feet to breathe. After a day of flying there could be up to an inch of sweated water in those boots, giving us athlete's foot problems and the like—kept us trim though! The unfortunate thing he did, however, was to tuck his socks inside the wrist seals, thereby acting as a wick to wet him thoroughly on the inside. Nearly all of us wore stockinette inside our neck seals to reduce neck chafing. However, this would be removed with a simple pull when descending in the parachute. Just prior to his fateful sortie he spent an hour playing squash. I saw him come into the changing room very hot and sweaty. He then only put a cotton roll-neck flying shirt under his immersion suit. At that time I had a vest, the flying shirt, pullover, bunny suit and the immersion suit. He was not well insulated!! We had a new type of Mae West about to be issued, but on his sortie he had the old version that required the Sarbe beacon to be removed from its stowage before pulling the operating toggle. He went to the wrong side of his Mae West and spent his last conscious moments removing the Sarbe battery instead of the beacon! The McMurdo light was also stored with its operating plugs in place, requiring removal to operate. He only managed to remove 2 plugs instead of the 4, giving only a few minutes' light. He also was found detached from his dinghy lanyard. Within a few days of the accident we were issued with the new Mae West. Both battery and beacon were placed on the same side and it did not require beacon removal to operate, just pull a toggle. The plugs in the light were also removed. I remember the dinghy drill briefing we all had on the Friday afternoon before his accident on I think it was the Monday night. He sat on a window ledge in the crew room paying scant attention, staring instead out of the window across the airfield.

There are always practical reasons for altering flying kit, and aircrew have done so through the years. Sometimes, however, it may simply be for aesthetics, but again with a practical aim. Steve Pickering, a survival equipment fitter stationed at Leuchars some years later, recalls:

A certain pilot on 43 was determined to get his 3C [Bone Dome helmet] painted white. However, SNCO I/C [Senior NCO in charge of] flying clothing was having none of it. A week after being rebuffed by the aforementioned Sgt; a BLACK, with silver stars, Mk 1a helmet was spotted being worn by the pilot. Upon landing, it went straight into his helmet box in flying clothing till next sortie. This went on for a couple of days till the SNCO spotted it, and we were told to get his 3C sprayed white.

April 1970 saw 11 Squadron take its turn on QRA again, using up virtually all its fuel allocation for the month on scrambles. As Steve Gyles further recalls in the following chronicle:

A Busy Month
Looking through my logbook, March and April 1970 evoke strong memories for a number of reasons. I was one of the junior first tourists on 11 Squadron. My mind was on many things, partly because in the May I was due to get married. But first the fighter game was to play a major role in my immediate future.

I guess it started on 4 March. I had just finished work for the day and was having a bath in the Mess before the bar opened when the crash alarm sounded. The voice over the tannoy stated that there had been an off-base crash. I dressed quickly and went back to the squadron to learn that our QWI had ejected following a double reheat fire off May Island in the Firth of Forth. As the evening wore on we all became increasingly worried for the pilot and before the bar had closed we learned that he was dead. The reason for his demise is another story for another place [as recounted above].

The next morning I led the first two-ship airborne in the traditional RAF manner to demonstrate that life must go on. The same day half of the squadron were grounded at the Missile Practice Camp at Valley so that integrity checks on the aircraft could be carried out. They were then recalled to Leuchars. At the end of the month, with the squadron now on QRA, I was sent over to Valley with one other pilot with the instruction to fire off all five of the squadron's allocated Red Top missiles. We had achieved one firing each when we were recalled immediately to base as the aircraft and ourselves were required for intense QRA activity from Soviet aircraft. The Soviets, it transpired, had decided to mark Lenin's centenary with a massive display of air power.

During April, the squadron then proceeded to fly its entire month's flying hours on QRA, with very little left for routine training. I completed about seven 24-hour stints in the QRA shed during the month, culminating in an epic mission on 23 April. When dawn was breaking on that morning I had, in the previous days, been scrambled on three occasions and bagged a couple of Bear Ds and a Danish Air Force Neptune.

It was about 0400Z hours that morning when the squawk box crackled into life with the familiar 'Leuchars, this is Buchan, alert two Lightnings'. In the event, only one aircraft was scrambled with my Flight Commander, Squadron Leader 'Chalkie' White, at the controls. However, mayhem was breaking out on the station. Squadron personnel were being called in to ready more aircraft. The crew of the Victor tanker on the ORP was brought to readiness, and I was getting inundated with telephone updates from Buchan.

Squadron Leader White had just returned from his sortie, shadowing two Bear Ds in the pitch black when the squawk box crackled into life again: 'Leuchars, alert two Lightnings and as many more as you can get. We have eighty unidentified tracks coming round the North Cape.' Within five minutes and in total RT silence I was thundering down the runway in the early dawn light. With the radar, nav aids and IFF also switched off, I headed off north to a position far, far north-east of the Scottish mainland. Twenty minutes later I reckoned I was there. On went the radio, radar and IFF. What I saw staggered me. My B-scope display was swamped with contacts from 20 miles out to 60 miles. An RT check with Saxa Vord determined that there were some sixty contacts in my area. At that point I made visual contact with the 'enemy'. There were finger-fours of Badgers and Bears everywhere. I did not need the radar any more. It was just a case of latching on to the nearest formation of Badgers and start photographing, moving up from the rear of the formation, one photograph either side and underneath of each aircraft. I had done three of that first formation when a shadow went over my cockpit. I glanced up to see another four-ship of Badgers cross me about 500 feet above.

At about this time I was advised that our tanker was in the vicinity. A check of my fuel gauge showed that a bit of juice would not go amiss. I asked for 'pigeons' [heading and distance] to the tanker, to which the controller replied that he had not a clue as he had some sixty contacts in close proximity and all heading south-west. I called the tanker to turn around 180 degrees, to which he asked if I could hold on for five minutes as he was intercepting three Bears! He eventually turned around; I got my fuel and returned to the mêlée, to be joined by another Lightning. For an hour and a half we again mixed with the huge formations with just the occasional interlude for fuel. When we all three had to break off and start back to base on minimum fuel I had intercepted and photographed three Bear Ds, six Badger Ds and one Badger C. The other Lightning, flown by Graham Clark, had intercepted seven aircraft, and the Victor had accumulated three. But that was not the end of the story.

Quite conveniently, the tanker reported that he was sitting with a Bear D that was heading straight for Leuchars and did we have any film left to record the event for posterity? So, over we went to join him and expended the last of our films in various three-ship formations. At about 200 miles to go to base, the Bear rocked his wings and turned gently away. Shortly after, two ships of our newly formed Phantom F-4 squadron [43 Squadron] could be seen going out to join in the fun.

Quite a sortie. My log book shows it lasted 3 hours 30 minutes.

We landed, debriefed, handed in our cameras and went for breakfast and a beer. Later that day I reported back in for night flying and asked if I could see my pictures from the morning sortie. 'No chance,' I was told. 'They have been sent down to MoD Intelligence.' Oh dear. I told the Squadron Commander that there were some 'additional' photos on the reel that could cause a problem but he did not seem concerned.

Well, come Sunday, I was sitting in the Mess reading the papers when, lo and behold, there was my picture of the Bear D with the Victor in echelon starboard and the other Lightning echelon port. And the story does not even end there. Apparently AOC 1 Group went through the roof. He banned his tankers from ever going within 10 miles of a Soviet bomber. When I retired from the RAF at Marham in 1990, the tanker boys there told me that ruling was still in force.

Yes, guys. You can blame me for all that.

The honour of providing one of five solo Lightning display pilots for the 1970 air show season was accorded to 11 Squadron, so of course a fair amount of time during the summer was spent practising whenever there was an aircraft available. Steve Gyles had the first of two close calls during his operational flying career when he climbed into the cockpit of a

11 Squadron Lightning and Marham Victor shadow Soviet Bear all photographed by *Steve Gyles* , this became more of an incident when the AOC in C No. 1 Group got to hear that one of his Tankers offered its services to assist with intercepting and shadowing an intruder. (*Barry G. Mayner*)

Two 11 Squadron Lightnings approach to land over the rise in the land at the 09 threshold. The vantage point from where this photograph was taken. This rise of land has been utilised by aircraft enthusiasts as a much favoured perch for decades. (*Jeremy Hughes*)

Lightning that had just been chucked about the sky by the picked soloist, Derek Nicholls:

> Derek Nicholls took over the aeros during my time there. On one occasion he had just done a practice over the airfield. The aircraft was refuelled and I jumped in to do a routine pairs sortie. I had lined up on the runway, run up to 92 per cent power and was waiting for my No. 2 to give me the thumbs-up for a pairs take-off. For some reason I gave the control column an extra full and free movement check [not normal practice at this point] and the tailplane ran away fully nose-down and went through its end stop, damaging the airframe!! The engineers found a hydraulic blanking plug had stuck in a valve in the 'Hobson' tailplane actuator. I have often thought how lucky I was, and of the consequences if I had not done that final check. More importantly, if it had happened while Derek was doing his sequence!

All the Leuchars-based squadrons were involved in official flypasts during the year, including a four-piece for the flypast at the opening of the Commonwealth Games in Edinburgh on 16 July. Four Lightnings were

The annual formal inspection, 8 May 1970, AOC 11 Gp, Air Vice-Marshal Ivor Broom CBE, DSO, DFC chats with ground crew on duty at the QRA shed. (*The National Archives*)

provided by 23 Squadron, led by Sqn Ldr M. A. A. Hobbs with Fg Offs J. S. Hinchliff and P. Cooper, and Flt Lt D. J. Willison. Furthermore, Flt Lt Russ Pengelly was called upon to fly his own solo aerobatic sequence at that year's Farnborough air show, interspersed through the week with another solo Lightning flown by a pilot from 226 OCU. This was unusual as Farnborough, like Paris, concentrates on showing off new aircraft yet to become operational or only recently so. In 1970, the Lightning, a startling performer throughout its service, was now past the sales market, especially as the RAF was now bringing in its interim replacement and looking to the long term.

No. 23 Squadron also deployed five aircraft to Sweden, involving air-to-air refuelling (AAR), where they were accompanied by Air Vice-Marshal I. G. Broom, AOC 11 Group. This was for the British-Swedish trade week from 21 to 28 September. The aircraft were flown out by Sqn Ldr Hobbs, Capt. Geiger, Flt Lt Brian Carroll, Wg Cdr R. D. Stone and Flt Lt Mike Streten. Upon returning, all had to divert to Lossiemouth due to bad weather. This month also saw 23 Squadron's Lightnings receive a new paint scheme, with an enlarged red eagle on the fin replacing the smaller one contained in a white disc.

Exercise 'Heartsease', an annual exchange exercise, brought a detachment of Italian F-104s in 1970, and the following year, in June, 23 Squadron sent four Lightnings to Dijon while Mirages headed from there to Leuchars. The GCI at Dijon was described as excellent and the low-level flying areas as extensive, but alas could not be fully exploited as only two serviceable

23 Squadron Lightning Demo team formation break over the river Eden this time, during their display at the 1971 Leuchars airshow. (*Charles E. MacKay*)

aircraft were available throughout the period of the detachment. The squadron was also billed on the programme for the Dijon Air Day, with one aircraft for the static display and one for the flying display. The latter was restricted to a non-aerobatic performance, there being no solo aeros pilot from either of the Leuchars Lightning squadrons that year. All went well, even though the servicing, albeit first line only, was carried out by the pilots themselves assisted by local ground crew. It was also found that the LOX hose and nitrogen and hydraulic adapters did not fit, and although this caused some frustrations, in itself it did not prevent flying. Furthermore, it gave the pilots a sense of satisfaction and confidence that they were able to carry out some servicing on the Lightnings. Dijon was described as 'eminently suitable for Lightning operations'. Having flown the Mirage IIIB, the British pilots were impressed with its manoeuvrability, while the French jockeys were equally impressed with the Lightning's acceleration and rate of climb.

However, the days of the Lightning were gradually coming to an end. (This period is dealt with more comprehensively in the next chapter.) The shortcomings of the beast in respect of its ability to reach great distances, loiter and engage targets from a distance were thrown into sharp relief when compared with the far more able F-4 Phantom, which by now was operating from Leuchars with 43 Squadron.

September 1972 was one of the most hectic months since 1966 for Leuchars QRA scrambles, with no fewer than twenty-five being flown by pilots of 23 Squadron between 9 and 17 September inclusive. No. 11 Squadron had left in March and 43 Squadron was on exercise. On 15 September, the commanding officer, Wg Cdr Bruce Hopkins, intercepted a Bear D, which was the subject of one of several iconic photographs, this time taken by a Phantom of 43 Squadron. The next day he was focused on leading the Battle of Britain four-ship formation at the air show, during which another of the QRA Lightnings was launched, flown by Flt Lt John Spoor. The interruption of the air show by the QRA launch was now a regular feature and would remain so until the end of the 1980s and, of course, the end of the Cold War.

There are many would-be fighter pilots who often wonder just what day-to-day life entails for those who make the grade. Former Lightning pilot Jerry Parr, who served on 23 Squadron at Leuchars from 1972 to 1975, recalls the past with frankness, as well as the healthy, light-hearted rivalry that existed between 23 and 43 Squadrons back in the day:

Like most, I scraped through the OCU and went on to become (in my opinion) a pretty good Lightning pilot; with over 1,000 hours on the ac, I never burst a tyre nor broke my probe.

10 May 1971, French Air Force Mirage IIIs visiting from Dijon airbase while four 23 Squadron Lightnings went in the other direction during exercise Heartsease. (*The National Archives*)

Another iconic Leuchars image and one of the last interceptions of a Bear by a 23 Sqn Lightning before re-equipping with the Phantom. (*Barry G. Mayner*)

Opposite above: Form 540 showing level of QRA activity during the month of September 1972, it shows 23 Sqn holding the duty for much of the month but 43 aircraft had to be diverted from exercise Strong Express. (*The National Archives*)

Opposite below: Continuation of the Form 540 for September 1972, showing the level of QRA activity. (*The National Archives*)

POD1402/446207/NO.300/W&W/H44/5

RAF FORM 540
(Revised May, 1965)

ANNEX 'A' TO
STATION FORM540
TED SEP 72

OPERATIONS RECORD BOOK OF (Unit or Formation) RAF LEUCHARS

Instructions for use of this Form are contained in QR 2137 and 2138 ; and AP 3040.

FOR PERIOD SEPTEMBER 1972

PAGE NO. 1
OF 2 PAGES

PLACE	DATE	LOCAL TIME	SUMMARY OF EVENTS	COMPILING OFFICER	REF TO ANNEXES AND FILES
Serial	Date	Sqdn	Tanker Support	Intercept	
1	4th	43	No	NIL	
2	5th	43	Yes	2 Badgers	
3	6th	43	Yes	2 Bear 'D's	
4	6th	43	Yes	2 Bear 'D's	
5	6th	43	No	NIL	
6	8th	43	No	NIL	
7	9th	23	No	2 Bear 'D's	
8	9th	23	No	NIL, STB, U/S.	
9	9th	23	Yes	NIL	
10	9th	23	Yes	2 Bear 'D's	
11	10th	23	Yes	2 Bear 'D's	
12	10th	23	Yes	1 Badger 'D' 1 Badger 'E'	
13	10th	23	Yes	2 Bear 'D's	
14	10th	23	Yes	1 Badger 'D' 1 Badger 'E'	
15	10th	23	Yes	2 Bear 'D's	
16	11th	23	Yes	2 Bear 'D's	
17	11th	23	Yes	1 Bear 'D'	
18	11th	23	Yes	1 Bear 'D'	
19	12th	23	Yes	2 Bear 'D's	
20	12th	23	Yes	2 Badgers	
21	12th	23	Yes	2 Bear 'D's	
22	12th	23	Yes	NIL	
23	13th	23	Yes	NIL	
24	14th	23	Yes	2 Bears	
25	14th	23	Yes	NIL	
26	14th	23	Yes	2 Bisons	
27	15th	23	Yes	2 Bear 'D's	
28	15th	23	Yes	2 Bear 'D's	
29	16th	23	Yes	NIL	
30	17th	23	Yes	NIL	
31	18th	23	NO S.T.B. U/S	NIL	
32	18th	23	Yes	NIL	
33	18th	43	DIVERTED FROM STRONG EXPRESS	2 Bisons	
34	19th	23	Yes	1 Bear	
35	19th	23	Yes	1 Bear 'D'	
36	20th	23	Yes	2 Bear 'D's	
37	21st	23	Yes	2 Bear	
38	21st	23	Yes	3 Bear 'D's	
39	21st	23	Yes	NIL	
40	21st	23	NO	NIL	
41	22nd	23	Yes	NIL	
42	22nd	23	Yes	2 Bear 'D's	
43	22nd	23	Yes	1 Bear	

POD1402/446207/NO.300/W&W/H44/5

SECURITY CLASSIFICATION SECRET

RAF FORM 540
(Revised May, 1965)

OPERATIONS RECORD BOOK OF (Unit or Formation) RAF LEUCHARS

Instructions for use of this Form are contained in QR 2137 and 2138 ; and AP 3040.

FOR PERIOD SEPTEMBER 1972

PAGE NO. 2
OF 2 PAGES

PLACE	DATE	LOCAL TIME	SUMMARY OF EVENTS	COMPILING OFFICER	REF TO ANNEXES AND FILES
Serial	Date	Sqdn	Tanker Support	Intercept	
44	22nd	23	No	NIL	
45	23rd	23	Yes	NIL	
46	24th	23	Yes	2 Bisons	
47	25th	23	Yes	4 Bears	
48	25th	23	Yes	2 Bear 'D's	
49	25th	23	No	2 Bear 'D's	
50	25th	43	DIVERTED FROM STRONG EXPRESS	2 Bear 'D's	
51	26th	23	Yes	NIL	
52	27th	23	Yes	NIL	
53	28th	23	Yes	2 Bisons	
54	28th	23	Yes	NIL	
TOTAL		SCRAMBLES 52, PLUS 2 AIRCRAFT 43 SQN DIVERTED FROM EXERCISE STRONG EXPRESS SORTIES.			
TOTAL		INTERCEPTS 66 - 4 BY STRONG EXPRESS AIRCRAFT.			
		HOURS FLOWN ON QRA TOTAL 141.57 HRS			
			15.43 by 43 Sqn		
			126.14 by 23 Sqn		
		OUT OF 52 SCRAMBLES FROM LEUCHARS ONLY 9 DID NOT HAVE TANKER SUPPORT			
		FROM EITHER LEUCHARS OR MARHAM			

Something you might consider are the wives. Vicky and I married in Jan 1973 six months after I joined the squadron; she put up with a lot, and I mean a lot. We're still together and sometimes we continue to disagree over my then edict to the boss: 'If I fail to return from a night sortie and am feeding the fish do not go and wake my wife to tell her; when in the morning she has slept then go and see her.'

Selfish or practical?

The number two, nay arguably the number one, Officers' Mess was the Sandford Hill Hotel run by Bruce and Mary Anne Robertson. We had some very drunken weekends there and worked off hangovers on Jock Howie's farm next door stacking bales, delivering lambs and generally helping out. It was a great environment, which would no doubt be disapproved of now. On a typical summer's day when on nights I'd arise about 10, shit, shower and shave, then walk my dog over the fields to the Sandford, arriving about midday to meet my wife for lunch. A couple of pints and a sandwich, then home for a kip and into work about 2100 hours. Always eight hours 'tween bottle and throttle.

My arrival check with the Squadron Commander [Bruce Hopkins] on 23 lasted 15 mins following a Hydraulic 2 failure. The T5 disappeared into the shed for a long time and I did my entire convex [conversion exercise] and op work-up including AAR in the single seater. Fantastic!

Because of a mysterious problem with the undercarriage on the T5—it sometimes collapsed when the drag chute was streamed from the left-hand seat—it was decreed that wherever possible the T5 was to be flown dual and the chute streamed from the right-hand seat.

Enter George Smith and the USAF exchange officer Gary Catren to fly in the tub—George in the left seat, Gary in the right. George flew the take-off in reheat but the bottom burner didn't light and the nozzle stayed open, thus less than 50 per cent thrust from the No. 1. With the No. 2 [top engine] delivering max poke, there was a substantial nose-down moment and the nose wheel would not come off as required; George struggled to raise it to no avail, cried 'Shit' and decided to abort. Gary, thinking George had said 'Chute', pulled the handle. The chute duly deployed and promptly burnt off in the No. 2 reheat plume. We now have a Lightning T5 heading for the world land speed record! Three quarters of the runway behind them still doing about 200 kts, the brakes burnt out as they did and the aircraft entered the barrier at about 180. The barrier tried to help but it was too much and the whole assembly was pulled from the ground, allowing the tub to continue on its merry way. Off the end, over a mound, it came to rest almost on the Guardbridge road, 50 yards from the Officers' Mess front door.

George and Gary dismounted, dusted themselves down and went for a coffee via the line hut where George declared the ac unserviceable: 'Number one RHT would not light'!! I think it was Cat 3 or 4.

In February 1974, 23 Squadron was preparing to set off for Malta. Indeed, the whole of the month was devoted to the deployment of the 'Red Eagles' to RAF Luqa. Exercise 'Bestface' tasked them with deploying ten Lightnings between 11 February and 5 March. This task was achieved, with nine aircraft returning on 6/7 March, but one being left behind temporarily, having suffered Category-3 damage after a tail scrape during landing from a sortie on 27 February. Naturally, IAF (Interceptor Alert Force, the new title for QRA) fell to 43 Squadron during the period. Wg Cdr Hopkins noted officially that the low price of alcohol in Malta called for some positive action, and that:

> … many a happy hour was lost consuming Cisk and Marsovin, the Maltese beer and grape juice. An occasion of some note was the squadron all-ranks party held at the Kalafrana Beach Club. It proved yet again that airmen have a higher booze tolerance than any other private [serviceman] in the Mediterranean!

23 Squadron on MPC in August 1973, *left to right* the pilots are: Grant Taylor, John Spoor, Euan Black, Peter Langham (Detachment Commander), Cliff Wilmer, Capt Lois Eon (FAF) and Jerry Parr, to the left and right of them are the Junior and Senior Engineering Officers who remain unidentified. (*John Spoor*)

Before the deployment, the 'Red Eagles' were holding a formal dining-in night on 8 February, which according to Jerry Parr was perhaps not unlike many others; that is to say, the event was carried off not entirely without incident. Many reading this will be familiar with the stories of high jinks emanating from many a mess function down through history, and the common gripe of the non-commissioned junior ranks has always been 'it's high spirits where the officers are concerned but vandalism where we're concerned'. One can feel some sympathy with this, but, to use a simple but extreme analogy, to conflate smashing a glass in someone's face in an argument with the idea of someone suffering injury while drunkenly obliged to somersault a line of furniture is to miss the point somewhat.

After all the fun and games of the February detachment and the preceding dining-in night had receded from the front page, the 'Red Eagles' were confronted with something of a headache. March brought serious engineering problems on the Mk 6 Lightnings, requiring immediate attention by the engineers. The early part of the year was dogged with fuel restrictions, which naturally limited routine flying, and on top of this a spate of preliminary warnings (PWs) were produced following inspections in light of a Lightning crash involving an aircraft from Wattisham together with further structural studies carried out at Farnborough. The PWs went as far back as mid-February and all concerned various investigatory checks, including security of screws on fuel pump connections, leaks from fueldraulic pumps, and fatigue cracks on the doubler at the mainplane centre joint (this refers to the wing centre joint). The most pressing PWs—checks for fatigue cracks on the reheat burner fuel feed pipes—came later, and had to be completed and any faults rectified before the next use of reheat.

This all took effect as soon as 23 Squadron returned from Malta, each aircraft having both engines removed. The squadron's engineers worked continuously for three weeks to deep strip each aircraft and managed to produce enough for the squadron to resume IAF by 25 March. Then, in April, the more serious problem of the reheat burner fuel feeds arose, requiring each aircraft to be cleared before taking to the air again. Jerry Parr recalls:

> The engineers worked very hard on mods as part of the fire integrity programme. Having removed both engines from all the aircraft and done the work, it was late on a Friday that another mod landed and the jet pipes (RHT system) had to come out of every ac! They worked bloody hard that weekend.

The operational presence of the Lightning as the principal interceptor of the RAF at Leuchars and elsewhere was now nearing the end, this being the year that saw a major shift in the RAF's tactical and defence fighter force. The squadron was given a boost in May with the arrival of three Mk 3 Lightnings from 111 Squadron to begin the work-up for the forthcoming Tactical Fighter Meet. By June, matters were looking up and fighter *v* fighter combat, which had been suspended earlier, had now restarted in earnest, initially with those pilots expecting to take part in the Fighter Meet. As for everyone else, they were gradually introduced into the much needed air combat training syllabus with the aim of all operational pilots achieving fully air combat qualified status by the end of the year.

By now, the Lightnings had been given a clean bill of health, fuel restrictions had been lifted and all was back to normal. The month was characterised by ECM training sorties and a chance at last to engage with 43 Squadron in dissimilar air combat. The preparation for the Fighter Meet included 1 *v* 1, 1 *v* 2 and 2 *v* 2 sorties being flown. A total of fourteen such sorties were carried out, the upshot of which was fourteen claims by 23 Squadron and ten claims by 43 Squadron.

The Tactical Fighter Meet held at Leuchars between 3 and 15 August was the first such staged by the RAF. No. 23 Squadron flew over fifty sorties before holding IAF for the rest of the month—an unusually quiet time, with only one live scramble and one practice. The operational debut of the Jaguar that year meant that, save for 43 Squadron, the first Phantoms hitherto engaged on offensive air and reconnaissance duties were now going to be replacing many of the Lightnings.

Fun and games aside, the serious aspect of the service's history is never forgotten, and on Sunday 15 September, 23 Squadron was on parade at St Giles' Cathedral in Edinburgh, where the squadron standard was borne by Flt Lt Parr.

In April 1975, the squadron received the Dacre Trophy for its success over the period from April 1974 to March 1975. A large Soviet naval exercise during this period upped the ante on IAF, with 23 Squadron being required to place two Lightnings at ten minutes' readiness, in addition to the Phantoms of 43 Squadron, which primarily held the reaction duty from 16 to 21 April to cater for the likelihood of the need to meet the requirements of a supersonic intercept. In the end, no Lightnings were scrambled.

In May, and only months away from disbandment, the 'Red Eagles' were off to RAF Wattisham on a bolthole deployment (when squadrons moved to temporary homes while runway resurfacing and other airfield construction works were afoot) where they took over Southern IAF from 9 May. During their stay at Wattisham, which lasted until July, they took part in a large number of four-ship exercises involving low-level combat air patrols, while a handful were detached further afield to 92 Squadron at Gütersloh. A further larger-scale exercise with the Wattisham-based Lightnings of 56 Squadron was planned during June in Exercise 'Crackforce', which involved both squadrons operating against each other. At one point there were about thirteen Lightnings in the air engaged in simulated combat, and one of 23 Squadron's pilots, Flt Lt R. D. Lapraik, engaged four Mirage Vs of the Belgian Air Force directly overhead the airfield. The squadron returned to Leuchars on 24 July and took over Northern IAF again from the following day.

The final moment for Lightning operations at Leuchars came towards the end of 1975. No. 23 Squadron was due to disband in October, so at the open day in September a notable finale was arranged. Six of the squadron's silver jets took to the air to form an arrow formation in a flypast, with four Phantoms from 43 Squadron bringing up the rear in card formation. They rounded off their display in spectacular fashion, the Lightnings running in to break along the display line, each pulling up and rolling out across the station in turn. On 31 October, 23 Squadron disbanded in order to re-form on the Phantom at Coningsby, after which it headed to Wattisham. Meanwhile, 111 Squadron was destined in the opposite direction. Having already left Wattisham for Coningsby and made the transition from Lightnings to Phantoms, its next move was to take up residence at Leuchars in November. By 12 January 1976, the new 23 Squadron was still at Coningsby, working up to the point where it would take up its definitive post at Wattisham.

Within the usual service rivalry, it has always been commonplace for the tactical ground attack pilot to look down (metaphorically) on his fighter brethren, the understanding being that the former relies on greater flying skill, facing greater demands on ability by spending so much more time at lower level with all the dangers inherent in flying into intense enemy air defences. The new CO, Wg Cdr Bill Wratten, noted with some humour the progress of the new 23 Squadron, as several of the new aircrew came from the Phantom in its hitherto air-to-ground role:

> It has been interesting to watch the ex-strike/attack Phantom crews coming to grips with the air defence role. Now that we are progressing on to the more complex sortie profiles, there appears to be a greater sense of respect developing for the 'scopies' amongst the ex-'mudmovers'. This is good to see.

8

The Mighty Phantom

Courtesy of its Cold War position as the most prominent air defence station in the UK, Leuchars was now at last due to receive a fighter that promised a combination of performance, range, weapons and radar, answering many of the concerns that could not be ignored regarding its predecessors. The range of the Javelin was respectable, but was unable to match the Phantom by any other yardstick.

The Lightning still had the edge in strict terms of airframe/engine performance, but was woefully inadequate in every other measure. As such, a policy statement regarding RAF Leuchars had been issued by the Ministry of Defence on 18 February 1969, giving planned dates for the formation of Phantom FG1 (F-4K) units at Leuchars. The plan also detailed the redeployment of both the current operational Lightning units based there at the time. The schedule proposed that, by 30 September 1972, the first half of a third Phantom FG1-equipped squadron would form, being complete by the end of that year. With the first Phantom squadron due to form by 31 December 1969, the strategy was that the first of the existing Lightning squadrons would move to Binbrook in the second quarter of 1971, with the next squadron moving in early 1972, thus ending over three years earlier than the Lightnings at Leuchars. A purely RAF Training Flight of eight Phantoms was also planned by mid-1971, dedicated to training for Phantom maritime air defence operations. Despite this order being acted upon initially that year, a change of government and a more sympathetic lean to the Navy meant that a compromise was afoot, so the idea of three squadrons of Lightnings at Binbrook and three with Phantoms dedicated to interceptor duties at Leuchars never quite materialised.

The plan had to be altered following the success of naval air ambitions. Had the arrangement gone ahead, it is entirely likely that 43 Squadron would have been joined by 74 Squadron, and either 65 or 85 Squadrons, to form the

Battle of Britain 4-ships from both 23 and 43 Squadrons, taken in 1971, a typical feature of the Leuchars airshow in the early 1970s was a co-ordinated display by the resident Lightning and Phantom squadrons beginning with a scramble then formation flypast together before splitting for their separate formation demonstrations. (*Charles E. MacKay*)

RAF's single F-4K Air Defence Wing. The three suggested number plates were the most logical options: 74 Squadron (the 'Tigers') was due to disband, and did so in August 1971; 65 was an available number plate following its ending as a Bloodhound missile squadron; and 85 would be available following its disbandment as the TFF squadron at Binbrook, also due in 1971.

There was enough concern at that time about the ability of Leuchars-based fighters—whether Lightnings or Phantoms—to cope with the volume of Soviet long-range incursions, from the point of view of endurance, that yet another good plan that failed to come to fruition was the idea of basing some if not all of the entire tanker fleet in Scotland once the Mk 2 Victors had been converted. The decision to continue with the one carrier, HMS *Ark Royal*, altered plans further still. The need for the Navy to retain a number of both Phantoms and Buccaneers meant that ultimately one Lightning squadron, 23, remained at Leuchars until October 1975. It was, however, joined by the FAA's 892 Naval Air Squadron. The Phantom Training Flight formed, but as a joint Navy/RAF unit.

Despite not having yet been officially formed or recognised as such, the first crews of 43 Squadron got to work at the beginning of July 1969. They were the third operational Phantom unit. Further south, at Coningsby in Lincolnshire, Nos 6 and 54 Squadrons had formed or were forming on the F-4M, known in UK parlance as the FGR2. The specific version for the RAF, it was assigned for now to the role of offensive air support and, until a dedicated squadron formed, armed reconnaissance as well.

On 10 September, the Minister of Defence (Administration), Roy Hattersley MP, visited the squadron and was described as showing a keen interest in the Phantom. Afterwards he chatted with both air and ground crews. Mr Hattersley was accompanied by the then Air Officer for Scotland and Northern Ireland, Air Vice-Marshal F. D. Hughes, and the Senior Air Staff Officer for 11 Group, Air Cdre E. W. Wootten. In the afternoon, the squadron was visited by the Phantom Flight Simulator Siting Committee. Nine days later, Air Vice-Marshal C. G. Lott visited the station. He had commanded the squadron from 1939 to 1940, through the Battle of Britain. Other senior figures, many ex-43 Squadron, visited over the Battle of Britain weekend, including Air Chief Marshal Sir Denis Spotswood, first AOC in C Strike Command. All were turning up for the ceremony on the Sunday.

Stn Cdr, Gp Capt Neville Howlett and OC 43 Sqn, Wg Cdr 'Hank' Martin, chat with just arrived Canadian CF-104 pilots, 19 June 1970, five RCAF jets arrived from 427 Squadron based at Baden Sollingen, while five of the Fighting Cocks F-4s went there. (*The National Archives*)

There was much to do as re-equipping 43 Squadron with the Phantom began that July. With Battle of Britain Week just around the corner, one would have thought that no demand for anything other than ground work and simple training sorties would be placed on them, having only just formed and yet to receive a full complement of anything, whether men or materials. Instead, with far from a full establishment of aircrew or aircraft, Sqn Ldr John Owen and navigator Flt Lt Nick Thurston were required to work up a solo aerobatic sequence for the Battle of Britain display on 20 September, a task at the time that perhaps would have been better undertaken by either the OCU or one of the other squadrons already formed at Coningsby. Overall, Sqn Ldr Owen and Flt Lt Thurston managed fifteen display rehearsals in the time available. However, the new squadron's first public outing was to provide two Phantoms to join nine Lightnings from 11 and 23 Squadrons in the flypast over St Andrews on 21 August, when RAF Leuchars exercised its Freedom of the town one year on from the initial ceremony. During the air show a number of guests were entertained in the new aircrew room.

The squadron is recognised as having formed officially on 1 September 1969, but as the station was stood down that day there were no ceremonies or functions of any kind. On 21 September, following the church service and re-formation ceremony, the squadron officers and their ladies and guests, totalling seventy-two, attended a reception and luncheon at the Officers' Mess. The entertainment followed on at the squadron hangar, and among the distinguished guests was a former First World War pilot, Gp Capt. F. Woolliams, who had served with the 'Fighting Cocks'. As a young RFC lieutenant, he had destroyed a German field gun during an attack on trenches on 3 May 1917, so there was a link with the squadron's recent operational task as a close support unit. Gp Capt. Woolliams and his wife had travelled up from Folkestone in order to be present. Three former Squadron Commanders also attended, as did the man who had led the Hunter aerobatic team in 1956, Gp Capt. Peter Bairsto.

The parade, commanded by Wg Cdr 'Hank' Martin, took place before the reviewing officer, Air Vice-Marshal C. G. Lott, now retired, who had commanded 43 Squadron at the outbreak of the war in 1939 and had lost an eye when leading a section of Hurricanes during the period leading up to the Battle of Britain. It was most fitting that such an outstanding alumnus was invited to review the parade. Towards the end of the month, one of the squadron's exchange officers, Capt. J. Hoffman, began a nine-week course at RNAS Yeovilton, and Sqn Ldr Cushman joined a two-week maritime air defence study group at Woolwich. On top of this, all the squadron's new crews were required to complete the Strike Command AAR course at Marham. Hitherto, 43 Squadron crews had been able to practise this all-important function.

With September and display commitments out of the way, there was some expectation that the squadron would achieve about twenty hours' flying per pilot in October. Flying hours per crew qualifications were going to be something else, as for half of the month the squadron would have only one navigator on strength, and two for the second half. Despite being a formed squadron, 43 had precious few pilots as well—only four at the time. Indeed, its total strength at the end of September had stood at four pilots (including the Squadron Commander, Wg Cdr I. R. Martin), three navigators, the senior and junior engineer officers and the squadron adjutant, together with eighty ground crew. Four more aircrew expected at the end of the month were coming straight from training, not at RAF Coningsby but at RNAS Yeovilton, given the version of the Phantom being flown by 43 Squadron.

Like so many of the RAF's more complex, demanding and indeed impressive aircraft, the Phantom was, due to its heavy numbers and the variety of crucial frontline roles being carried out as of 1971, placing such a demand on training and resources that every effort was made to ensure that all those selected, up until this stage at least, were hand-picked individuals. Eventually, however, it had to rely increasingly on those coming straight from flying training. Over a period of barely three years the demand was to put together and maintain eight frontline squadrons by early 1972, covering tactical strike, offensive air support, tactical reconnaissance, and with 43 Squadron at Leuchars, maritime air defence. But to maintain such a high posture with such numbers meant the day when courses of pilots and navigators would go straight through the OCU from flying training was not too far away. A typical RAF squadron of just about any description usually maintains a higher ratio of trained aircrew to aircraft, but this was not being achieved with the early Phantom units. A ratio of 1.5:1 of aircraft to aircrew was more likely the case, particularly in the strike squadrons based in Germany.

One proposal was to shift a degree of OCU training onto the frontline units in the form of additional training flights. Various other schemes were introduced to try and address the predicament, such as opening up ranges for weapons training at weekends, which resulted in the inevitable rise in complaints about noise, on top of which were the greater demands placed on personnel. The air force was in many respects a 9-to-5 organisation during peace time, or Cold War-style peace time anyway. All these problems were resulting in a low utilisation rate, the one exception to the rule however being 43 Squadron, which was making heavy use of its aircraft. This was attributable to its unique maritime air defence role and, in due course, QRA commitment.

Following the decision to wind up, to all intents and purposes, the Navy's carrier force but to continue running on at least a single angled-deck carrier until 1978, the issue of tailoring the level of flying training for fixed-wing naval aircrew, specifically those destined to fly the Buccaneer and Phantom, was being addressed. The future layout meant effectively subordinating the FAA's fixed-wing fleet to the RAF, while increasingly moving RAF air and ground personnel into various former naval slots, as the time would come when these aircraft would become wholly land-based and therefore under complete RAF control. The first step was to wind down the Navy's own equivalent of the RAF's OCUs. This included two FAA HQ training squadrons: 736 Squadron, based at what was then RNAS Lossiemouth and responsible for operational conversion of the Navy's Buccaneer crews; and 767 Squadron, based at RNAS Yeovilton, which in turn produced RN Phantom crews of a high standard.

What was to happen now was that while no new Navy fixed-wing training would be taking place prior to the introduction of the Sea Harrier some years hence, refresher training to provide a healthy rotation of existing crews was to be maintained with carrier qualifications in mind until 1978. This then meant the continuation of the already established post-OCU Training Flight in order to ensure that Phantom crews so assigned could proceed to carrier qualification while it was required. The intuitive logic of this might suggest setting up such a unit at RAF Coningsby, right next to the RAF's own principal F-4 training unit. However, by July 1971, the decision had been taken to retain the Phantom Training Flight (PTF) at Leuchars. The then Vice-Chief of Air Staff, Air Marshal Sir Denis Smallwood, had taken into consideration the unique nature of compatibility; that is to say, both 43 Squadron and the Navy operating the F-4K. There was the need to train landing signals officers and provide instrument ratings for carrier pilots as well, as aircraft embarked on the *Ark Royal* were not dual-stick control aircraft. So all pilots going to Coningsby who would subsequently be going to Leuchars, would need to undergo the post-OCU conversion to the F-4K before joining the 'Fighting Cocks' or the last naval F-4 unit, 892 Naval Air Squadron (NAS). Those assigned to the latter, of course, received carrier deck training.

Training for Navy ground crew was also deemed best carried out at Leuchars, where they could be introduced to the so-called Flexi-Ops techniques designed to give servicing personnel of various specialisations practice on the aircraft, extending their range of expertise. Furthermore, for this the unit would be made up of RAF aircraft, commanded by an RAF officer and staffed as far as possible with RAF flying instructors drawn from those who had the carrier qualification and would be able to instruct on deck landing and other naval procedures. Of course, this was quite a hard stipulation to meet at the time, and inevitably some instructors came from the FAA. The Flexi-Ops training requirement for deck aircraft servicing crews meant that the majority of maintenance staff on the PTF would also come from the Navy.

Lock up your Daughters! The Navy's in town, 892's newly arrived F-4K Phantoms, October 1972. (*The National Archives*)

Gp Capt Mike Swiney welcomes 892 Naval Air Squadron to their new dis-embarked home for the next 6 years. (*The National Archives*)

Air Marshal Smallwood outlined seven main advantages for basing the new unit at Leuchars:

1. All F-4K Phantoms (FG1s) would be concentrated on one base, resulting in savings in overheads, test equipment, spares and so on;
2. All FG1s would be under the command of the AOC in C Strike Command (Coningsby's Phantoms were under the direct command of AOC in C Air Support Command at the time), who would be able to use the aircraft for air defence when necessary;
3. Any additional training capacity would be used for the RAF's own needs;
4. Navy personnel would be confined to only three airfields—Leuchars, Lossiemouth and Honington (Lossiemouth was already being earmarked for handover to the RAF in 1972);
5. All naval training (except the basic OCU course) and operations would be concentrated in one Command, thus providing a single link with the Navy;
6. It would avoid the problem of installing deck landing equipment at Coningsby, leaving that station free from the deck landing task;
7. The FG1 flight simulator would be located at Leuchars.

An alternative would have been for all Phantom training to be co-located at Coningsby, but the advantages outlined above were seen as more than ample to outweigh this. Strike Command was therefore tasked with working out the detailed arrangements necessary to fit all this into the organisation at Leuchars. Until 1974, 43 Squadron was unique among the RAF interceptor units, as the others, up to this stage, had been flying Lightnings. Courtesy of the restructuring of defence policy in respect of the aircraft carrier and land-based naval units, it was shortly joined by 892 NAS from the end of 1972 in order to centralise all operations and training, as described. This rendered some assistance to 23 and 43 Squadrons, who were a fighter squadron short since 11 Squadron had left for Binbrook in March. Therefore, whenever 892 NAS was not embarked on the *Ark Royal*, it was a further contribution to the Northern QRA force, taking its place on the rotation with the others.

The presence of an RAF station can provide many unusual opportunities, although these are not always necessarily available to the public. However, that does not stop some from trying to make use of the fact that, for example, an air base on the doorstep can be a ready source of weather forecasts and reports, provided one does not let on that the enquiry is not flying-related. Eric Lothian used to work near St Andrews in the early 1970s. He had a boss who was a golfing enthusiast and who would

Returning from Baden Sollingen in Germany, five 43 Sqn Phantoms, the first four breaking over the station, the photograph was taken by *Daily Telegraph* photographer, Peter Stephenson on 22 June 1970. (*MOD/Crown copyright*)

routinely check with the Leuchars Met office for a heads-up on the forecast before heading off to the golf course in the evening in order to practise his swing. As Eric Lothian recalls, he was:

> ... a complete golf nut who had no interest in his job. He could (and, unfortunately, did) talk through an entire game from years ago and could describe not just scores but every lie, every ball, etc, of a foursome in great detail!
>
> He lived near St Andrews and went golfing every night if the weather was at all suitable. His office window looked north from Glenrothes, so much of the sky over north-east Fife was visible. Normally he could tell from the view whether or not to arrange a game, but sometimes when it looked iffy he made a phone call to check the weather.

Calls seemed to go on for longer than one would expect for just 'rain likely' or 'staying clear' sort of thing, and he kept repeating acronyms and numbers—strange.

He seemed to get quite pally with the chap at the other end of the line, until one day he became hesitant and eventually said he didn't have a plane. 'A plane?' I thought! Voice at the other end became increasingly louder, then he slammed the phone down in a panic, saying that they wanted his name and address for possible prosecution! Only then did he admit he had been calling Leuchars Met office because of its proximity to the Old Course.

He went about in terror for a few days but all phones went through a switchboard with hundreds of users, so he never heard anything more.

The new year began well for 43 Squadron. Not only had the target of 336 hours' flying been achieved—the total being 342.5—but this had translated into a record number of sorties being flown. The squadron's previous best had been 199, but on this occasion it had accumulated 216. From 12 January, the squadron held the IAF commitment until the end of the month. It also fell to 43 Squadron to again represent the Command, and indeed the RAF, with the 1973 Phantom solo aerobatic display pilot task, Sqn Ldr Brian Clifford being appointed. He flew two practice sorties that month, in the back seat of 1972's solo man Roger Beazley, who was posted on the Empire Test Pilots' course. This left the squadron strength at fifteen pilots and seventeen navigators. In March, a full month-long detachment to Malta involving the entire squadron took place under the codename Exercise 'Ablution'.

In May, Sqn Ldr Clifford received partial (down to 1,000 feet) display authorisation and demonstrated the Phantom's thunderous performance publicly at Dyce, at Church Fenton, for the SSAFA air display, and at Henlow. The squadron was also visited by Duff Hart-Davis of *The Sunday Telegraph*, who was flown on two sorties: one a low-level navigation exercise and one in a chase aircraft for an IAF sortie in which two Bears were intercepted.

The following month, Sqn Ldr Clifford was fully cleared by HQ 11 Group as the Phantom solo pilot, and 43 Squadron was involved in flying tactics it was not necessarily familiar with. This was in connection with the new NATO Air Defence Ground Environment (NADGE) computer-controlled system, but the squadron's involvement under Exercise 'Tardy Spectre III' was regarded as being of little training value. NADGE was a relatively new and close-controlled way of micro-managing sorties, with parameters programmed into NADGE that were not really compatible with the Phantom and its greater autonomy to hunt with its two-man crew and long-legged radar. A larger than usual number of navigation sorties were flown during June, involving hi-lo navexes from Rygge in Norway to Ørland, and Aalborg in Denmark, a total of eighteen being flown between Leuchars and Rygge. There were more 'Tardy Spectre' sorties with NADGE, but again the upshot was that the sortie profile was seen as inflexible, prompting the suggestion that 'extensive reprogramming of the NADGE computer and a great deal more training for aircrew and controllers would be required to produce an effective operational combination'.

Fuel restrictions were in place at the start of 1974, resulting in reductions in flying time each week. These amounted to three 12-hour periods and one 8-hour period, so maintaining operational currency was rather difficult. All the same, 43 Squadron was meeting its allocation of tasked flying, even when ending up with just nine serviceable Phantoms at the end of the month. As might be expected, each squadron maintained a store of live missiles at the base for immediate use. At this time, the allocation was 298 Sidewinder heat-seeking missiles and 283 Sparrow collision-course missiles for 43 Squadron alone, with about 176 and 229 serviceable respectively. A ban on flying on Fridays did have an efficacious effect in one way, as it allowed the ground crew to catch up with recovering aircraft for the following week's flying.

A film company called Anvil sent a team to film the IAF during February. From the end of March, the Phantoms had to replace the Lightnings on IAF temporarily, owing to the grounding of the Mk 6 Lightnings due to a search for a common fault affecting the Avon engine described in the previous chapter.

The annual 'Heartsease' detachment or exchange that year was with the USAF 496th Tactical Fighter Squadron from Hahn in West Germany. The fuel restrictions were still in place, but the squadron was nevertheless tasked as usual with providing an aerobatics pilot, Flt Lt A. M. 'Sandy' Davis. He was only cleared for practice down to 500 feet in May, with a view to his first public appearance scheduled for July; ordinarily this would have been May.

The still very early development of the Tornado multi-role combat aircraft (MRCA) brought to the station a delegation from BAC to examine the air-to-air refuelling probe used by the British Phantom with a view to incorporating it in the new design. A survey was also carried out for a possible forced deployment in 1975, as the runway was again due to be resurfaced. This, of course, would affect everyone, but the least likely to be found looking for a new home, one might expect, would be the Navy's 892 Squadron, and initial calculations for 43 Squadron determined that about 180,000 lb of equipment would need to be moved off the base to support just that one unit. April brought preparations for the bolthole deployment for runway repairs, with everyone away to Kinloss by the end of the month in order to assume IAF, the squadron operating from there until the end of June. Before that, Marian Pallister of the *Sunday Mail* visited the squadron and flew in a Phantom.

Another round of visitors came in June, including the stage manager of the Dundee Repertory Company to borrow the squadron bugle for use in a stage production. At the end of the month, DACT (Dissimilar Air Combat Training) with 23 Squadron's Lightnings was planned as the fuel situation began to improve, and Flt Lt Davis flew to second place in the Embassy-sponsored aerobatics competition at Greenham Common IAT on 2 July. This was no mean achievement, as anyone with any idea of the standard of flying and the variety of high-performance types from various other international air arms at this air extravaganza would concur.

By now, the era of the Lightning was rapidly drawing to a close at Leuchars and the height of F-4 operations was at hand. No. 23 Squadron would disband in October and be replaced the following month by 111 Squadron with the McDonnell Douglas F-4M Phantom, the third F-4-equipped operational unit. The Navy's 892 Squadron was in and out, spending the time embarked on the *Ark Royal*, and 43 Squadron was involved in trials to track the Martel anti-ship missile, designed to equip both the RAF and RN Buccaneers, during Exercise 'Negritto' in October.

While 111 Squadron was settling in, the BBC took the opportunity in 1976, while there was still time before the last 'proper carrier' was decommissioned, to make a fly-on-the-wall documentary of the *Ark Royal* and all embarked on her, including 892 Squadron, on tour down the coast of America and into the South Atlantic. Many will recall Rod Stewart singing 'Sailing' as the theme to *Sailing*!

Although made up largely of experienced pilots and navigators, 111 Squadron was still finding its feet. However, unlike previous squadron arrivals at Leuchars who had had to find their feet gradually while aircraft and often fresh aircrew pitched up in piecemeal fashion, the 'Tremblers' turned up on the doorstep fully staffed with thirty aircrew. Perhaps bearing testament to the idea of forming a new unit elsewhere before relying on them on operational assignment while they existing little more than on paper, they had formed on the Phantom, initially in 1974, and so had been put together comprehensively and cohesively over the preceding year. They benefited at the time from having a US Marine Corps pilot, Capt. T. Wilkerson, who, unsurprisingly for the time, brought priceless experience of Vietnam from not too far back. He was able to coach the new squadron on visual ident procedures and tactics, and, as 111's commanding officer Wg Cdr Park hoped, had learned something of radar intercept tactics. In

March 1976, he was posted out and replaced by Capt. D. A. Stamper, also from the US Marine Corps. As 43 Squadron had hitherto been the only F-4 unit in the RAF wholly assigned to the air defence role, this meant that quite a few former Lightning pilots provided the lion's share of experience.

The squadron managed to get its teeth into more trade while holding the Northern IAF, intercepting three Bear Delta aircraft on 12 April. Much of the month saw the crews practising air combat manoeuvring, starting with 1 *v* 1 daytime tactics and then gradually increasing the demand until a detachment from the Hunter Tactical Wing at Wittering turned up for two weeks on 26 April, and finished up with two Phantoms versus one Hunter. The valuable training provided by the Hunters from Wittering could not be overstated. Having such a thing as what the Americans call an aggressor unit or squadron to provide regular dissimilar tactics and

Phantom FG1, XV591, seen over the Tay Bridge, November 1982. (*MOD/Crown copyright*)

evasive action training so easily available is worth its weight in gold to any serious fighter outfit.

An insight into the mindset of RAF aircrew according to type came in August 1976. The RAF concluded a report essentially on aircrew satisfaction/dissatisfaction with their role and the aircraft they were provided with in which to do it. Predictably, enthusiasm waned more among those who flew the less glamorous aircraft, and the level of satisfaction could be judged according to who flew what. While most of 23 Squadron's Lightning pilots who were interviewed were generally content, two were unhappy with their role, and nine disliked what was described as excessive rules and regulations. All fourteen Phantom crew (seven pilots and seven navigators) were content with the aircraft and their role, although six were again unhappy with excessive rules and regulations. When those flying larger and heavier aircraft, including the iconic Vulcan, were asked to give a frank response to the same questions, approximately half were unhappy with the aircraft and a greater proportion disliked irksome rules and regulations. Interestingly, the one aircraft given praise across the board by the crews who flew it was the Buccaneer, which was also thought to be the best for its particular role. However, most criticism was reserved for the politicians, who, in the opinion of the aircrew of the day, had depleted the RAF. (If only they could have been given the opportunity to peer into a crystal ball and see how things are in 2015!) It was also noted that the RAF was considered to be the poor relation of the other two services, and was not quite what it ought to be in the opinion of its junior officers. Many of them compared their service unfavourably with the Army, which, it was said, had 'real officers'.

Silver Jubilee year, 1977, saw no great functions in the pipeline save the obligatory street parties around the married quarters in June, but the involvement by Leuchars personnel at the RAF's Silver Jubilee Review was quite substantial. The review, held at RAF Finningley, aimed to have all current operational squadrons of the day represented by a single aircraft on static display, with a very similar representative line-up for the flypast itself. No. 111 Squadron provided its quota of two Phantom FGR2s, one for each, and 43 Squadron also provided a single aircraft for the static display. However, due to the take on how to represent the roles and responsibilities of the squadrons in the flypast, it was called on to provide two of its FG1s to join the maritime section in the flypast.

Before summer was out, a well-reported incident took place at the base. AOC 11 Group had just called Exercise 'Ricochet' on 4 August, which involved generating live armed aircraft. During the day's proceedings, a Sidewinder missile happened to leave the rails of a stationary Phantom while on the tarmac and shot across the airfield and over the Eden Estuary.

All arming was stopped and the errant aircraft—an FGR2/F-4M belonging to 111 Squadron—was taken away to be gone over with the proverbial fine-tooth comb. There was no clear evidence to link the event to any individual, and on the aircraft's return to the squadron a disagreement over procedure arose when putting the jet in the Q-shed for QRA/IAF duty. Keith Arkwright, who was serving at the station at the time, recalls what happened with mixed feelings about the event. He told me that he would be honoured (if embarrassed) for his experience to go into print with his name attached. Here is what he recollects:

> Further to this incident the aircraft was put into quarantine for six months with every man and his dog investigating why it should have fired a missile on the ground, but they never gave out any reason.
>
> Shortly after it was released back to service I was taking over QRA for a week and this particular aircraft was on the 'arming point' undergoing acceptance checks by the pilot and navigator, with the aircraft fully armed with all the safety and arming pins removed and the engines running. The pilot then asked me to attach the tractor/towing arm to the front and push him back into the QRA hangar with the engines running to keep the INAS [Inertial Navigation and Attack System] on-line. I told him that I would need to put the rocket motor safety pins into the Sidewinders before I would go in front of this aircraft.
>
> He told me that I couldn't do that as it would mean taking the aircraft off 'Q-Readiness'. I explained why I wouldn't do this, at which he ordered me to push him back as is. I refused. He then informed me that he was going to have me court-martialled for disobeying a direct order and radioed for the Squadron Wing Commander to attend.
>
> I sat and waited.
>
> The Wing Commander came out and asked me what was going on. I explained why I was not willing to sit on a tractor in front of this aircraft without at least the Sidewinder motor pins in. He borrowed my headset and spoke to the pilot. He then told me to put any safety pins I wanted in and push the aircraft into the shed. I did.
>
> For some reason the pilot was taken off QRA for that week, and I am still waiting for my court martial.

Steve Gyles had experienced problems with hydraulics on the point of take-off when serving at Leuchars some years earlier as a Lightning pilot on 11 Squadron. He had by now returned, having converted to the Phantom and since been posted to 43 Squadron. On 21 November 1977, he experienced a quite hairy incident, involving a Phantom this time around, which required very quick reactions to escape a doomed situation:

This story, while a major happening in my own life, rates very low amongst Martin-Baker ejectee survival stories—particularly as the aircraft lived to fly another day. Also, with the benefit of hindsight, I may have escaped with fewer injuries had I stayed with the aircraft. There again, there have probably been many aircrew who chose the latter option and did not survive to tell their story.

The drama began on the take-off roll at 0930 hours on a wintry but calm November morning at RAF Leuchars. I was number two of a pair of Phantom FG1 air defence aircraft in a 30-second stream take-off. As I was accelerating fast through 100 kts the aircraft started to veer off to starboard. I attempted to correct first with rudder and a dab of left brake but then with nose wheel steering as response was only minimal. The aircraft was not feeling right and I was struggling with the directional control when it suddenly snapped sharply to starboard, out of control. I aborted take-off.

The aircraft left the runway in a slight slide with the speed in the region of 100 to 120 kts. As it hit the grass my left rear-view mirror seemed to explode in a ball of flame. Instinctively I glanced over my shoulder expecting to see the left wing area on fire but almost immediately realised that I had seen either the rear cockpit canopy ejectors fire or the navigator's ejector seat rocket pack ignite.

My brain raced and, curiously, three statements printed themselves on my mind: firstly, what did the navigator know that I did not; secondly, I was going to face a Board of Inquiry regardless of whether I stayed or ejected; and finally, I had always wanted to own a Martin-Baker tie!

My decision to eject was now made, but I delayed for what seemed to me like three or four seconds before pulling the seat pan handle. My reason for delay was to ensure that the navigator's seat had cleared the aircraft, as in a previous F-4 accident the navigator had been killed when the pilot's canopy hit him during the ejection sequence. I was told at the subsequent inquiry that both seats had been seen to leave the aircraft within one second! This meant that my initial observation of flames, my three thoughts, my ejection decision and deliberate delay were all played out in less than half a second.

The force of the ejection threw my head sharply down. I had a snapshot image of the canopy arch and then blackness. A roaring sound and a series of sharp jerks were reminiscent of a London Underground train at high speed in a tunnel. There was then a brief view of forest above my head and then tranquillity as I viewed St Andrews Old Course the right way up and my navigator's parachute in front and below me. In a flash I realised that I was fast overtaking him. I was still holding on to the ejector seat bottom handle and, therefore, still attached to the seat. I had just time to let go before the ground rushed up to meet me. I hit the ground extremely hard on my backside, fracturing my spine, although I did not realise it at the time.

I lay there on the runway on my back for what seemed an eternity. The impact had knocked every bit of air out of my body and for some time I was unable to catch my breath. However, my worst nightmare was yet to unfold.

With air finally back in my lungs I released the parachute Koch fasteners and dinghy pack clips, disconnected and removed my helmet and struggled to my feet. The aircraft was bogged down in the ground about 40 m away. One engine was still turning over at idle RPM—I had stop-cocked the other before ejecting. Some 60 m back up the runway I could see parachute silk and my navigator's legs. Above the engine noise I heard the sound of a fast-approaching fire vehicle. It was a foam tender—a long-wheelbase Land Rover tasked with being first on an accident scene to rescue any survivors. I gave the crew a 'thumbs-up', pointed to the navigator and started running in pursuit. I then observed, in what seemed slow motion, the vehicle draw up alongside my navigator, the crew get out and run over to the body. One crewman then walked back to the vehicle, collected a blanket and draped it across the body. Convinced that I had killed my navigator (Andy Moir), I stopped running, turned around and started to walk away. Other vehicles were by now rushing all over the place. No one seemed at all interested in me. The Station Commander swept by in his car without even a glance in my direction. I felt totally alone, distraught and depressed. I also now became aware that my back was screaming with pain, so I lay down on the ground and waited for transport to cart me off to the medical centre.

For the next two or three hours, lying in a hospital bed, I felt alone, sick and miserable. I had killed my navigator, crashed the boss's aircraft (fleet letter A) and my own body was broken and bruised. Eventually a doctor came to tell me that I had multiple fractures to my lower spine and a dislocated coccyx, but more importantly my navigator had a broken leg and was now conscious. He seemed totally amazed when I told him I thought he was dead. Do we ever get good at communications?

The following day I was told by the President of the Board of Inquiry that I was not to blame for the accident. Evidence showed that moisture had got into the nose wheel steering electrics, shorting it out and causing the nose wheel to run away 70 degrees starboard. To put this into context, imagine driving down the M6 at about 130 mph and the steering wheel starts to turn involuntarily to the right; despite pulling against the wheel you can only slow down the rate of turn and the wheel finally goes to full right lock. Oh yes, you are in a tanker, not a car. You have 16,000 lb of volatile fuel all around you.

The incident did have an amusing postscript. A week after the accident, Andy and I were transferred to RAF Ely hospital. Andy was wheeled into our side ward first. A young nurse approached his bed, took the name plaque from his bed post and proceeded to write while speaking: 'Flt Lt Moir, RAF Leuchars. Oh, you are the young man who ejaculated.' Andy burst into laughter and the blushing nurse made a quick exit. I was then wheeled in. Andy related the story and we were still having a good laugh when Nurse Stewart walked in again. Not daring to look at Andy, she walked over to my bed, took my plaque and began the same process: 'Flt Lt Gyles, RAF Leuchars. Oh, you are the other boy who ej... ej... ej... baled out.'

Four months later both Andy and I were declared fit to fly, although in separate aircraft for our respective first sorties. My trip was a check-out with the squadron flying instructor. Twenty minutes into the flight the left-hand engine banged and surged. We shut it down, put out an emergency call and landed. For the next week navigators mysteriously disappeared or went sick whenever they were scheduled to fly with me ...

I went on to complete the tour without further major drama. My regular navigator, Bob Lawley, stuck with me and I do not believe I ever frightened him. When I left the squadron he crewed up with another pilot and almost exactly a year later (26 January 1981) ejected on take-off. Yes, the good old nose wheel steering problem again. This time the pilot did not abort but performed the first ever Phantom soft ground take-off, apparently leaving twin gouges in the soil from the stabilators!

The recently arrived SAR Wessex HC2 helicopters of 22 Squadron's 'B' Flight had been kept busy, as one might expect, with scrambles of their own since their arrival in 1976. They had a busy month in July 1977, with no fewer than eleven callouts up to the 27th, during which all bar one were resolved without any loss of life. However, the Flight was called to respond to a report of a body in the water off Kinghorn, but a search of the area turned up nothing. It may have been a prank call, or the reported object might not have been as claimed. Suffice to say, no follow-up reports reached the squadron.

The most auspicious, if brief, event of the month was a visit from HM Queen Elizabeth The Queen Mother. Later, at the end of the year, it was announced on the national news that the Navy's last Audacious-class carrier, HMS *Ark Royal*, was for the chop by the end of 1978. This would have little, if any, impact on Leuchars, save for 892 Squadron, of course,

Steve and Andy's Phantom seen after it came to rest following the nearly fatal crash on take-off. (*Steve Gyles*)

whose whole *raison d'être* was about to go, rendering it surplus to naval requirements. At least the aircraft had a future in due course, as they would be used to replace the F-4Ms of 111 Squadron, given that the ex-Navy F-4Ks would bring commonality with 43 Squadron.

January 1978 brought a DACT exercise for 111 Squadron with Norwegian F-5As at Sola, on Exercise 'Whisky Troll', designed to provide RAF and Royal Norwegian Air Force crews with experience of each other's operating procedures. For the first time, Leuchars-based Phantoms were allowed to carry out a 2 *v* 2 sortie with the Norwegian F-5s. The latter, being small and nimble in comparison, were found to be highly manoeuvrable and ideally simulated the Soviet MiG-21 Fishbed. After such a sortie on 12 January, one of the Phantoms, XV410, burst a tyre on landing and damaged its undercarriage, the other one returning home.

Before disbandment, 892 Squadron was planning to mark its final year of operations with the Phantom, 1978, with a solo display of its own, but tragedy intervened. During an aerobatics practice on 12 May, aircraft XT868 crashed on the airfield, killing the observer, Lt J. Gavin, and seriously injuring the pilot, Cdr C. C. N. Davies, who was rushed by a Wessex of 'B' Flight to Dundee Airport for transfer to hospital. This was the last flight of an aircraft of 892 Squadron from Leuchars, as the squadron was otherwise embarked at the time.

In June 1978, the Leuchars squadrons between them launched fifteen times on live QRA, intercepting twenty-seven Tu-95 Bears and three Tu-20 Badgers. This could have been any month, give or take the odd exception, from 1966 to 1990, which can be seen as a truly defining era of the Cold War. But to put matters in perspective, in this same month the amount of activity affecting the RAF's then three other UK interceptor stations involved little or nothing with regard to the interception of intruders. Binbrook, near Grimsby in Lincolnshire, recorded no QRA involvement at all, the three main operational commitments that month being Exercise 'Aiming Fist', a synthetic exercise sponsored by NATO that involved only Wing Ops on their computers; Exercise 'Tapper Blow', an offensive support exercise in which Binbrook's Lightnings attacked a variety of bomber aircraft, involving in-flight refuelling; and Exercise 'Cavalcade', in which the base's Lightnings made surprise attacks on aircraft from 1 Group, essentially the RAF's main offensive air element.

Further south, at Wattisham, 23 and 56 Squadrons undertook routine training commitments that could be fitted in with royal duties such as providing a diamond-16 formation for HM The Queen's birthday flypast on 3 June and a visit by HRH the Duke of Edinburgh nine days later.

Coningsby-based 29 Squadron was also involved in 'Tapper Blow', intercepting 1 Group's Buccaneers and Jaguars operating at low level, as well as Operation 'Active Edge' on 2 June, during which it generated seven armed aircraft in 6 hours and nine by the end of the exercise, which lasted a total of 8 hours and 30 minutes. The squadron also flew in an electronic warfare exercise—'Coffee Charlie'—involving the provision of four aircraft under the control of the Neatishead Sector Operations Centre near Cromer, to intercept Canberra aircraft from 360 Squadron attempting to jam the Neatishead radar. It also had the responsibility for the Southern QRA, for a statutory nineteen-day period from 26 May. During the first two weeks of June—indeed, throughout the whole nineteen days—five practice scrambles were ordered off, with no live ones. I point this out in order to give some idea of the difference between the three bases in England, which had the luxury of rotating the task between them, and the two squadrons in Fife that rotated their lot between them. This is not, of course, to impugn the reputation of those serving at the English bases. Several would have served at Leuchars at some stage, either through choice or the luck of the draw. It makes for a logical analogy to regard Leuchars as the Biggin Hill of the Cold War.

This was also the year that the RAF reached its Diamond Jubilee. In recognition of this, 43 and 111 Squadrons marked the occasion at that year's 'at home' day with a diamond-9 formation that also flew over Edinburgh Castle as part of the closing ceremony of the Military Tattoo. That year's air show was particularly good, the flying content including an appearance by the USAF F-15 and displays by both the Red Arrows and their French counterparts, La Patrouille de France.

The Royal Dutch Air Force, which was celebrating the 65th anniversary of military aviation in its country, was also represented in the display, with an F-104 (in anniversary markings) and an F-5. Among the official visitors were the Chief of the Air Staff, Sir Michael Beetham; AOC in C 11 Group, Air Vice-Marshal Peter Latham; and the Air Officer for Scotland and Northern Ireland, Air Vice-Marshal Jock Kennedy. Surviving members of the RFC living in Scotland were also invited.

A few changes were afoot at the 1978 air show. In particular, more of the airfield was made available for car parking, this being one of the ever-present problems at air shows of all descriptions. Even with the extra space for cars, the airfield was full early on and some latecomers had to be turned away. At the other end of the day, the weather started to turn, the arrival of rain prompting long queues to form in a rush to leave the station. Some cars did not get away until 8 p.m. after darkness had fallen. Amidst all of this, another major NATO exercise was in progress, Exercise 'Northern Wedding'. The demands of this required that squadrons be made ready to participate by 6 p.m. on the day, while many of the station personnel were still to clear the airfield and then carry out the obligatory 'fod plod'—an inspection for foreign object debris.

The first F-15 to appear at the Leuchars airshow as a flying participant certainly was this one on 2 September 1978. (*Peter Nicholson*)

A Lightning makes a high speed low pass with tongues of reheat visible, during the 1978 airshow. This time the aircraft came from 5 Squadron at Binbrook. Lightnings having long since left Leuchars. (*The National Archives*)

Towards the end of the year, yet another runway resurfacing was at hand, and just before the RAF's 60th anniversary year was out, 111 Squadron notched up another milestone while on deployment to Luqa in Malta by flying 111 (eleven?) sorties in the space of two days. On the downside, a tragedy had occurred when one of the squadron's recently delivered FG1s (F-4Ks), XT598, was lost during a recovery to Leuchars from 30 miles east over the North Sea on 23 November, the two crew lost being both graduate entrants. Flt Lt C. L. Jones, the pilot, had previously flown Lightnings with 111 Squadron at Wattisham and with 19 Squadron at Gütersloh; his navigator, Flt Lt M. H. Stephenson, had flown the Phantom both in the strike role with 17 Squadron at Bruggen and as an air defence fighter with 19 Squadron at Wildenrath before joining 111 Squadron in July 1977.

During the Christmas period, both squadrons shared the QRA duty, but it was a crew from 111 Squadron, Flt Lts Goddard and Mahoney, who flew the only live intercept of the festive season, at 0030 hours on 16 December, when two Bear Ds en route to Cuba on a heading of 240 degrees were intercepted at 65°05'N and 09°05'W at 29,000 feet. The intercept position was so far out to the north-west that it was controlled by the Royal Danish Air Force's 'Pole Star' radar station on the Faeroes, and by a US AWACS Viking aircraft.

There was an ominous start to 1979, with yet another loss of a F-4K Phantom from 111 Squadron, XV578, flown by Sqn Ldr Mal Gleave (a former Lightning pilot) and his navigator, Fg Off. Al Lewry. However, both ejected safely after an engine failure just off the Scottish coast.

The Phantoms from 43 Squadron began leaving Leuchars on 9 April for Kinloss on another bolthole deployment. Two days later, at 0930 hours, QRA duties were continued by 43 Squadron alone, from Kinloss, while 111 Squadron headed south to Coningsby. On 12 April, the last Phantoms of 43 Squadron departed at 1340 hours, the contractors starting the major work on the runway four days later, although some preliminary work had already been done. As part of the contract, the runway was still to be made available, somehow, every fortnight.

With Leuchars now out of action for at least eight months, its role as a master diversion airfield (MDA) had to be transferred and it was agreed that HMS *Gannet*, more familiarly known as Prestwick, was to take on the duty until the fresh tarmac was set at Leuchars. The terms of MDA transfer, ratified on 17 May, clearly accommodated a little flexibility, as the practice of using Troon airfield as a temporary MDA had been effective since 12 April. (Interestingly, the MDA role will continue at Leuchars even after the Army moves in during 2015.) The nine months of the bolthole detachment were typical of the era.

Now that 43 Squadron essentially bore the responsibility of 'meeting and greeting' all intruders into UK airspace from the north, an unofficial badge was designed, the 10 Bear badge. Rodney 'Budgie' Burgess was serving on the squadron at the time and recalls:

> We originated the idea of the 10 Bear badge whilst on bolthole at Kinloss in 1979 when everybody on the squadron had made a Q Intercept, mainly to piss off the Southern squadrons. My wife did all the original artwork for the badge, calligraphy for the certificate and the design for the tie. We still have the originals. I got my certificate and badge on 1 August 1979.

Ian McBride, who flew with 74 Squadron during the earliest such intercepts of Soviet aircraft, was the commanding officer of 43 Squadron at the time and noted that they:

> … intercepted so many Soviet aircraft that virtually every operational crew member earned membership of the 10 Bear club. The actual number of interceptions is probably still classified but it was not far short of 300! I believe it is still the record.

As Rodney Burgess further recalls:

> The bolthole period was particularly active because the Russians were sending round droves of Bear Foxtrots. We even got up to Q 12, all of which flew and made intercepts in a 65-hour period.

The end of the bolthole deployment from Leuchars came about on 18 December 1979, and 111 Squadron was first to resume Northern QRA (as it was once again being referred to after the brief period of the Interceptor Alert Force). Four scrambles were ordered on Christmas Eve and Christmas Day, netting one NATO Orion maritime patrol aircraft, the fourth scramble at 1515 hours returning to base shortly after take-off with serviceability problems.

During the early part of 1980, QRA responses continued as usual, with 111 Squadron having the Northern 'Q' responsibility during most of April. Between 9 and 30 April, this coincided with a Soviet naval exercise with a resulting high volume of QRA scrambles: no fewer than thirty-eight Bear Ds, sixteen Bear Fs, seven Modified Bear Fs, two Bison Bs and three Badger Ds. There were also a number of live scrambles resulting in no intercept and some practice scrambles, a total of thirty-three in all, so it is hard to imagine how the two squadrons at Leuchars found time to do anything else. The biggest haul went to Flt Lts Watling and Pike, both

A selection of Leuchars related patches; 10 Bear Badge, 43 Sqn shoulder patch, Falklands patch, 23 and 43 Sqn official badges. (*Paul Warren*)

of 'A' Flight, who launched at 0915 hours on 21 April, the second launch that morning. They intercepted four Bear Ds, two Fs and one Modified F. As if this was not demand enough above normal peacetime squadron operations, Exercise 'Elder Forest' took place on 15/16 April, during which thirty sorties were flown, including a survival scramble.

A number of visitors were also received during this period. Members of the Edinburgh and Heriot-Watt University Military Education Committee visited on 10 April and were briefed by the Squadron Commander, Wg Cdr D. C. Read, on the squadron's history. On 23 April, the Rector of St Andrews University was escorted by Sqn Ldr Rick Peacock-Edwards during a further visit, and five days later ten members of a Norwegian Parliamentary Committee 'with eight others' were entertained by one of the practice scrambles.

With the runway at Leuchars now resurfaced, the next phase of development at the airfield was ready to take place. In his Christmas address in 1979, the Chief of the Air Staff, Sir Michael Beetham, had stated that six RAF stations—Coningsby, Honington, Leuchars, Lossiemouth, Marham and Wattisham—would all have new hardened aircraft shelters built in order to provide protection for frontline aircraft against conventional attacks. The HAS sites were already long established at the RAF bases in West Germany, but for the years ahead, well into the 1980s, the squadrons at Leuchars would continue to operate from the old austerity C-type hangars at the west end of the base. Amazingly, the HAS site was not ready for occupation, or at least was not occupied, until early 1986.

Two sites were eventually built, either side of the main runway at the east end. The one on the north side was assigned to 43 Squadron, which moved its eighteen Phantoms into the twelve shelters it had been allocated. Ideally, just one aircraft of this size should occupy each shelter, but two can fit in at a squeeze, so the squadron had to persevere somewhat. The HAS on the other side of the runway was allocated to 111 Squadron. Barry Mayner had joined 43 Squadron just as the new sites were made ready for occupation. This marked the end of the old Q-sheds built back in 1965, as designated shelters on the south side of the airfield were set aside for the purpose of QRA.

When QRA was moved at Leuchars from the tin sheds at the 09 threshold to the southern (111) HAS site, two HAS's were allocated to QRA and a purpose-built Ops/Domestic facility was built.

The two HAS's picked were pointing in different directions and the Q2 HAS was some 50 yards from the exit of the Ops building. A corridor was built from the Ops/Admin building to the Q2 HAS.

It was not possible to put two armed aircraft in the one HAS because if the front aircraft failed to start, the rear one would be trapped. The

RTU-95 Bear being shadowed by an F-4K, January 1985. (*Barry G. Mayner*)

taxiway was used to the right from both, being the shortest route to the main taxiway.

Shortly after returning from the bolthole at Coningsby, 111 Squadron received the first of its repainted Phantoms in the new 'Ghost Grey' scheme. By the end of June 1980, the 'Tremblers' had seventeen jets on charge, all FG1s, three of which—XT870, XT872 and XT865—were in the new toned-down grey paint scheme. It appears that this was effective during the DACT exercises during a detachment to the US AFB at Alconbury that month when it was found that the new camouflage was quite advantageous, the pilots of the USAF 527th Aggressor Squadron flying F-5E Tigers confirming that it was more difficult to keep a track of the Phantoms in this scheme during air-to-air combat training. However, at the same time, the effectiveness reduced the definition of the aircraft outline to the point that the Aggressor pilots hesitated for a few seconds before reacting, and while this may seem no time at all, just a couple of seconds, as Sqn Ldr Rick Peacock-Edwards wrote in his report, 'would be enough to mean the difference between a quick kill and a successful "Bug Out" '.

In order to make the camouflage effective, the recommendation was for all Phantom squadrons to continue to operate a mix of 'Ghost Grey' and 'Lizard' aircraft, the latter being the 50:50 application of sea green and sea grey to the upper surfaces with full colour roundels. The Ghosts had toned-down service markings. The reason for the mix of paint schemes was, of course, to provide a choice of camouflage for different tactical situations, i.e. low-level over land, etc. Whatever the decision at the time, it became clear as the years wore on that the 'Ghost Grey' camouflage trumped all in the eyes of the Air Staff, and clearly that of other air forces, as just about every tactical aircraft you see today is in some form of light grey.

Following a hiatus after 1978, the air show returned to Leuchars on 19 September 1981. The home-based units were to the fore once again, providing the additional show of frontline hardware over and above the officially assigned display aircraft seen at the other three remaining Battle of Britain displays. This year it fell to 111 Squadron to provide the now traditional home formation display team. Led by Sqn Ldr Cliff Spink, and with Flt Lts Paul Richard, John Norton, Ian Simmons, David Jones, Pat Watling, Graham Bond and Chris Knight making up the pilot/navigator crews, they practised every other day for the preceding four weeks and, while not fully an aerobatic display team in the sense that the Red Arrows are, they provided spectacular demonstrations relying on the brute power and performance of the aircraft. A regular and unique feature of the Leuchars air show for many years, the Battle of Britain quartets provided by the resident squadrons certainly had the edge over the established

111 Sqn Phantom with ground crew, November 1982. (*MOD*/Crown *copyright*)

polished display teams in terms of dramatic demonstrations of noise and
speed. Typically, this required about eighteen practice sorties (remember
the scant three for the 11 Squadron Lightning team in 1967!) spread over
the month leading up to the big day. Sqn Ldr Spink and his team concluded
their sequence with low-level, high-speed runs across the airfield before
pulling into the near vertical from 500 feet to 24,000 feet.

There was always, however, the added impact on serving personnel. The
run-up to the air show in 1974 had coincided, or rather run back to back,
with Exercise 'Northern Merger' requiring 43 Squadron's maintenance
personnel to be placed on 12-hour shifts for a two-week period. There was
also the coinciding demand of air show and Exercise 'Northern Wedding'
in 1978. The 1981 display season saw 43 Squadron providing the solo
Phantom display once again, this time flown by Sqn Ldr Ray Dixon and
Flt Lt Colin Bond.

Sqn Ldr Dixon had had a narrow escape a couple of months earlier, when during a night exercise he had made a hasty exit together with his navigator (on that occasion, Fg Off. Matt Syndercombe) as their Phantom, XT866, crashed during final approach. The scarce warning afforded meant that both ejected at hardly any height above the runway and certainly well outside the safety parameters, but both their lives were saved by the effectiveness of the Martin-Baker seats' ample ascent before the chutes deployed. Fg Off. Syndercombe suffered minor burns and was off for nine months before he was medically cleared to fly again, but Sqn Ldr Dixon was back flying very soon after the accident.

With the Cold War still very much the prime concern of western defence planners in 1979, the Air Force Board determined that an additional three air defence fighter squadrons were needed to fulfil the RAF's responsibilities in the UKADR (UK Air Defence Region), EASTLANT (Eastern Atlantic Area) and SACLANT (Supreme Allied Commander Atlantic) command areas. To address what had been a serious rundown of the UK's air defence capability throughout the previous two decades, many interim solutions were being sought by the new government, including a purchase of more up-to-date American fighters. In order to flesh things out further, the idea of arming Hawk advanced jet trainer aircraft with AIM-9L Sidewinder heat-seeking missiles was also considered and accepted.

The proposal at this stage, at a point of rising tension with the Warsaw Pact, was to deploy thirty-six Hawk jets, equipped to carry the Sidewinder missiles, to Leuchars, Wattisham, Coningsby, Binbrook, Stornoway and St Mawgan. Apart from the latter two, the rest would be shepherded by the resident all-weather fighters. Even so, the introduction of the Tornado ADV (air defence variant) was expected to see a decline of the operational interceptor strength from 116 to 100. Among the various options, apart from the purchase of foreign fighters within the available budget that was concentrating the minds of the air chiefs, was the idea of expanding the number of Lightning aircraft remaining, meaning using up the airframe hours more quickly. Another proposal was to maintain a number of Phantoms for a longer period and accelerate the Tornado programme. In addition to this was a NATO recommendation to deploy forty-eight more Tornado fighters within the UKADR, bearing in mind that the criterion at the time was for a maximum of two fighter squadrons per airfield, requiring four minimum, with a fifth for a single squadron to be deployed (expected to be Brawdy). So a further airfield had to be retained that would normally have been expected to be placed in reserve. This airfield was Binbrook, and serious thought was given to deploying the Tornado OCU there or basing it at Leuchars. Although Binbrook was seen as the less expensive option, Leuchars was deemed to have all the training and operational advantages.

The renewed priority for the air defence of the UK expanded beyond the requirement for additional fighters. A bolstered surface-to-air missile screen, as much as could be managed, was under way also. For Leuchars this included the arrival of 27 Squadron RAF Regiment. A much misunderstood outfit, the RAF Regiment had never quite received the press it deserved, often being regarded as no more than an armed guard force. The unit, which arrived and began its work up to operational status at Leuchars in November 1975, had been formed on the Rapier low-level surface-to-air missile system in January at RAF North Luffenham in Leicestershire. Guided by the DN 181 radar, its short range suited the local defence requirements of individual airfields.

By April 1987, Leuchars had experienced a further increase in tempo with more active units than it had seen since the early 1950s. With the two resident fighter units, the RAF Regiment Rapier Squadron, the SAR Flight, University Air Squadrons and Air Experience Flight, the station now had a new outfit to accommodate, as 228 OCU was returning for the first time since disbanding at the end of 1966. Following a year and bit in the wilderness, 228 OCU had re-formed again in 1968 at Coningsby as the Phantom OCU, doing sterling work providing aircrew over a period of less than four years to work up from scratch eight operationally declared squadrons covering strike, closer air support, tactical reconnaissance and, latterly, interceptor fighter roles. From the mid-1970s it increasingly concentrated on the latter as the Phantoms transferred to the air defence remit to allow the standing-down of most of the Lightnings.

With the Phantom now also winding down in favour of the Panavia Tornado ADV, the OCU moved back to Leuchars in order to better utilise space both on the ground as well as in the air, and to take advantage of the often tranquil Fife coast with its reputed better weather. With the shadow identity of 64 Squadron, 228 OCU took up residence and continued to turn out aircrew for the then remaining six air defence squadrons and, as was now the case, the Battle Flight in the Falkland Islands at RAF Mount Pleasant. This was expected to continue with a minimum reduction to four squadrons, the last of which was not expected to disband before around 2003 or 2004.

In the event, thanks to the crumbling of the Berlin Wall, the subsequent defence review ensured 228 OCU's second stay at Leuchars was short-lived yet again. 'Options for Change', the government's strategic defence and security review of the age, together with the Treaty on Conventional Armed Forces in Europe, which prompted reductions either side of the now defunct Iron Curtain, hastened the decision to disband the remaining Phantom squadrons, and all were gone by April 1993, there now being little justification for their retention. The OCU's fate was to disband on

A Rapier missile team of 27 Squadron, RAF Regiment, keep a watchful look out for approaching raids during a live exercise, the two Phantoms getting airborne on runway 27 are from 111 Sqn, *c.* 1978. (*MOD/Crown copyright*)

22 April 1987, Welcome arrival for 228 OCU. *From left to right*: Gp Capt Ian McFadyen (Leuchars CO), Wg Cdr David Roome (OC 228 OCU) with OCU instructor staff; Jim Jackson, Barry Clephane, John Teager, Gerry Woodley (OC Eng Wg at RAF Coningsby), Dave Lewins, Paul Marskell and Ian Morrison. The old Gentleman in the foreground is a veteran pilot who was stationed at Leuchars in the 1920s. (*Royal Air Force Museum Archives*)

31 January 1991, but until that time it continued to have its work cut out supplying the remaining squadrons.

However, the early years, which had required separate courses for pilots and navigators, were long gone. The course syllabus had initially included ground attack courses split into pilots on one course and navigators on another, rather than determining future crews by role as was later to be the case. Air defence Phantom crews were essentially what the OCU produced from 1973/74 onwards, this period heralding the arrival of the BAC Sepecat Jaguar strike attack/reconnaissance fighter and the transfer of all remaining Phantoms from all these duties to the interceptor and air superiority fighter remit.

When Paul Warren, an ab initio F-4 pilot, arrived at Leuchars on posting to 43 Squadron in September 1980, due to the fact that 228 OCU remained equipped with F-4Ms while 43 and 111 Squadrons had all the F-4Ks originally intended for the FAA, there remained a good deal of conversion training left to do. Paul's log book shows that he flew a total of thirty-one convex flights during the period from October 1980 to 16 February 1981 in order to be classed as limited combat available:

> At some point around then I must have been declared combat ready as my first QRA launch was on 5 March 1981.
>
> There were some other requirements to cater for the 'war role' of the squadron, by practising TASMO [Tactical Air Support for Maritime Operations] exercises. My distant memory leans me towards recall that the squadron's wartime role was for it to be allocated to the Navy, to be directed by and used for their benefit. Never sure how that was going to work in practice, as most of the pilots spent their routine flights practising LLOLPIs [low-level over land practice intercepts], 1 *v* 1,1 *v* 2 or 2 *v* 2 ACT [air combat training] or routine medium- to high-level head-on intercepts know as 'randoms'. Intercepting Bears, Badgers and Bisons was one thing, but occasionally intercepting ships was not unprecedented. On one occasion, when responding to a QRA scramble, and an 'almost' intercept that had evaporated at over 150 nm away when the targets turned back to Murmansk, after hanging around for a while we shortly after carried out what was to prove an unnecessary AAR and were sent home by the fighter controllers. However, there had been some interest in two Soviet vessels that were cruising just off the coast of Scotland, and we were tasked to approach from behind the hills, so they couldn't see us coming, and take some low-level photos.
>
> So assuming we were doing around 480-500 kts, i.e. at around 8 nm per minute, for a vessel only 3½ miles off the coast, it would give them less than a minute's notice before we pitched up with our camera. I cannot recall the reason, but the USAF exchange officer in the rear ended up using his own camera with colour film rather than the RAF issued B&W camera; hence the photos looked a little different, inasmuch as the red decks showed up a bit better than on the standard old B&W photos. Unfortunately, questions were asked about the height we flew past to get the photos, but thankfully the years dim the memory of the resultant inquiry by the killjoys and the grown-ups.

Another officer who later qualified for the coveted 10 Bear badge, and who later commanded 228 OCU, was John Walmsley. He had a fair tally of Bear and other Soviet long-range aircraft intercepts, not to mention a few others besides.

John Walmsley's log of intercepts while serving on 43 Squadron at Leuchars reads:

Tail Gunners' position on the TU-95 Bear, taken on 12 March 1982. (*Paul Warren*)

111 Sqn Phantom 9-ship formation, put together to celebrate the Squadron's 70th Anniversary in 1987. (*Michael Clarke*)

Sep 13 83	2 × Badger D, 2 × F-16
Oct 5 83	1 × Bear E, 1 × Bear A
Mar 3 84	2 × Bear D
Mar 5 84	2 × Bear D
Mar 6 84	1 × Bear A, 1 × Bear E, 1 × May, 1 × Sea Harrier
Mar 7 84	2 × Bear D, 1 × Orion
Jul 11 84	1 × Bear B, 1 × Bear C
Jan 16 84	2 × F-14, Mediterranean Sea

23 Sqn Mount Pleasant

| Jun 13 86 | 1 × Elint 707 (Argentinian), Falkland Islands |

My most memorable Q scramble was the 6 March 1984 one with my nav 'Ned' Kelly. We intercepted a formation of one Bear A and one Bear E which we shared with an RN Sea Harrier. Eventually the Victor tanker had to leave and topped us up to full before he did. So there we were in the Iceland/Faeroes gap with three full external tanks, and Saxa Vord GCI said that we could continue to shadow the Bears to the 'prudent limit of our endurance'. I decided that we would escort them all the way to North Cape (to prove a point), which would still have left us with tons of fuel, probably handing them over to Norwegian F-16s and then returning to Leuchars.

By this flight I already had earned my 10 Bear badge, but this put Ned up only to nine. He remarked that with his luck he would probably never see another one and not get his badge. However, as we headed up the coast of Norway with our two Bears, with the radar in standby mode, some electronic noise appeared on the scope just right of the nose. Always inquisitive, we switched on the radar and saw a moderate-sized blip on a reciprocal heading about 4 miles displaced to starboard. The size of the blip meant that it was probably not a Norwegian F-16 which had been my first guess. At the appropriate range I executed a sharp 180-degree turn to the right, we turned off the radar transmitter and rolled out in formation with the unknown aircraft. To our delight it was yet another Soviet aircraft, this time a military version of the Coot airliner, known to NATO as a Coot-A. The Coot-A was a dedicated strategic Elint/reconnaissance aircraft fitted with side-looking radar, cameras and other optical sensors [the Soviet equivalent of the USAF Boeing RC-135]. Ned was over the moon, since the Soviets had handed him his 10th Bear [the Coot also counted for the badge] on a plate; this was probably the easiest QRA interception ever! We shadowed him down towards Saxa Vord, then broke away and returned happy to Leuchars, completing a 5 hour 20 minute QRA sortie. It was almost as if the Soviets were using the same line on the map for the day's flying effort. Perhaps we should have named their impromptu airway as 'RED ONE!'

John Walmsley flew Lightnings with 5 Squadron initially and then converted to Phantoms for much of his flying career. His last flying tour was as OC 228 OCU/64 Squadron at Leuchars.

In addition to numerous detachments (and weather diversions) to Leuchars, I served as OC 'A' Flight and deputy squadron commander on 43 Sqn from '83 to '86 (serving under Harry Drew, Tony Bagnall and Al Winkles). My command of 64 Sqn was relatively short, from '89 to early '91, as the unit was closed down (with only six weeks' notice) right at the start of the air war in Iraq1.

Barry Mayner was back on 43 Squadron, having returned to Leuchars after a tour on the Phantom in Germany:

On Saturday 5 September 1985, I was on QRA at Leuchars with a newly qualified first tour pilot—Tony Andrews. This was Tony's first day on QRA. We had taken over our aircraft at 0830Z. At 0900Z we were standing on the apron in the sunshine going over the best way to get airborne if we were scrambled.

1987 encounter over the Outer Hebrides. (*Barry G. Mayner*)

Our discourse was rudely interrupted by the scramble hooter and the Q-shed doors started to open, the Q2 crew ran out of the domestic area and we passed them as we headed for our aircraft 'R' XV579. We checked in with Wing Ops and the Buchan controller came on line and gave us our scramble instructions and airborne time.

At 0920Z we lifted off and set heading towards the Benbecula area to rendezvous with a tanker out of Marham.

The Victor 2 had been scrambled earlier for his transit north. We refuelled to full as soon as possible and set off north-west to find the Bears. The Russians had routed through the Iceland/Faeroes gap and we joined up about 200 miles west of Benbecula. Before leaving the cover of Benbecula Radar we were instructed to fly to PLE [prudent limit of endurance] with the Bears. Our tanker had also been refuelled by a second Victor who had followed up from Marham. This was a new event for us as this procedure had not been discussed or anticipated.

The two Bears, 19 and 35, were heading 210 (SW) at the correct height for the heading and in a loose offset trail of about 2 miles. The FG1 Phantom was not equipped with HF radio, so we were soon dependent on the Victor for communications back to Buchan. Also the FG1 navigation equipment was far from ideal for the area we were entering. I asked the Victor to provide me with an accurate position every 15 minutes to keep me up to date.

We were 220 miles west of Shannon, still heading 210 and in formation with the trail Bear, when I noticed that the moon was behind the Bear's wing and decided to take a couple of pictures. As I was looking through the camera viewfinder and asking Tony to fly with the moon on the Bear's wingtip I was aware that a contrail had appeared in the viewfinder. I took two frames quickly and then looked up at the aircraft making the trail. It was Concorde—the BA morning flight from Heathrow to Washington.

Some time later, as we approached 45 degrees North latitude and 18 degrees West longitude, we were advised by the tanker that he could fill us to full one more time and would then have to return to Marham.

I decided that Tony and I would stay with the tanker and head back towards the UK and talk to Predannack Radar as soon as possible to request further instructions. We were told to maintain an east/west racetrack 50 miles south-west of the Scilly Isles. Later we were cleared to return to Leuchars and a pair of Lightnings and another Victor were scrambled to take over. We landed back at Leuchars 7 hours and 35 minutes after take-off, having circumnavigated Ireland.

This was a one-off sortie, and I am not aware that anyone else has done it. [It is possible that Dave Nelson and Steve Green flew a similar sortie a few years earlier, but I have no details.] I made enquiries later and found out that our Bears had visited the sea trials of the latest American super-carrier, *Dwight D. Eisenhower*, and then landed in Cuba.

The decision to proceed was made by Wg Cdr Joan Hopkins, the OC Operations at RAF Buchan. I had known Joan for many years during my tours in the ground radar world.

During 228 OCU's second reincarnation at Leuchars, the mantle of providing the F-4 Phantom solo display came about again, the unit having previously covered the requirement while at Coningsby in 1979 and 1980. In 1988, Flt Lts Chris Lackman and Jack Thompson toured across Europe demonstrating the agility of the big heavy fighter. This particular year was marred by a number of tragic and other serious incidents at air shows or during practice by display teams. Earlier in the year, one of the Red Arrows pilots ended up in hospital after an incident on take-off at RAF Scampton, and a tragic event at Ramstein involving the Italian Air Force aerobatic team, Frecce Tricolori, hit the front pages in August, sparking an unhealthy media focus on air shows, particularly in respect of military aircraft. But for Leuchars and 228 OCU, this was a particularly sad year, as Flt Lts Lackman and Thompson were both killed during an aerobatics rehearsal over RAF Abingdon on 23 September. While practising for the Battle of Britain display the next Saturday they came to grief when their Phantom struck the airfield tail-first at the bottom of a loop. Before the incident, the crew and their aircraft, XV428, had been deployed to RAF Lyneham in preparation. Both were experienced fliers and instructors, being from the staff of the OCU.

Before converting to the Phantom, Chris Lackman had seen service during Operation 'Corporate' in the Falkland Islands. He had both the Vulcan and the Lightning under his belt. His navigator, Jack Thompson, had served on 44 (Rhodesia) Squadron, flying Vulcans from Waddington before making the leap to the world of the fast jet and the F-4 in 1978, serving with 19 and 23 Squadrons. Chris Lackman transferred in 1983, and after the OCU course served with 43 and 23 Squadrons. The subsequent report into the fatal incident determined that:

The aircraft was well to the right of the crowd centre after completing a 360 degree hard turn since no allowance appeared to have been made for the strong wind. It was seen to roll out of the turn and immediately enter a very hard pull-up using full reheat. As it approached the top of the loop, the aircraft appeared to be slower and lower than usual and, at the apex, it was seen to fly in the inverted position for several seconds; the pilot appeared to be 'pushing' and maintaining level flight. During the second half of the loop, the initial pitch rate to the vertical appeared slow, and at the vertical the aircraft was alarmingly low. From there on, the pull became increasingly hard and some wing rock occurred. Just before impact the aircraft achieved a nose-up attitude of 10-15 degrees but with a massive rate of descent. The crew were killed in the impact.

An experienced Phantom pilot noted:

They were caught out by the strong wind and tried to compensate for this by delaying the second half of the loop, flying inverted to move across to the crowd centre. This was fraught with danger, irrespective of whether they achieved sufficient height for the second half of the loop. I suspect that they achieved the correct minimum height since the navigator would have monitored the peak altitude very closely. Flying inverted, to maintain height requires a push of minus 1 g; the aircraft would be at slow speed and minus 1 g which is not easily achieved at slow speed. Thus it could have been descending, losing valuable altitude. The second result of this manoeuvre is the delay in rotation rate to enter the second half of the loop [as mentioned in the MoD report]. Normally at the top of a loop an aircraft is continually rotating in the vertical and if you stop the rotation, the restart of rotation will lose precious altitude, compounding the problem. At the vertical it was all over, the aircraft

Chris Lackman and Jack Thompson get airborne in style, 17 September 1988, to provide the finale to the 1988 airshow. (*Fergal Goodman*)

was too low, and no matter how hard you pull the end result is the same. The wing rock indicated that the pilot knew of his dilemma and gave it his best without departing from controlled flight. Tragically his best was insufficient for him to pull out in time. The navigator would have had to hope that the hard pull would work, and just before impact he would not have achieved a safe ejection with such a high descent rate.

Following the incident, the RAF suspended displays by Phantom aircraft until a review of display parameters had been completed. Individual aerobatics in the Phantom resumed in 1990, with the minimum height for the top of a loop being raised to 6,000 feet. That year the OCU again provided the solo aerobatic display, with Flt Lts Steve Howard and Nige Marks.

9

The Tornado Years, Cold War Thaw

Of the two squadrons at Leuchars in early 1989, 43 Squadron was the first to disband, in July, in preparation to be the first to receive the Tornado F3 in September. No. 111 Squadron stood down shortly after in order to begin re-forming on the Tonka (the nickname for the Tornado) from early 1990, in accordance with long-term planning. Soon to become surplus to requirements was 228 OCU, the inevitable 'Options for Change' review concluding that in order to comply with the limitations imposed by the Treaty on Conventional Armed Forces in Europe now in place, existing older airframes should logically bear the brunt. This in turn presaged the rapid rundown of the remaining F-4 units, leaving the Tornado F3 as the RAF's sole air defence fighter for the foreseeable future. Certainly, the shift toward downsizing could not be described as heel-dragging. By April 1993, the last of the F-4s were gone, the last having left Leuchars by January 1991.

And so, on 23 September 1989, there was an added attraction to the annual Battle of Britain air show. On this occasion the station received its first two pristine, factory-fresh Panavia Tornado F3s in 43 Squadron markings. Both aircraft arrived in gin-clear weather at 3.30 p.m. and taxied in front of the VIP enclosure. In the rear cockpit of the lead aircraft was the squadron's new commanding officer, Wg Cdr Andy Moir (he of the famous encounter with the nurse at Ely following his short-notice exit from a Phantom in 1977). His pilot on this auspicious occasion was Sqn Ldr Jim Davidson, who had flown the Phantom on 43 Squadron previously and had subsequently flown the Tornado GR1 with 617 Squadron before returning to the air defence world and converting to the F3. The other aircraft taxiing in before the crowd was piloted by Sqn Ldr Nick Willey, a veteran of the Lightning, and his navigator, Sqn Ldr Ken Thompson, another former Phantom man. Jim Davidson and Ken Thompson were, respectively, the squadron's first appointed commanders of 'A' and 'B' Flights.

The arrival of the F3 at Leuchars took place before the revolution that brought down the Berlin Wall. Leuchars was the last station in line for the planned replacement, the plan at the time being to work up seven squadrons in total but retaining four squadrons of Phantoms—two at Wattisham and two at Wildenrath. However, the 'Fighting Cocks' were scarcely up to strength with their allotted complement of F3s when a sad and poignant task befell them. This was to provide a flypast at the funeral of a former squadron CO, Air Vice-Marshal George Lott, who had passed away on 31 December. At the funeral on 9 January 1990, a single Tornado F3, flown by Sqn Ldr Davidson with Wg Cdr Moir in the navigator's seat, flew overhead as the coffin was lowered.

Back in 1975, the Standing Committee formed to review the concept of the air defence variant of what was still the MRCA had felt doubtful that the idea was prudent even then, given the confines of NATO's new strategy of flexible response at the time. That there was a need for a new air defence aircraft to replace the Lightning and Phantom was not in doubt, and there was also no doubt that the ADV, with its lack of 'stretch' and relatively lacklustre performance, was seen in some ways as inferior to the American aircraft that would be available at about the same time that the ADV would be delivered to the RAF. It was therefore not seen as the preferred military option, were the RAF to be given a choice with impunity.

However, as is always the case when British defence choices are made, financial and political advantages had at least to be outweighed by the ADV's shortcomings before a different course could be followed. Bearing in mind just how subjective a goal this would be immediately places matters clearly in perspective. To this end, the Under-Secretary of State for Air regarded the performance of competing aircraft to be, at best, only marginally superior. Alas, while objecting on other grounds, the idea of, for example, having F-15s based at Leuchars or elsewhere was outranked ultimately by adherence to financial, political and industrial concerns. Of greatest concern was the damage that would be done to the international consortium building the MRCA, and to the likelihood of any other independently produced European combat aircraft, plus the additional cost of £2-£3 billion, even with the most favourable terms with the Americans. There was also a third alternative, which was to limit the number of Tornados to the lowest acceptable level, whatever that might be.

Indeed, the projected performance of what became the Tornado F3 was so poor that, as far back as 1975, demands were being made that the proposed replacement for the Harrier and Jaguar 'must have an adequate air combat capability, to balance the relative ineffectiveness of the MRCA ADV in this respect'. So, despite what has been said in defence of the Tornado F2/3 at the time of its inauguration into RAF service, it was accepted, to some degree at least, that a high-agility fighter was still desirable, if only in the mainland European theatre. Yes, it was a long-range interceptor with all-weather capability, but an air combat fighter? Did it need to be? Yes, it did, if it was to be relied upon outside of chasing Bears and Badgers from Leuchars.

Interestingly, the then Chief of the Air Staff, Sir Andrew Humphrey, felt that the ADV could meet the principal elements of the threat, and that while other aircraft might be able to carry out some tasks more effectively, none could counter the whole range of possible threats. He was very much of the opinion that the weight of air defence expenditure—indeed, the bulk of resources—should go on the production of fighter aircraft, in an almost reciprocal position to the Sandys air defence policy of 1957, which had done so much to emasculate UK air defences at that time by regarding surface-to-air missiles as nothing more than complementary to the manned fighter, rather than the other way round. However, Sir Andrew also believed that the introduction of what he saw as a specialised force of aircraft at the expense of the total number of ADVs would not be realistic. Furthermore, the planned 165 ADV Tornados were seen as the absolute minimum and, interestingly, it was felt that cancelling them in favour of anything American, in part or in whole, would bring about the collapse of the entire MRCA programme.

While 43 Squadron was working up to operational readiness with the pointy, pale grey Tonkas, 111 Squadron soldiered on for a few more months with the Phantom, flying the last F-4 sortie on 25 January 1990, before it too disbanded to re-form on the Tornado. The collapse of the Berlin Wall, which precipitated the end of the Cold War, was a real game-changer. Almost overnight, the routine incursions into UK airspace by Soviet Badgers, Bears and Bison stopped. As early as 1990, by the time the first of the F3s were operationally ready at Leuchars, the rate of incursions into Britain's Northern Sector had reduced considerably.

The next steps taken by the UK Government, among others, was to determine just what kind of defence posture would be justifiable in the coming years. The review that followed was to settle what the requirement would be in the long term, and as far as the RAF was concerned, it occurred to those charged with the responsibility that any remaining old airframes should be got rid of where duplication could be identified. This put two aircraft from the frontline inventory in the firing line: the Buccaneer and the Phantom. These would go, and the defence of UK airspace would rest on the now fully deployed Tornado ADV.

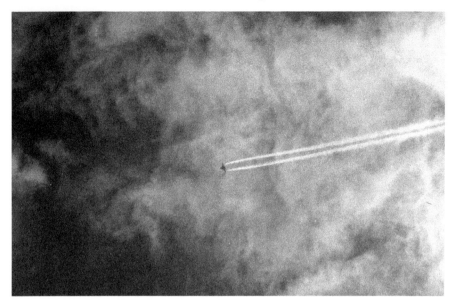

Fl Lt's Steve Howard and Nigel Marks disappear vertically over Finningley, 50th Anniversary Battle of Britain airshow, before returning to display over the homestead, 22 September 1990. (*Author's Collection*)

However, no sooner had the Cold War begun to thaw than problems started to materialise elsewhere. In July 1990, the month in which the details of the 'Options for Change' defence review were announced, President Saddam Hussein of Iraq invaded neighbouring Kuwait. Although few would have thought it at the time, this was to be the start of a new age of conflict. Within days of the Kuwait invasion, an Allied taskforce led by the US began a build-up in Saudi Arabia on a scale not seen on the world stage since the Second World War. Among the first RAF contingent as part of Operation 'Granby' were Tornado F3s from Leuchars.

Aircraft and crews from Coningsby-based 29 Squadron deployed initially and were later joined by crews and aircraft from 43 Squadron, but the perceived shortcomings of the Tornado F3 influenced the decision on just how the aircraft were deployed in theatre. All F3s were assigned to a purely defensive posture in relation to Saudi airspace, such was the fear that their alleged relatively sluggish performance at altitude would find them wanting. This did nothing for the reputation of what was very shortly to be the RAF's only defence fighter. Just how the F3 would have acquitted itself will remain forever a matter for conjecture given the absence of Iraqi fighters during the conflict, almost certainly on the orders of the President, whose concern about and appreciation of the overwhelming weight of the Allied air forces was by no means misplaced.

The immediate post-Cold War era did produce a positive result for the air show enthusiast, as the newly founded good relations between East and West meant that Soviet and other Warsaw Pact military aircraft were no longer prevented by political disagreement from appearing at events in the UK. To this end, the Soviet Air Force aerobatic team, the Russian Knights, made their only appearance in the UK, in September 1991. Flying six Sukhoi Su-27/30 Flanker fighter aircraft, the team arrived at Leuchars against the backdrop of a possible reversal of the political ground gained so far. An attempted military coup in Moscow had taken place just prior to the event, threatening to reverse the new climate of international relations. As it happened, the coup failed and the goodwill visit of the Russian Knights went ahead, the display team providing a most impressive highlight to the Battle of Britain displays at both Leuchars and Finningley that year.

The continuing round of defence cuts meant a notable reduction at Leuchars. The RAF Regiment Rapier Squadron, No. 27, was set to move, and the F-4 Phantom OCU, now surplus to requirements, was of course gone. Some may think it ironic that at a time when the RAF was going to war in earnest on a bigger scale than at any time since Suez, defence cuts, and quite substantial ones at that, were being pressed ahead with.

A little-debated point was that increasingly the whole rationale of Leuchars as a quick-response fighter station was harder to justify to the layman, and at least one senior military figure questioned the wisdom of having a Northern fighter force ready to race toward the Arctic Circle to meet intruding bombers bearing red stars when that now seemed unlikely. One very senior Army officer, the Director of Defence Programme Staff, was invited to Leuchars to meet personnel and experience a trip in a Tornado and despite being impressed with the professionalism of the aircrew, he left Leuchars no more convinced of the need for quite so many fighter aircraft of this level of performance. With Russian long-range patrol/reconnaissance bombers now almost non-existent, it was getting harder to make the case.

Once the implications of the defence review 'Front Line First' had been applied, matters settled only for a short while, as history has now proved. With every subsequent defence review, the RAF has faced further significant cuts, specifically to the frontline fleet, with the addition of piecemeal trims in between. However, life continued for a time as it otherwise had at what was still the home of the Northern QRA, Tornado F3s of 43 Squadron taking part in a reinforcement exercise to Norway entitled 'Strong Resolve' in February 1995. This also involved Harriers and Tornado GR1s, and had the whiff of a typical Cold War exercise. Later, in June that year, the Cold War-era TACEVAL exercise returned, having been suspended as far as RAF

An historic milestone, Sukhoi SU-27 Flankers of the 'Russian Knights' aerobatics team from the Soviet Air Force, seen here on the flightline, 21 September 1991. (*Colin Lourie*)

111 Sqn Tornado F3 shadows a TU-95 Bear, this time under more agreeable circumstances, and rare sight during the F3 era, they were both *en route* to the International Air Tattoo at Fairford, July 1993. (*Peter R. March*)

squadrons were concerned due to greater demands of operational flying during the Gulf War of 1991, in which 43 Squadron played a significant part. Since then, no-fly zones over the Balkans and Iraq have also made use of RAF and other fighter units. Rather than reducing, the demands on military air operations in the post-war era have, with some irony, at least remained constant and perhaps become more stretched, given the continued severe rounds of cuts.

On 30 October 1995, two of 43 Squadron's F3s suffered a mid-air collision some miles east of Leuchars during an exercise requiring the practice of visual identification. As one aircraft approached the other from the rear, difficulty in seeing the aircraft in front in time resulted in a nose-to-tail collision. One F3 crew, Flt Lts Kevin McCarry and John Booth, were forced to eject but were later picked up by an SAR Sea King from RAF Boulmer (Leuchars having lost its SAR Flight in 1993). The other crew managed to limp back to Leuchars and had to wait 40 minutes while the ground crew removed the cockpit canopy.

The advantage of flying the same aircraft in the same role between units co-located at a single air base allowed for inter-squadron co-operation, once the rivalry, banter and occasional open war between them was pushed aside. From 1975 to 2009, Nos 43 and 111 Squadrons enjoyed such mutual support due to operating the same or similar types, first with the Phantom and then with the Tornado F3. This allowed personnel from one squadron—left behind while most of their unit headed off on exercise, or increasingly since the 1990s, to support operations overseas—to supplement the other unit in residence and help fulfil whatever flying programme they were seeking to achieve, including QRA.

Back to the ceremonial, and on 30 November 1996, the Stone of Destiny, the coronation stone of Scottish kings, was returned to Edinburgh Castle from Westminster Abbey in London. Although it did not seem so at the time, there was another issue stirring that could yet have long-term implications for the defence structure of the UK—that of Scottish independence.

As part of the day's ceremonies, it had been planned for a formation of four Scottish-based RAF jets to perform a flypast as the stone passed through the outer portcullis of the castle, which is framed on either side by the statues of William Wallace and Robert the Bruce. In order to keep the affair as Caledonian as possible, the formation was crewed entirely by Scotsmen, almost all coming from 43 Squadron, flying Tornado F3s ZE342, ZE207, ZE834 and ZE296. The formation was led by the Leuchars OC Ops and Deputy Station Commander, Gp Capt. David Hamilton (in order to meet the requirement for an all-Scottish formation) with Sqn Ldr Allan Goodison as his navigator. After the castle flypast, 'Braveheart Formation' flew on over Turnhouse Airport, the Forth Bridges (the backdrop for many formations of Leuchars fighters down the years) and then on to St Andrews before heading back out over the North Sea on routine training. In all, the sortie lasted 90 minutes.

The formation was made up as follows:

1. ZE342—Gp Capt. David Hamilton and Sqn Ldr Allan Goodison;
2. ZE207—Flt Lts Sandy Gordon and Gary Dunlop;
3. ZE834—Flt Lt Ian McCombie and Sq Ldr 'Mac' McNeil-Matthews;
4. ZE296—Flt Lt Simon Clark and Sqn Ldr Keith Cowieson.

World affairs were starting to have a more noticeable effect on the station and its routine, the conflict in the Balkans having seen Leuchars squadrons once again called upon to deploy overseas. But operations in Iraq and Kosovo permitting, more time was now being spent on training to meet a wider range of possible operational scenarios. One such exercise, in November 1997, involved eight Leuchars-based Tornado F3s acting as aggressors in an attempt to attack a target on the North Sea coast defended by Tornado F3s from RAF Leeming. During the simulated attack, some aircraft exceeded the speed of sound, and at quite low level, resulting in a subsequent investigation following the auto-shutdown of Hartlepool nuclear power station.

With the arrival of the new millennium, planning for the 60th anniversary Battle of Britain display was afoot, although the event was nearly cancelled at very short notice. It was all the more significant, given that Leuchars was now the sole station to host such an event primarily commemorating the success and sacrifice of 'The Few'. That it took place at all was something of a miracle, as it coincided with a display of public disaffection with government fuel policy. Blockades of fuel distribution centres across the country meant that many engaged in panic buying of fuel, which in turn brought about a shortage of fuel and long queues of motorists—whether in desperate need or merely hoarding what they could. Despite this, the good folk of Scotland and visitors from near and far were treated to a flying display that would have done the Royal International Air Tattoo proud.

The following year, the air show was under threat of short-notice cancellation once again. This time, just four days before it was due to take place, at shortly after 2 p.m. the British people were having brought to their attention early reports of events in America of one of the most tragic and historically defining moments in history. It was 11 September 2001, the day when two hijacked airliners were flown into the twin towers of New York's World Trade Center, one more was flown into the Pentagon, and a fourth, believed hijacked as part of the same operation, was brought down before it could reach its intended target.

The phrase 'The world will never be the same again' is too lightly used, but on this occasion it was a perfectly fitting one. The US Government placed that country on a war footing and flights in and out were suspended, and amidst this maelstrom of events it appeared that such a trivial matter as an air show would not figure as being of any importance. No other country, including the UK, could see the rationale for preparing for all-out conflict, but the security situation was certainly tense and brought added concerns about the safety of military bases. This posed something of a dilemma, but matters were dealt with in a measured fashion. So, while the air show planned for the following Saturday was subject to renewed security concerns, nothing beyond what had already been arranged was seen as indispensable. There was undoubtedly the question of just how comfortable everyone was with pressing on under the circumstances, but the decision was ultimately taken to go ahead with the event. The tragedy of what has long since been referred to as 9/11 was recognised during the afternoon, with a one-minute silence observed by about 50,000 people.

Terrorism had not normally been seen as a concern for those charged with defending national airspace from attack, but following 9/11 the relevance of the manned interceptor gave much needed justification for the maintenance of round-the-clock QRA when it became clear just how devastating a hijacked airliner could be in the age of the suicide bomber. This is the nature of defence posture—it is not about preparing for certainty, but preparing for any conceivable possibility.

The response to the 9/11 attack, as we know only too well through no end of inquiries instigated mainly to examine the conduct of the Prime Minister and others, was to launch an invasion of Afghanistan in 2001, and Iraq in 2003, the latter largely in response to dubious claims that Saddam Hussein was harbouring Weapons of Mass Destruction (WMD). The invasion of Iraq became the second Gulf War, and air defence operations over Saudi airspace were again contributed to by the Leuchars Wing just as during Operation 'Granby' in 1990/91. On this occasion, 111 Squadron led the deployment.

Leuchars-based squadrons had been involved in a large number of operations between the first and second Gulf Wars—whether as part of Operation 'Southern Watch', requiring combat air patrols over southern Iraq, or patrolling Bosnian airspace, or undertaking operations over Kosovo—but the terror attacks of 9/11 placed an even greater demand on air defence units and were to have long-term consequences. The manner in which those attacks were carried out caused such concern that during the Olympic Games in 2012, Typhoons were deployed to RAF Northolt in the suburbs of west London. (While it was home to Hurricane squadrons during the Battle of Britain, it is a most unlikely modern fighter base, surrounded by the metropolis of Greater London.) In addition, a further demand on the Leuchars Wing in recent times has seen routine deployments, with other NATO interceptor squadrons, to Lithuania. Since the Baltic state's entry into NATO, responsibility for its defence has been continuously managed under this arrangement. The case for maintaining high-performance fighter aircraft at an immediate state of readiness is therefore finding some justification again.

Recently, the SNP MP Angus Robertson asked how many times fighters had been scrambled in response to approaches by Russian military aircraft. The figures for the years 2010, 2011 and 2012 were eleven, ten and eight scrambles respectively—nothing like the 1970s and '80s, but an increase, if only marginal, on the 1990s. In addition, scrambles to intercept airliners indicating some problem or distress have, since 9/11, attracted the attention of the media. However, whatever the justification for the continued presence, contraction has continued, with the UK-based interceptor force of nine squadrons in 1990 down to five in 2001. By 2005, it was down to three, with two squadrons based at Leuchars and one at Leeming. Coningsby was in the process of preparing to train the first operational Typhoon pilots at this time, the Operational Evaluation and Conversion Units at BAE Warton later moving to the Lincolnshire base. The future held considerable promise for Leuchars at this point, the base having long been earmarked to become the second of what was expected to be three Typhoon bases by the end of the decade or soon after.

During 2003, when 56 Reserve Squadron, the Tornado F3 OCU, moved up from Coningsby, it brought a further 300 RAF personnel to the station. Leuchars also became a base for 137 military personnel, deployed under Operation 'Fresco', which was the military response to the firefighters' strike. In addition to this, aircraft were deployed from time to time on Operation 'Resonate', this being the continued policing of the airspace over southern Iraq, and Tornado F3 crews were flying missions totalling sixteen hours a day under Operation 'Telic'. Some crews were flying sorties that put them aloft for as long as eight hours, supported of course by in-flight refuelling.

However, the lack of any kind of reaction by the Iraqi Air Force resulted in the Leuchars Tornado F3 deployment and associated personnel returning home from 11 April 2003, although other station personnel were required to remain. Among those who did were personnel from 612 (County of Aberdeen) RAAF Squadron, whose volunteer personnel provide emergency surgical and other medical services, an RAF version of the 4077th MASH. One of their members, Sqn Ldr Gavin McCallum, was personally credited with saving the lives of six people and was presented with the Sir Andrew Humphrey Memorial Medal. The six had all been wounded when the Chinook helicopter they were being flown in was shot at. Sqn Ldr McCallum's fortitude was all the more admirable, as he continued working after receiving a gunshot wound.

Despite the heavy reliance on a comprehensive range of military personnel and equipment, the Treasury axe fell heavily again. This time, the remainder of the Jaguar fleet was chopped from the RAF's dwindling battle order, leading to the closure of another venerable old RAF station, Coltishall in Norfolk. However, the review had no immediate impact on Leuchars, which by now housed the largest concentration of interceptor aircraft in the RAF, although any optimism for the future was misplaced. The promised arrival of the Typhoon fighter was not yet in doubt, but it was quite clear that it would form a larger chunk of a much smaller air force. As far as Leuchars was concerned, this brought about an immediate restructuring of the resident University Air Squadrons camped at the base. Aberdeen, St Andrews and East Lothian squadrons were amalgamated to form the East of Scotland Universities Air Squadron.

In 2007, when the runway at Leuchars was again resurfaced, the secondary cross-runway was in use by the resident Tornados for as long as possible before the three home-based units dispersed to their bolthole airfields.

56 Sqn aircrew prior to fly their own disbandment flypast on 18 April 2008, just 17 days after the RAF's 90th Birthday. (*MOD/Crown copyright*)

All were back in 2008, but 56 Squadron was due to stand down as a precursor to the eventual retirement of the Tornado. The next expected step was for the first Typhoons to take up station, but before this could happen the delivery rate of the new fighters was slowed, partly as a result of the diversion of seventy-two aircraft to Saudi Arabia. A further saving was accrued by accelerating the rundown of the Tornado ADV force. By 2009, Leuchars had gained the distinction of being the last operational base for the 'Flying Scissors', as far as the interceptor role is concerned, of course. Coningsby, by now operational with the Typhoon, deployed the first two squadrons, at least notionally, as multi-role or rather swing-role squadrons.

Further piecemeal defence cutting ahead of the arrival of the Eurofighter Typhoon affected Leuchars once again. This time it was the unit with the greatest affinity with station and the local area, 43 Squadron, that was facing premature disbandment. The news was compounded by tragedy only some ten days before the official ceremony, when two of the squadron's members were lost on a training sortie in Tornado F3 ZE942. The pilot, Flt Lt Kenneth Thompson, and his navigator, Flt Lt Nigel Morton, were lost on 2 July 2009, and the squadron's official disbandment ceremony went ahead under this cloud on Monday 13 July.

The promise at the time was that the 'Fighting Cocks' would live again, equipped with the Typhoon, but as of 2013, this was yet to happen, and those tasked with determining the unit identity and make-up of Britain's military followed instead the precedent of retaining the oldest squadron numbers with the longest consecutive active history, save for those with a particularly distinguished background. There is only one squadron that has truly enjoyed this distinction—617, the 'Dambusters'—therefore, the fifth operational Typhoon squadron, recently formed, bears the insignia of No. 2 Squadron. This unit was previously operational with Tornado GR4s at RAF Marham.

As a result of these far-reaching cutbacks, squadrons with a more recognisable fighter pedigree, including many that served at Leuchars, have almost all disappeared. Sadly, their distinct squadron markings no longer adorn the RAF's frontline interceptor fighters: the unique black and white checkerboards of the 'Fighting Cocks', 43 Squadron; the yellow-edged black lightning flashes of the 'Black Arrows', 111 Squadron; the tessellating light orange and black triangles of the 'Tigers', 74 Squadron; the red and white checkerboards of the 'Firebirds', 56 Squadron; and the red and blue alternating bars of the 'Red Eagles', 23 Squadron. All of these have operated from Leuchars in the past fifty years, and in the last fifteen have disappeared, with little hope that any future fighter in RAF service will carry their markings again.

9 Tornado F3s, all from the Leuchars wing, photographed on 11 July 2008, they were taking part in the RAF's 90th Anniversary Royal Review flypast before HM Queen Elizabeth II at RAF Fairford, the formation comprises four aircraft each from 43 (Black & White checks on fins), 111 Sqn (Yellow Lightning Flash on fins) and one from 56 r Sqn (Red & White checks on fin). (*Peter R. March*)

23 June 2007, 111 'Tremblers' celebrate their 90th Birthday with invited guests inside one of the HAS. Note the model Hunters used to re-created the famous 22 strong Pterodactyl loop performed over Farnborough in September 1958. (*MOD/Crown copyright*)

On 11 September 2010, 6 Squadron officially formed on the Eurofighter Typhoon FGR4, on the occasion of the annual Battle of Britain air show. A considerable effort was made by the base personnel and others, to a degree that is just not seen at such events any longer. The last remaining F3 squadron, No. 111, provided a four-ship formation, and the new squadron's stand-up ceremony was graced, somewhat ironically, with a flypast by a Spitfire, a Tornado F3 and a Typhoon, billed as 'Past, Present and Future'. In keeping with the Leuchars air show's retention of past traditions, the sunset ceremony was held with marching pipes and drums before the Station Commander and Air Officer Scotland, Air Cdre R. J. 'Harry' Atkinson, all culminating in a low-level, high-speed run by a Tornado and a Typhoon of the resident squadrons, the Tiffy carrying on into the sunset while the Tonka pulled up to the vertical and disappeared into the stratus. The end of an era!

10

Defence and Security Review, Typhoon and the Future

The official formation of 6 Squadron at Leuchars on the Typhoon was, some might say, long overdue. The previous five years had seen a radical shift in the way that the new Typhoons assumed the role of their predecessors, which essentially boiled down to two existing types: the Tornado F3 in the air defence role, and the Jaguar force. Usually the transition from old to new was seamless, but the takeover by the Typhoons from the older two jets was piecemeal, to put it as fairly as possible.

Ordinarily, a squadron with an air defence pedigree would have been a more likely selection, but what most people would not have understood was that, even in those pre-SDSR days, the long-term plan was already for far fewer frontline operational squadrons on the RAF's inventory than was even evident from the 2004 review. Therefore, the earliest numbers were being allocated to form on the new aircraft, while later numbers with a longer line of antecedent air defence fighter types were facing disbandment. Instead, 6 Squadron appeared as the first Leuchars-based Tiffy unit, a former close air support squadron whose nickname, the 'Flying Tin Openers', was earned during its service in the Western Desert and Mediterranean campaigns where it was heavily employed flying tactical offensive air sorties against German armour. Hence the moniker that was adopted and maintained, along with the ground attack role, through the post-war era. The squadron had the luxury of being largely able to maintain this unbroken history with successive tactical fighter or bomber types in the past—Canberras in Cyprus, and then Phantoms, before no fewer than thirty-three years of operating the Jaguar!

Also known as 'Shiny Six', the squadron had originally formed on 31 January 1914 at Farnborough, so was a truly venerable unit, pre-dating the outbreak of the First World War. Like the previous Leuchars residents, 11 Squadron, it had spent most of its existence overseas before re-forming at Coningsby as the RAF's first operational Phantom squadron in 1969. Now, as of July 2010, having been disbanded since 2007 (the only period in history when it did not form part of the RAF orbit, either forming or formed), it was working up to strength as the service's third operational Eurofighter Typhoon squadron, with the first of the Tranche 2 aircraft. Their destination, as was clearly the long-term plan, was Leuchars.

As matters stood, Leuchars was still on course to operate three frontline Typhoon squadrons, the infrastructure at the station having been prepared at some expense in anticipation of this. The squadron was officially formed at Leuchars on 11 September 2010, having arrived over the preceding weeks with its brand-new Typhoon FGR4s, already bearing the squadron's light blue bars containing the zigzag red emulating the pattern on the back of an adder and with the now traditional winged can-opener on the fin.

However, the new government's SDSR was not too far away. Rumours were already rife, but the idea of Leuchars, or the planned build-up of the Typhoon Wing, falling into the Treasury's cross-hairs was not expected. When it came, the axe initially fell elsewhere and, while the announced loss of two Tornado GR4 squadrons would still leave five squadrons and the GR4 OCU based equally between Lossiemouth in Moray and Marham in Norfolk, there was still a fear among the local community that Lossiemouth would be the one extra RAF base closure that the government was still seeking.

Officially, Lossiemouth also had its future spoken for at this stage, as the home of the future F-35 force. Moray is SNP heartland, and the local MP Angus Robertson is that party's spokesman on Defence. Now the mention of this is not entirely irrelevant. The response of the UK Government to the people of Lossiemouth was probably motivated not simply by visible protests and concern about the loss to the economy but also by the need to prevent the area becoming a more significant anti-Union thorn in its flesh, agitated by media coverage. No sooner had the SDSR initial findings been published than the local populace of Lossiemouth—without any seeming cause, but clearly spooked by the abrupt dismissal of the Nimrod MRA4, which in turn presaged the closure of RAF Kinloss—were shortly taking to marches and demonstrations, telling David Cameron and Liam Fox to keep their hands off the base. The local concerns were to a point justified. Nearby Kinloss, an unexpected casualty of SDSR, was now to close as it was surplus to requirements following the unforeseen and highly controversial decision to leave this island nation in the unique position of having no maritime patrol aircraft. Nevertheless, the local reaction seemed to spur paranoia, which was fed by the usual press reports erring towards a bleak assessment.

Clearly concerned about the situation at Lossiemouth, the government seemed to want to be seen to be doing the right thing. Not too many years before, the RAF had faced an uphill struggle trying to convince communities across the country to accept its presence on their doorsteps, especially if it meant the arrival of noisy jets. But in 2010, people were more exercised by the economic cost of losing an air base. Up until then, the idea of Leuchars no longer being an RAF station seemed about as far-fetched as the Army no longer being the official residents of Aldershot barracks.

The Army's future, post-SDSR, was that it would leave Germany, and while things had not yet been fully decided, the search for bases back home could be presented as a silver lining of sorts for the residents of Moray. That the government could have emphasised this possibility to allay the fears of the residents, but did not, remains something of a mystery. The simple logic was that if the RAF were to leave Kinloss and Lossiemouth, the Army returning from Germany would meet all economic concerns with the minimum cost by moving to both stations.

However, within days of SDSR being announced and with no further base closures revealed, people at Lossiemouth were marching to the main gates of the RAF station and lobbying the government not to close it. Very soon after, the suggestion that RAF Leuchars could close instead was mooted and quickly gathered credibility. The idea of the Army moving in anywhere was still far from settled, and the greater fear was that Leuchars could simply end up with a rusting chain padlocked around the main gates of a ghost station. This nevertheless suited the government's economic agenda which, given the now radically altered political face of Europe, enabled the remainder of the BAOR to be brought home. However, the idea of moving Army personnel to Lossiemouth did not appear to meet with much enthusiasm, so the long-term solution would be to move them to Leuchars instead. What is also undeniable, and I say this with the greatest respect to those who serve in the Army, is that the public have a wariness, always unfounded, of finding a number of boisterous, fit young men with an instilled sense of unit pride and an esprit de corps on their doorstep, which may lead to problems in town on a Friday night.

Indeed, the impending arrival of the Army at Leuchars prompted quite a reaction in some quarters, given the particular circumstances of the area. St Andrews, an unlikely garrison town, has rubbed along well with its air force neighbours over the years since the airfield first appeared and has, of course, established a link through its University Air Squadron. That apart, the Army differs from the RAF as a military service in a number of ways. Principally, the Army is more manpower-intensive, by far the greater part of which is made up of the aforementioned young men, mostly junior ranks. The typical RAF fighter squadron operates using a different balance of personnel, but the still higher ratio of junior ranks is nevertheless relatively small compared to the number of commissioned officers. All the pilots on a squadron are officers (which conveys an expectation of gentlemanly and thoughtful conduct!) while the junior ranks are, for the most part, skilled and semi-skilled tradesmen: avionics technicians, armourers, aircraft airframe and engine fitters or ATC staff, supply staff, clerks and communications/signals staff.

These points may not be well understood by the layman in detail, but the overall perception, whether justified or not, is that the RAF represents a less volatile proposition. Just before this book was published, the Army was already having to refute claims that the two communities—soldiers and students—might not get on. At the start of 2014, the local newspaper, *The Courier*, quoted an unnamed source as saying:

> We need to see how the two groups are going to mix, because there could be a clash of lifestyles. There is anecdotal evidence of what has happened at other university towns. Students and squaddies could mix like oil and water.

The Courier claimed that the above quote was officially denied but had come from sources within the local police. Apart from such claims being dismissed by the Army, with some justification, the attempts to push such concerns aside by Fife Council were not exactly wholly reassuring for the locals. However, one councillor at least, Tim Brett, who is on the Defence Transition Task Force, was quite resolute, saying:

> The Army are no different from anybody else. They've got families and children, and to suggest they are a lot of tearaways is not accurate. I don't think these suggestions are helpful … The community of Leuchars is looking forward to welcoming them.

However, St Andrews councillor Dorothea Morrison said:

> The RAF have obviously been very welcome and we hope the Army will also come into the area without any problems. I certainly hope we don't have any problems with the squaddies coming in because we do on occasions have problems with the students.

The Defence Secretary, Dr Liam Fox, had announced his decision on 18 July 2011, after some delay brought on by events to do with phone tapping by elements of the popular press. Leuchars was to become a base for what was described as two major Army units and a Brigade HQ. Interestingly, this took place while Typhoon pilots and ground crew were just returning from taking part in air attacks against the armed forces of Colonel Gaddafi in Libya. This had provided an opportunity for the Typhoons from Leuchars and Coningsby, while still to fully develop the ground attack role, to demonstrate the aircraft's ability in this regard. In all respects, the aircraft and their pilots enjoyed some success.

Under the circumstances, it may have seemed to some that the cuts were either being taken too far or could stand being held in abeyance for a while. Furthermore, 6 Squadron, now the sole occupant of Leuchars, was getting its feet under the table rather than preparing to leave as one might have expected following the announced closure of a base. In fact, it had been chosen by Air Command to provide the Typhoon solo display for the 2012 air show season, and its executive officer, Sqn Ldr Scott Loughran, was picked for the second time as the display pilot, his previous tour being in 2009 when he was an instructor on 29 Squadron(OCU) at Coningsby.

It may not seem that relevant, but additional tasks requiring such commitment are not typically given to units that are meant to be preparing for a permanent move elsewhere. This, together with unconfirmed reports that the eventual total of Typhoon squadrons could rise from five to six or even seven, produced a degree of false hope, and there was more to come when it was announced that the next and fourth operational Typhoon squadron to form was going to move to Leuchars as well. No. 1 Squadron was then, as 6 Squadron had done two years before, getting to grips with the Typhoon at Coningsby, while the aircraft it was to be issued with would follow in due course. When the first pilots of 1 Squadron arrived at Leuchars they borrowed 6 Squadron's airframes for a short time until sufficient of their own were made available. Indisputably the oldest squadron in the RAF, 1 Squadron can trace its lineage back to 1878 as a balloon unit, so it is claimed, but its history firmly holds from 1912 when it formed as No. 1 Airship Company, operating first as a naval unit before becoming the airship detachment of the RFC. It did not form with powered fixed-wing aircraft until January 1914, when it was equipped with the Avro E.

Alumni of the squadron include Col. Robin Olds of the USAF, who flew P-51 Mustangs, F-86 Sabres and F-4 Phantoms respectively in the three significant conflicts for American forces: the Second World War, Korea and Vietnam. Col. Olds served as commanding officer of 1 Squadron at Tangmere in 1948, when it flew the Meteor F4. Another alumnus is Flt Lt Alan Pollock, the first pilot to fly a jet aircraft beneath the upper span of Tower Bridge, who was serving with the squadron at the time and also flew Hunters with the 'Fighting Cocks' in Aden. So this was the next venerable RAF unit to arrive at Leuchars, albeit under less than promising circumstances for the station this time.

On what was to be the penultimate open day, 15 September 2012, the proceedings opened with four of 6 Squadron's Typhoons getting airborne to return over the top of the old Air Traffic Control Tower (one-time headquarters of 23 Squadron) and the official re-formation ceremony of 1 Squadron on the apron in front, presided over by the Chief of the Air Staff, Air Chief Marshal Sir Stephen Dalton. Later, without a hint about the future, eleven more of the based Typhoons flown by pilots of 1 and 6 Squadrons were launched, with the last two rotating into the vertical, reminiscent of the Lightning era, to bring down the curtain on what had also been billed as the official Royal Diamond Jubilee event for the RAF.

In 2013, Typhoons were scrambled from Leuchars to intercept an Egyptian Airways flight following the finding of a message on board by someone threatening to set fire to the aircraft. In the present jittery climate since 9/11, most air forces meet any indication of a hijacking of any sort by scrambling interceptors, and the Egyptian Airways aircraft was escorted by two of Leuchars' finest into Prestwick. As it was en route from Egypt to New York, it is not difficult to conclude that Leuchars was, albeit by a slender margin, better placed to react on this occasion than fighters based at Lossiemouth.

During a visit to Leuchars in January 2013, Air Marshal Richard Garwood, Deputy Commander-in-Chief (Operations), had met personnel of 1 Squadron, describing the move away from sharing accommodation with 6 Squadron to its own on the base as the next logical step. This was about eighteen months after the post-SDSR announcement from Dr Liam Fox, offering a further glimmer of hope that a change of heart had taken place and that Leuchars was, perhaps, not going to see the end of its days as an RAF station and therefore an end to its link with aviation after all. However, speculation that Air Marshal Garwood's visit was something to be optimistic about was misplaced. It had been said that this all added up to the RAF mounting something of a rearguard action to retain Leuchars on a fully operational basis, and indications were that it may have won a partial victory of sorts, but everyone was put out of their misery and speculation ended on 5 March 2013, when the new Defence Secretary, Philip Hammond, announced that the two major units of the Army mentioned back in July 2011—the Royal Scots Dragoon Guards (moving from Fallingbostel in Germany) and 2nd Battalion, Royal Electrical and Mechanical Engineers—would indeed move in, but not the Brigade HQ as had been mentioned initially.

Another story was released at the same time by *The Courier* newspaper, which had itself been at the forefront of the campaign to retain the status quo and the RAF presence at Leuchars. It reported that station personnel had been told that the last of the Typhoons would leave in September 2014, with the Army moving in sometime early in 2015. A couple of weeks later, the same paper revealed that Defence Chiefs had further confirmed that the first Typhoons would be leaving at the end of 2013, to take the place of the Tornados at Lossiemouth as they in turn were removed. So the die was cast, and 103 years of military flying from Leuchars was set to slip into history. Six decades as the most northerly fighter station standing guard over the Northern approaches to British airspace since 1950 were now at an end.

The concern now was the availability of diversion airfields. With Lossiemouth located on the Moray coast and no other military airfields between it and Yorkshire, Typhoon pilots returning from sorties taking them north of Scapa Flow, with or without an attendant tanker each time, are going to be placed in an unenviable position. Andrew Robathan in answer to a question from Menzies Campbell (himself a tireless campaigner for retaining the RAF at Leuchars) about whether any Typhoon-related mission infrastructure/equipment would remain after the redeployment of the squadrons to Lossiemouth, said that 'the airfield at RAF Leuchars will be retained for other flying roles, including as a diversion airfield'. Previously, when the RAF had relinquished control of an airfield to the Army, usually in England, the question of a diversion had not arisen and therefore this all-important requirement had never been debated in public. For example, when RAF Abingdon closed, active airfields at Benson, Wittering, Odiham, Lyneham and Brize Norton were all to hand. When Finningley and Scampton (the latter since reopened) were abandoned by the junior service to make it a leaner and fitter fighting force following the 'Front Line First' defence review, alternatives for diversionary requirements were equally close at hand, with Waddington, Coningsby, Cranwell, Leeming, Church Fenton and Linton-on-Ouse to fall back on.

However, the decision to retain Leuchars and Kinloss as active airfields seems to be something of a spanner in the planning works. It is clear that this has prevented the aim of relinquishing both airfields for financial savings, which has been proved for all reasons of aviation safety to be out of the question. Only time will tell exactly what the long-term future holds, but as the exercise is purely in the interests of preventing economic disaster (and nobody can deny it), avoidable expenditure is now being incurred on shuffling everyone around. With the need to retain intact the airfield, when the principal aim was to reduce airfield infrastructure rather than the number of units flying from them, it certainly seems that this has all been managed with quite simplistic thinking. In June 2014, 6 Squadron left for Lossiemouth, 1 Squadron following in September. The Army will begin to arrive from 2015.

There is, of course, one more loss to the community, which while not crucial to military and defence planning has nevertheless become iconic in the aviation world—the annual air show. I mention this as it had become the second most popular outdoor event in Scotland after football. Furthermore, the air show, or 'Battle of Britain 'at home' day to use the official title, is the responsibility of the Air Force Board, not any private company or charity. The RAF's own in-house management, the Air Staff, are the originating authority. On 6 September 2013, on the eve of that year's show, the dreaded announcement for fans of the air show—that it would be the last—was made during the afternoon while Scottish Television and other media companies were at the station to preview the event. The Station Commander, Air Cdre Gerry Mayhew, pointed out that by September 2014, half of the then station strength would have moved to Lossiemouth, but keen to allay disappointment, he also announced an ongoing comprehensive review of air show commitments by the RAF, with consideration being given to finding a replacement for the Leuchars air show forming part of that review. When asked if the air show could, if the

FOD PLOD, Station Commander, Air Commodore Clive Bairsto and SAC Emma Walker join the rest of the available Station personnel in the fod plod (Foreign Object Damage Patrol) across the airfield following the 2008 airshow. (*MOD/Crown copyright*)

airfield were maintained, ever return to Fife, he said he believed it was in the mix.

The display has been held at Leuchars in this format, i.e. commemorating the Battle of Britain, each year since the first occasion on 15 September 1945, with six notable exceptions: 1956 and 1957 (runway resurfacing and extension); 1979 (runway resurfacing); 1980 (no reason given); 1999 (projected operational commitments concerned with the conflict in Kosovo); and 2007 (runway resurfacing and preparation for arrival of Typhoons). This, incidentally, made the 2013 show the 63rd rather than the 65th, as claimed on the front of the souvenir programme. From 1995, Leuchars hosted the Battle of Britain 'at home' day alone, which was somewhat ironic considering that the campaign being commemorated took place predominantly over the South East of England.

Another casualty of the closure of the base was 58 Squadron of the RAF Regiment, a field infantry unit that had disbanded in 1992 as part of ongoing cuts. It re-formed at Leuchars on 1 April 2010 and, except for the Mountain Rescue Team, was the first recognisable unit at Leuchars to go. However, instead of relocating it was due to disband—a curious development given the emphasis on mobile light assault infantry in UK defence policy. Not surprisingly, the squadron disbanded soon after returning from its last deployment to Afghanistan. The good news was that it was just the unit identity that would disappear, the personnel of 58 Squadron having been offered postings elsewhere, including Lossiemouth, Leeming and the RAF Regiment Depot at Honington, which is now home not just to the training unit but also to the bulk of the remaining RAF Regiment squadrons. True to form, as with many other units across the armed forces, the disbandment was already planned ahead of its last deployment to Afghanistan from October 2013 for six months.

A recent innovation has been to provide a regular flypast of aircraft from Leuchars and Lossiemouth at the Edinburgh Military Tattoo. This was organised initially for the 2011 event, with a single Typhoon pulling up sharply into a steep climb directly over the esplanade each day, often masked by low cloud. The following year, the flypast became more ambitious and a four-ship of two Typhoons and two Tornados brought complaints, some of which were typically flippant and absurd. One local, clearly not fully abreast of current affairs, complained that she thought the Germans were bombing the city! The reaction of the authorities, not at all unexpectedly, was to be accommodating and try to find a compromise, the solution being that the formation that had been engaging reheat over the city was to carry out the remaining runs in dry power. It is a shame that this spectacular overture to the tattoo was not thought of and authorised many years earlier, other than for the one-offs like the diamond-9 flown in

On 14 September 2012, the French Air Force Chief of Adla Commands, Lt Gen Guillame Gelee, was flown on a low-level sortie from Leuchars in the rear cockpit of a 6 Sqn Typhoon T3, piloted by Leuchars CO Air Commodore Gavin Parker, while Air Vice-Marshal Stuart Atha AOC 1 Group RAF was flown in the back of a Rafale B by piloted by Cne M Gerard, a French Air Force exchange Officer with 1 Sqn at Leuchars. (*MOD/Crown copyright*)

1978. It now comes literally when Leuchars' days as a fighter station are numbered.

Much of the run-up to closure from the start took place against the backdrop of the possibility of Scottish independence, the campaign for which continues by hook or by crook, despite the result of the Independence Referendum. As recent wild predictions over the 2015 UK General Election have suggested, it may yet prove successful eventually. What would happen then to the RAF presence north of the border, and just what would an independent Scottish Air Force in reality be composed of? Herein lies another interesting debate. The SNP reacted to the implications of both SDSR and the further planning round that confirmed the base closures and personnel movements by criticising the government on the grounds of neglect. Should independence become a reality, the future defence structure in Scotland will be a real headache for Nicola Sturgeon and her party to think through.

The SNP suggested during the independence campaign that they would be able to rely on a single squadron of twelve Typhoons, presumably passed to Scotland by agreement with the UK. In 2015, the RAF fields a force,

Scott Loughran blasts off the runway at the Fairford 2012 RIAT as a prelude to his aerobatics display. (*Trevor Thornton*)

at Lossiemouth, of thirty-six Eurofighter Typhoon aircraft (the number planned originally for Leuchars), whereas the two countries that the SNP most closely feel an independent Scotland would emulate, Denmark and Norway, each field a force of around fifty F-16 fighters. While not quite comparable to the Typhoon, being a previous-generation design, the F-16 does possess a tactical radar, supersonic speed, high agility and in-flight refuelling, and is also relatively cheap and economical. However, its drawbacks are short legs and a single engine, but it is a sensible alternative, and while the governments of Denmark and Norway are currently seeking its replacement with the F-35 Lightning II, it will continue to be operated by these countries' air arms for some time yet.

And so the future beckons. For now, it seems that Britain's hitherto longest continually serving military airfield will be retained in active mode but with no operational assets. The station will gradually assume the character of a barracks rather than an air base, but its longer-term future is far from clear. The prospect of a return to the very same defence posture determined by the Cold War appears increasingly likely, given the developments on the back of problems in the Ukraine. During 2014, more than 100 scrambles of RAF Typhoons from both Leuchars and Lossiemouth to intercept Russian military aircraft encroaching on UK airspace were recorded, according to the Defence Secretary, Michael Fallon, in a report in the *Daily Mail* on 15 December that year. Since the move from Leuchars to Lossiemouth has been completed, more provocative sorties by Tu-95 Bears (yes, the same aircraft, with various upgrades, that tested the Leuchars Wing from the late 1960s to the end) have been flown as far south as the English Channel coast, prompting alarm in the press, not to mention difficulty in maintaining diplomatic language on the part of the UK Government. But I will leave the final words for now to the postscript!

Last knockings, four Typhoons of 1 Sqn break in to the circuit on return from another Joint Warrior exercise, 8 April 2014. (*Author's Collection*)

Postscript

In April 2014, 6 Squadron's celebrations of its 100th anniversary on the station included a display by a Hurricane from the Battle of Britain Memorial Flight, an aircraft synonymous with its tank-busting days. One of the squadron's Typhoons had its spine and fin resprayed in the light and dark desert camouflage of the age, and four Typhoons overflew the ceremony. On 10 May, RAF Leuchars paraded through the town of St Andrews for the last time, with all operational units and station personnel represented—1 (F) Squadron, 6 Squadron, and 58 Squadron RAF Regiment—while a single Typhoon flew low across the parade on South Street, where the station had first exercised its Freedom of St Andrews in August 1968.

But perhaps the most poignant farewell took place at the last Leuchars air show. As 1700 hours passed on Saturday 7 September 2013, a week earlier than tradition would usually dictate, Air Officer Scotland and RAF Leuchars Station Commander, Air Cdre Gerry Mayhew, saluted from the dais as the band marched off. A single Typhoon from the then still locally based 1 Fighter Squadron, and a single Tornado from the Lossiemouth-based 617 'Dambusters' Squadron, flew past low in close formation before curving north and roaring out of sight as the sun set on Royal Air Force station Leuchars.

Up up and away, a Typhoon gets airborne demonstrating its short field performance, or rotation take off, by rotating the nose through almost 90 degrees on leaving the runway and climbing vertically while still a good furlong away from the end, the last RAF aircraft to hold a reputation for this kind of effortless spectacle was the Lightning. (*Author's Collection*)

Appendix I

Squadrons based at RAF Leuchars

Unit	Dates	Type Operated
Fleet School of Aerial Fighting & Gunnery 203 Squadron	01/03/20-18/09/23	Sopwith Camel & Nieuport Nightjar
205 Squadron	15/04/20-01/04/23	Parnall Panther
3 Squadron	01/10/21-08/11/22	Sopwith Snipe
401 Fleet Fighter Squadron	01/04/23-08/05/23 26/07/23-30/08/23 01/09/23-10/02/24 20/10/24-16/01/25 02/04/25-04/07/25 24/08/25-07/09/25	Fairey Flycatcher
402 Fleet Fighter Squadron	01/04/23-04/03/24 25/12/24-01/02/25	Fairey Flycatcher
403 Fleet Fighter Flight	01/06/23-14/03/24	Fairey Flycatcher
404 Fleet Fighter Flight	01/06/23-13/09/25	Fairey Flycatcher
421 Fleet Spotter Flight	01/05/25-23/06/25 06/09/28-19/10/28	Blackburn Blackburn Avro Bison
441 Fleet Reconnaissance Squadron	01/04/23-17/07/23 27/08/23-08/03/24 28/05/24-13/11/24	Fairey IIID

442 Fleet Reconnaissance Squadron	01/04/23-08/05/23 26/07/23-29/07/24 21/10/24-16/01/25 05/06/25-04/07/25 31/08/25-02/26 14/06/26-26/06/26 12/10/26-27/10/26 23/03/31-27/04/31 30/05/31-13/09/31	Fairey FIIID
443 Fleet Reconnaissance Flight	21/05/23-28/06/29	Fairey FIIID
444 Flight Reconnaissance Flight	02/25	Fairey FIIID
461 Fleet Torpedo Flight	14/09/26-16/09/26 09/28-26/10/28 17/06/29-05/11/29	Blackburn Dart Blackburn Ripon
462 Fleet Torpedo Flight	30/09/26-21/10/26 09/28-26/10/28 17/06/29-04/10/29	Blackburn Dart Blackburn Ripon
443A Fleet Reconnaissance Flight	07/27-10/27 16/05/28-13/06/28	Fairey IIID
445 Fleet Reconnaissance Flight	01/09/27-07/11/32	Fairey IIID/Fairey IIIF
446 Fleet Reconnaissance Flight	01/09/27-10/09/30	Fairey IIID/Fairey IIIF
447 Fleet Reconnaissance Flight	28/06/29-03/07/29	Avro Bison
449 Fleet Reconnaissance Spotter Flight	30/04/29-23/04/31	Blackburn Blackburn/ Fairey IIIF
450 Fleet Reconnaissance Spotter Flight	02/06/29-12/08/31	Blackburn Blackburn/ Fairey IIIF
36 Squadron	10/30	Horsley I & III
822 Squadron	10/33	Fairey IIIF
811 Squadron	10/33 06/35-07/35	Blackburn Ripon Blackburn Baffin
802 Squadron	10/34	Hawker Nimrod I & II/ Osprey I & III
810 Squadron	14/05/34-08/10/34	Blackburn Ripon/ Blackburn Baffin
800 Squadron	10/34 24/05/36-06/06/36 13/06/37-29/09/37	Hawker Nimrod/Hawker Osprey

801 Squadron	10/37	Hawker Osprey I, III & IV
224 Squadron	01/09/38-15/04/41	Avro Anson I/Lockheed Electra Hudson I
223 Squadron	01/09/38-08/12/40	Avro Anson I/Bristol Blenheim IV/Lockheed Electra Hudson I
605 Squadron	02/40	Hawker Hurricane I
320 Squadron	01/10/40-18/01/42	Avro Anson I/ Lockheed Hudson I
114 Squadron	13/05/40-19/07/41	Bristol Blenheim IV & V
86 Squadron	02/02/41-03/03/41	Bristol Blenheim IV
42 Squadron	01/03/41-18/06/42	Bristol Beaufort I & II
107 Squadron	03/03/41-11/05/41	Bristol Blenheim IV
455 Squadron	28/04/42-14/04/44	Hampden I/ Beaufighter X
144 Squadron	22/04/42-08/04/43	Bristol Blenheim IV & V
489 Squadron	12/08/42-05/08/42	Hampden I/ Blenheim IV
489 Squadron	06/10/43-08/04/44	Hampden I/ Beaufighter X
206 Squadron	11/07/44-31/07/45	B-24 Liberator VI & VIII (VIII from 03/45)
547 Squadron	01/10/44-04/06/45	B-24 Liberator VI & VIII
203 Squadron	19/03/46-16/01/47	B-24 Liberator VIII/ Avro Lancaster GR3
120 Squadron	01/10/46-14/12/50	Avro Lancaster ASR/GR3
237 OCU	15/04/48-03/10/51	DH Mosquito PR34/ Supermarine Spitfire XVI & XIX
43 Squadron	11/11/50-29/07/54 29/07/54-21/06/61	Gloster Meteor F4 & F8 Hawker Hunter F1, F4, F6
222 Squadron	09/05/50-01/12/54	Gloster Meteor F4 & F8
229 OCU	15/12/50-28/03/51	DH Vampire FB5 & T11
809 Naval Air Squadron	08/09/52-13/10/52	DH Sea Hornet F21
811 Naval Air Squadron	19/08/53-02/02/54	Hawker Sea Hawk F1
151 Squadron	15/09/51-08/53 08/53-10/55 10/55-15/06/57	Vampire NF10 Meteor NF11 Venom NF3

222 Squadron	01/12/54-01/08/56 01/08/56-01/11/57	Hawker Hunter F1 Hawker Hunter F4
275 Squadron 'C' Flight	30/06/55-01/04/59	Sycamore HR13 & HR14/ Whirlwind HAR4
151 Squadron	15/06/57-01/09/61	Gloster Javelin FAW5
29 Squadron	22/07/58-01/03/63	Gloster Javelin FAW6 & FAW9
228 Squadron 'C' Flight	01/09/59-28/08/64	Sycamore HR14/ Whirlwind HAR2, 4 & 10
25 Squadron	31/10/61-31/12/62	Gloster Javelin FAW9
23 Squadron	09/03/63-31/10/64	Gloster Javelin FAW9
74 Squadron	01/03/64-12/06/67	English Electric Lightning F1, F3 & F6
202 Squadron 'C' Flight	29/08/64-08/04/76	Whirlwind HAR10
23 Squadron	31/10/64-31/10/75	English Electric Lightning F3 & F6
228 OCU/11 Squadron	01/05/65-23/12/66	Gloster Javelin FAW9 & T3 English Electric Canberra T11
11 Squadron	03/04/67-28/03/72	English Electric Lightning F6
43 Squadron	01/09/69-01/07/89 01/06/88-01/07/89	McDonnell Douglas F-4K Phantom II McDonnell Douglas F-4M Phantom II
892 Squadron Fleet Air Arm	17/07/72-04/04/78	McDonnell Douglas F-4K Phantom II
Phantom Training Flight	1972-1978	McDonnell Douglas F-4K Phantom II
111 Squadron	03/11/75-31/01/90	McDonnell Douglas F-4M & F-4K Phantom II
22 Squadron 'B' Flight	08/04/76-1993	Wessex HC2
228 OCU/64 Squadron	22/04/87-31/01/91	McDonnell Douglas F-4M Phantom II
43 Squadron	23/09/89-13/07/09	Panavia Tornado F3
111 Squadron	01/06/90-22/03/11	Panavia Tornado F3
56 (R) Squadron	03/2003-25/04/08	Panavia Tornado F3
6 Squadron	11/09/10-06/2014	Eurofighter Typhoon FGR4
1 Squadron	15/09/12-09/2014	Eurofighter Typhoon FGR4

Appendix II

Station Commanders

Appointed Commander	Date/Year of Appointment
Wg Cdr R. P. Ross	16/03/1920
Gp Capt. C. S. Burnett, CB, CBE, DSO	01/04/1922
Gp Capt. P. H. L. Playfair, MC	15/11/1922
Gp Capt. A. W. Bigsworth	05/08/1925
Gp Capt. W. R. Freeman, DSO, MC	07/10/1928
Gp Capt. F. E. T. Hewlett, DSO, OBE	07/09/1929
Gp Capt. L. J. E. Feinnes	16/05/1933
Gp Capt. L. F. Forbes	02/05/1936
Gp Capt. O. Grenfell, MC, DFC	01/08/1938
Gp Capt. B. E. Baker, DSO, MC, AFC	01/09/1938
Gp Capt. S. L. G. Pope, DFC, AFC	01/05/1940
Gp Capt. B. V. Reynolds	17/11/1941
Gp Capt. G. W. Tuttle, OBE, DFC	05/09/1942
Gp Capt. R. L. Wallace, AFC	31/01/1943
Gp Capt. J. Constable-Roberts, CBE	01/05/1944
Gp Capt. P. F. Canning, CBE	27/08/1944
Gp Capt. R. W. K. Stevens	16/04/1945
Gp Capt. C. R. Taylor, OBE	15/07/1945
Gp Capt. G. K. Fairclough	06/04/1946
Gp Capt. R. G. Forbes	01/02/1948
Gp Capt. M. W. S. Robinson, CBE	26/04/1950
Gp Capt. G. A. Brown, DFC	27/07/1951
Gp Capt. P. G. StG O'Brian, OBE, DFC	21/07/1953
Gp Capt. D. F. Beardon, AFC	17/10/1955
Gp Capt. E. G. L. Millington, CBE, DFC	03/01/1958
Gp Capt. E. Plumtree, OBE, DFC	16/12/1959

Gp Capt. A. N. Davis, DSO, DFC	02/10/1961
Gp Capt. W. Harbison, DFC	21/01/1963
Gp Capt. A. S. R. Strudwick, DFC	14/08/1965
Gp Capt. J. M. Nicholls, DFC, AFC	09/06/1967
Gp Capt. N. S. Howlett	23/01/1970
Gp Capt. M. J. E. Swiney, OBE	28/01/1972
Gp Capt. G. A. White	21/09/1973
Gp Capt. R. L. Davis	17/10/1975
Gp Capt. W. B. Maish	20/05/1977
Gp Capt. J. J. Cohu	03/08/1979
Gp Capt. M. J. Graydon	28/08/1981
Gp Capt. T. C. Elworthy	11/08/1983
Gp Capt. I. MacFadyen	05/07/1985
Gp Capt. P. T. Squire	01/01/1988
Gp Capt. A. J. C. Bagnall	08/01/1988
Gp Capt. L. A. Doble	1990
Gp Capt. S. M. Nicholl	1992
Gp Capt. N. J. Sudborough, CB, OBE	1993
Air Cdre J. Haines	18/12/1995
Gp Capt. R. B. Hodgson, MIA, BA	1998
Gp Capt. P. A. Coker	04/10/1999
Air Cdre M. Routledge	25/06/2001
Air Cdre S. Bryant	23/04/2003
Air Cdre J. Stinton	04/03/2005
Air Cdre C. A. Bairsto	13/04/2007
Air Cdre R. J. Atkinson	13/03/2009
Air Cdre G. D. A. Parker, OBE, ADC	12/09/2011
Air Cdre G. Mayhew	12/02/2013

Note: The appointment was a dual one from Air Cdre Routledge onwards, with the additional responsibility of the post of Air Officer Scotland. Air Cdre Haines had been the first to hold both appointments, but the situation seems to have reverted for a while. The appointment of AOC Scotland also included Northern Ireland, when it warranted the rank of Air Vice-Marshal, before the role was split and the CO Leuchars carried the responsibility for the RAF in Scotland, hence the promotion to Air Commodore (one-star rank).

Appendix III

Leuchars-based Lightning, Phantom, Tornado and Typhoon solo display pilots and crews

As the frontline jet fighter has leapt ahead in performance and sophistication over the years, particularly during the 1950s and '60s, an unexpected development has been that the new jets have proved less suitable for formation aerobatics than their simpler, lighter and more numerous predecessors. The Hunter was very much the half-way house, considered the best in terms of the balance of performance, complexity, size and the resources needed in respect of operational and training requirements. With the arrival of the English Electric Lightning, the improvement in all respects was staggering. The Lightning was therefore the last frontline type to be used for formation aerobatics, the thinking for the future being for the prowess of the Mach 2 fighter to be demonstrated in the air in solo form only. Given the much reduced numbers of the new third- and fourth-generation jets, the allocation of even solo displays decreased rapidly, to the point where just one or two were authorised per type. As such, the Leuchars-based units have over the years provided a significant number of officially sanctioned solo display crews, from the Lightning through to the Typhoon:

Lightning solos

Variant	Pilot	Unit	Year
F3	Flt Lt Glyn Owen	74 Squadron	1964
F3	Flt Lt John Hind	23 Squadron	1965
F3	Flt Lt Dave Mitchell	74 Squadron	1965
F3	Flt Lt Al Turley	23 Squadron	1966
F3	Flt Lt David Liggitt	74 Squadron	1966
F3	Flt Lt Al Turley	23 Squadron	1967

F6	Flg Off. Richard Rhodes	11 Squadron	1967
F6	Flt Lt Mike Laughlin	11 Squadron	1968
F6	Flt Lt Tony Craig	23 Squadron	1968
F6	Flt Lt Mike Donaldson	23 Squadron	1968
F6	Flt Lt Kevin Mace	11 Squadron	1969
F6	Flt Lt Derek Nicholls	11 Squadron	1970
F6	Flt Lt Russ Pengelly	23 Squadron	1970

Phantom solos

Variant	Pilot Navigator/WSO	Unit	Year
F-4K/FG1	Sqn Ldr John Owen Flt Lt Nick Thurston	43 Squadron	1969-71
F-4K/FG1	Flt Lt Roger Beazley Flt Lt J. McNeil-Matthews or Flt Lt Norman Browne	43 Squadron	1972
F-4K/FG1	Sqn Ldr Brian Clifford Flt Lt Norman Browne	43 Squadron	1973
F-4K/FG1	Flt Lt Sandy Davis Flt Lt Nick Reffold	43 Squadron	1974
F-4K/FG1	Flt Lt Sandy Davis Flt Lt Norman Browne	43 Squadron	1975
F-4K/FG1	Sqn Ldr Ian MacFadyen Flt Lt Norman Browne	43 Squadron	1976
F-4K/FG1	Flt Lt Mike Bell Flt Lt Nick Reffold	43 Squadron	1977
F-4K/FG1	Flt Lt John Spoor Flt Lt Andy Moir	43 Squadron	1978
F-4K/FG1	Sqn Ldr Ray Dixon Flt Lt Colin Bond	43 Squadron	1981-82
F-4K/FG1	Sqn Ldr Simon Lloyd- Morrison Flt Lt Dave Clark	111 Squadron	1983
F-4K/FG1	Sqn Ldr Simon Lloyd- Morrison Flt Lt Gary Hewitt	111 Squadron	1984
F-4K/FG1	Sqn Ldr Barry Doggett Flt Lt Dick Hansen	43 Squadron	1986
F-4M/FGR2	Flt Lt Chris Lackman Flt Lt Jack Thompson	228 OCU/ 64 Squadron	1988
F-4M/FGR2	Flt Lt Steve Howard Flt Lt Nigel Marks	228 OCU/ 64 Squadron	1990

Tornado solos

Variant	Pilot Navigator/WSO	Unit	Year
F3	Flt Lt Tim Freeman Flt Lt Steve Kilvington	56 Squadron	2003
F3	Flt Lt Tim Freeman Flt Lt Neil Crawley	56 Squadron	2004
F3	Flt Lt Richard Moyes Flt Lt Gareth 'Gaz' Littlechild	56 Squadron	2005

Typhoon solos

Variant	Pilot	Unit	Year
FGR4	Sqn Ldr Scott Loughran	6 Squadron	2012

Bibliography

Beedle, Jimmy, *The Fighting Cocks* (Barnsley: Pen & Sword, 2010)

Cummings, Colin, *RAF Accidents since 1945* (various)

Dannatt, General Sir Richard, *Leading from the Front* (London: Corgi Books, 2011)

White, Alan, *Lightning Up: The Career of Air Vice-Marshal Alan White* (Barnsley: Pen & Sword, 2009)